Globalisation, Policy and Comparative Research: Discourses of Globalisation

Globalisation, Comparative Education and Policy Research
12-volume Book Series (Springer)

Series editor: Joseph Zajda (Australian Catholic University, Melbourne Campus)
http://www.springeronline.com/sgw/cda/frontpage

Book series overview

The *Globalisation, Comparative Education and Policy Research* book series aims to meet the research needs of all those interested in in-depth developments in comparative education research. The series provides a global overview of developments and changes in policy and comparative education research during the last decade. Presenting up-to-date scholarly research on global trends, it is an easily accessible, practical yet scholarly source of information for researchers, policy makers and practitioners. It seeks to address the nexus between comparative education, policy and forces of globalisation, and provides perspectives from all the major disciplines and all the world regions. The series offers possible strategies for the effective and pragmatic policy planning and implementation at local, regional and national levels.

The book series complements the *International Handbook of Globalisation and Education Policy Research*. The volumes focus on comparative education themes and case studies in much greater scope and depth than is possible in the Handbook.

The series includes volumes on both empirical and qualitative studies of policy initiatives and developments in comparative education research in elementary, secondary and post-compulsory sectors. Case studies may include changes and education reforms around the world, curriculum reforms, trends in evaluation and assessment, decentralisation and privatisation in education, technical and vocational education, early childhood education, excellence and quality in education. Above all, the series offers the latest findings on critical issues in comparative education and policy directions, such as:

- Developing new internal strategies (more comprehensive, flexible and innovative modes of learning) that take into account the changing and expanding learner needs
- Overcoming 'unacceptable' socio-economic educational disparities and inequalities
- Improving educational quality
- Harmonizing education and culture
- International cooperation in education and policy directions in each country

For other titles published in this series, go to
www.springer.com/series/6932

Joseph Zajda • Val Rust

Editors

Globalisation, Policy and Comparative Research: Discourses of Globalisation

 Springer

Editors
Joseph Zajda
Australian Catholic University
Melbourne Campus
Australia

Val Rust
University of California
Los Angeles
USA

ISBN 978-90-481-8152-0 e-ISBN 978-1-4020-9547-4

DOI: 10.1007/978-1-4020-9547-4

Printed on acid-free paper

springer.com

To Rea, Nikolai, and Dorothy

Preface

Globalisation, Policy and Comparative Research, which is the fifth volume in the 12-volume book series *Globalisation, Comparative Education and Policy Research*, presents scholarly research on major discourses in comparative education research. It provides an easily accessible, practical yet scholarly source of information about the international concern in the field of globalisation, and comparative education. Above all, the book offers the latest findings to the critical issues concerning major discourses in comparative education in the global culture. It is a sourcebook of ideas for researchers, practitioners and policy makers in education, globalisation and equity and access in schooling around the world. It offers a timely overview of current issues affecting comparative education and education policy research in the global culture. It provides directions in education, and policy research, relevant to transformational educational reforms in the twenty-first century.

The book critically examines the overall interplay between comparative education discourses, globalisation, dominant ideologies and education. It draws upon recent studies in the areas of globalisation, equity, social justice and the role of the State (Zajda et al., 2006; Zajda et al., 2008a). It explores conceptual frameworks and methodological approaches applicable in the research covering the State, globalisation, equity and education. It demonstrates the neo-liberal ideological imperatives of education and policy reforms, and illustrates the way the relationship between the State and education policy affects current models and trends in education reforms and schooling globally. Various book chapters critique the dominant discourses and debates pertaining to comparative education discourses and the newly constructed and reinvented models of neo-liberal ideology in education.

The book explores the ambivalent and problematic relationship between the State, globalisation and social change. Using a number of diverse paradigms in comparative education research, ranging from critical theory to globalisation, the authors, by focusing on globalisation, ideology and democracy, attempt to examine critically both the reasons and outcomes of educational reforms, policy change and transformation, and provide a more informed critique on the Western-driven models of accountability, quality and school effectiveness. The book draws upon recent studies in the areas of equity, cultural capital and dominant ideologies in education (Zajda, 2005; Zajda et al., 2008b).

Equality of educational opportunity is difficult to achieve in highly stratified societies and economic systems. Coleman (1975), Levin (1978) and others have argued that education alone was not sufficient to overcome significant SES differences in the society divided along dimensions of class, power, income, wealth and privilege. Globalisation, in most developing countries (the majority of humanity), is articulated in the form of finance-driven policy reforms concerning efficiency and effectiveness. Their effect on education systems is likely to 'increase' educational inequalities and access (Carnoy, 1999; Zajda, 2008).

Furthermore, a lack of emphasis on the relationship between policy, poverty and schooling, and the 'withdrawal of the state as a major provider in the field of education in many parts of the world' raise serious human rights and ethical questions (Soudien and Kallaway, 1999; Zajda, 2005, 2008). The growth of global education policy hegemony defining accountability, standards, quality assurance and assessment fails to respond to the changing relationships between the state, education and social justice in the global economy.

Equality of educational opportunities, labelled by Coombs (1982) as the 'stubborn issue of inequality' (Coombs 1982, p. 153), and first examined in comparative education research by Kandel in 1957 (Kandel, 1957, p. 2), is 'still with us' according to Jennings (2000, p. 113). Furthermore, the prospect of widening inequalities in education, due to market-oriented schooling, and substantial tolerance of inequalities and exclusion, are more than real. Access and equity continue to be major issues in education. The policy shift away from the progressive and egalitarian vision of education that characterised the 1960s and the 1970s has serious implications for human rights, social justice and democracy.

The general intention is to make *Globalisation, Policy and Comparative Research* available to a broad spectrum of users among policy makers, academics, graduate students, education policy researchers, administrators and practitioners in the education and related professions. The book is unique in that it:

- Explores conceptual frameworks and methodological approaches applicable in the research of the State, globalisation and education reforms
- Illustrates how the relationship between the State and education policy affects current models and trends in schooling globally
- Demonstrates ideological imperatives of globalisation, neo-liberal ideology and the State
- Evaluates the ambivalent and problematic relationship between the State, education reforms and outcomes in education globally
- Provides strategic education policy analysis on recent shifts in education, and policy research
- Gives suggestions for directions in education and policy changes, relevant to democratic and empowering pedagogy in the twenty-first century

We hope that you will find *Globalisation, Policy and Comparative Research* useful in your teaching, future research and discourses concerning schooling, social justice and policy reforms in the global culture.

Australian Catholic University (Melbourne Campus)   Joseph Zajda

References

Apple, M.W. (2004). *Ideology and Curriculum* (3rd Edition). New York: Routledge Falmer.

Carnoy, M. (1999). *Globalization and Educational Reform: What Planners Need to Know*. Paris: UNESCO, International Institute for Education Planning.

Coleman, J. (1975). What is Meant by 'an Equal Educational Opportunity'? *Oxford Review of Education*, 1, 27.

Coombs, P. (1982). Critical World Educational Issues of the Next Two Decades. *International Review of Education*, 28(1), 143–158.

Jennings, Z. (2000). Functional Literacy of Young Guyanese Adults. *International Review of Education*, 46(1/2), 93–116.

Kandel, H. (1957). Equalizing Educational Opportunities and its Problems. *International Review of Education*, 3(1), 1–12.

Soudien, C. and Kallaway, P. (1999). *Education, Equity and Transformation*. Dordrecht: Kluwer.

Zajda, J. (2005) (Ed.). The *International Handbook of Globalisation and Education Policy Research*. Dordrecht: Springer.

Zajda, J. (2008). Globalisation and Implications for Equity and Democracy in Education. In Zajda, J. Davies, L., and Majhanovich, S. (Eds.), *Comparative and Global Pedagogies: Equity, Access and Democracy in Education* (pp. 3–12). Dordrecht: Springer.

Zajda, J. Majhanovich, S. and Rust, V. (2006) (Eds.) *Education and Social Justice*. Dordrecht: Springer.

Zajda, J. Biraimah, B. and Gaudelli, W (2008a). (Eds.), *Education and Social Inequality in the Global Culture* (pp. xvii–xxvii). Dordrecht: Springer.

Zajda, J., Davies, L. and Majhanovich, S. (2008b) (Eds.). *Comparative and Global Pedagogies: Equity, Access and Democracy in Education*. Dordrecht: Springer.

Acknowledgements

We wish to thank the following individuals who have provided invaluable help, advice and support with this major research project:

Harmen van Paradijs, Publishing Editor, Springer

Bernadette Ohmer, Springer

Marianna Pascale, Springer

Dorothy Murphy, Associate Editor, Educational Practice and Theory, James Nicholas Publishers

Rea Zajda, James Nicholas Publishers

We also want to thank numerous reviewers who were prepared to review various drafts of the chapters. These include:

Ari Antikainen, University of Helsinki

Alberto Arenas, University of Arizona

Jill Blackmore, Deakin University

Malcolm Campbell, Bowling Green State University

Mark Bray, International institute for Educational Planning (Paris)

Paul Carlin, Australian Catholic University (Melbourne Campus)

Phil Clarkson, Australian Catholic University (Melbourne Campus)

Holger Daun, University of Stockholm

David Gamage, University of Newcastle

Yaacov Iram, Bar Ilan University

Kyu Hwan Lee, Ewha Womans University (South Korea)

Kas Mazurek, University of Lethbridge

Marie-Laure Mimoun-Sorel,Australian Catholic University (Melbourne Campus)

Wolfgang Mitter, German Institute for International Educational Research

Christopher McIntosh, UNESCO Institute for Lifelong Learning

Gabrielle McMullen, Australian Catholic University (Melbourne Campus)

Val Rust, UCLA

Anne Scott, Australian Catholic University (Melbourne Campus)

Caroline Smith, Australian Catholic University (Melbourne Campus)

Sandra L Stacki, Hofstra University

Margaret Secombe, University of Adelaide

Rea Zajda, James Nicholas Publishers

We are particularly grateful to Harmen van Paradijs, Publishing Editor, Springer, who supported this project, and who took the responsibility for the book production process, and whose energy and enthusiasm ensured that the book was published on time.

Contents

Chapter 1
Globalisation, and Comparative Research: Implications for Education

Joseph Zajda

1.1 Globalisation and Implications for Education

Globalisation and competitive market forces have generated a massive growth in knowledge industries that are having profound effects on society and educational institutions. In the global culture, the university, as with other educational institutions, is now expected to invest its capital in the knowledge market. It increasingly acts as an entrepreneurial institution (Sabour, 2005). Such a managerial and entrepreneurial reorientation would have been seen in the past as derogatory and antithetical to the traditional ethos of the university which was to provide knowledge for its own sake (Delanty, 2001; Sabour, 2005; Zajda, 2005). Delanty (2001) notes that 'with business schools and techno-science on the rise, entrepreneurial values are enjoying a new legitimacy … the critical voice of the university is more likely to be stifled rather than strengthened as a result of globalisation' (Delanty, 2001, p. 115). It can be said that globalisation may have an adverse impact on the higher education sector, and on education in general. One of the effects of globalisation is that the university is compelled to embrace the corporate ethos of efficiency and profit-driven managerialism. As such, the new entrepreneurial university in the global culture succumbs to the economic gains, which seem to be offered by neo-liberal ideology.

As the humanistic, social justice and human rights tradition, so influential in the 1960s, began to weaken, the economic and techno-determinist paradigm of the Internation Monetary Fund (IMF), the World Bank and the Organisation of Economic Cooperation and Development (OECD) gained in prominence. In short, neo-liberal and neo-conservative ideology has re-defined education and training as investment in 'human capital' and 'human resource development'. This in turn has familiar social indicators in the global economy discourse.

Education in the global economy, espousing neo-liberal and neo-conservative ideology, is likely to produce a great deal of discontent and conflict. We are reminded of the much-quoted words 'All history is the history of class struggle'

J. Zajda
Australian Catholic University, Melbourne Campus

(Marx and Engels, 1848). However, Nyberg, like Dahrendorf, argues that power more than social class defines the essence of inequality. Globalisation has an evolving and growing complexity of a new dimension of social stratification of nations, technology and education systems during the twenty-first century. This is due to unequal distribution of power and other socially valued commodities. It has a potential to affect social conflict (see also Dahrendorf, 1958, 1988; Nyberg, 1981; Apple, 1995, 2004).

Until recently 'the big eight' nations symbolised the global economy and development. A total of 210 economies, including 148 economies with a population of more than one million, existed in the world in 2001 (*World Development Indicators*, 2001). They consisted of many poor nations, with gross national product (GNP) per capita and income as low as $80 in Mozambique in 1996, giving it 130th rank in the global economy. By comparison, Australia was 13th, with its GNP per capita of $20,090 in 1996. In Sierra Leone, a former British colony in Africa, life expectancy was 37, and in Afghanistan adult illiteracy rate was 69% in 1995. It was demonstrated in the latest survey by the World Bank that in 2008 there existed an unequal income distribution between nations, which widened and consolidated economic inequalities globally:

> The richest 20 percent of the world's population spent more than 75 percent of the world total, while the poorest 20 percent spent less than 2 percent. (*World Development Indicators*, 2008)

When discussing the complex, and often taken-for-granted symbiotic relationship between consumer production and consumption in the global economy, we can refer to Marx's famous theory of the fetishism of the commodity. We could also include the 'production fetishism', or the illusion created by 'transnational production loci, which masks translocal capital', and the 'fetishism of the consumer' or the transformation of the consumer's social identity through 'commodity flows' or global consumerism, which was made possible by global advertising. Appadurai (1990) suggests, that through advertising in the media and commodities, the consumer has been *transformed* 'into a sign', both in Baudrillard's sense of a *simulacrum*, and in the sense of 'a mask for the real seat of agency, which is not the consumer but the producer and the many forces that constitute production' (Appadurai, 1990, p. 308). In a post-modern sense, a post-industrial global culture can be considered as a new hybrid of *global* cultural imperialism (see also McLaren and Farahmandpur, 2005).

There is a trend in educational systems around the world to shift the emphasis from the progressive child-centred curriculum to 'economy-centred' vocational training (Walters, 1997, p. 18), as well as forms of governance, requiring 'intense production', and the use of performance indicators (Daun, 2005, pp. 102–104). This was discovered in comparative studies of education in China, Japan, the USA, Great Britain, Germany, Russia, the Scandinavian countries and elsewhere. Although these nations are vastly different in terms of politics, history and culture, and *dominant ideologies*, they are united in their pursuit for international competition in the global market. Hence, curriculum reforms and school policies increasingly address the totalising imperatives of the global economy discourse-competition, productivity and quality.

Schools are only too keen to promote international links and globalisation. The International Baccalaureate, as an alternative to local secondary education certificates, is offered by some elite private schools. In Australia, for example, an article in *The Weekend Australian* newspaper titled 'Baccalaureate: a School Test for Global Villages' linked 'parental concerns about curriculum with the push for Australia to think globally', August 1 & 2, 1992). The head teachers quoted in the article referred to the *transferability* and the international recognition potentially offered by the certificate and its value for students who wish to be geographically mobile (Zajda, 2007, p. 106). This global mobility is increasingly relevant in the global culture. The issue of *globalisation*, or as Giddens defines the term 'the intensification of worldwide social relations which link distant localities in such a way that local happenings are shaped by events occurring many miles away' (Giddens, 1990, p. 64; see also Giddens, 2000), has been taken up in school promotion. A vivid example of this is a photo of a former girl student leaning on a large mounted globe. Her words 'My school put the world within my reach' signify the 'value of taking the world view' and suggest a 'world of career options open to her' (Zajda, 2007, p. 107). She, like other products of the global culture, will presumably become part of a new class of cosmopolitans, or individuals with credentials which consist of 'de-contextualised cultural capital', which allows them to participate in many cultures, particularly 'transnational cultures' related to the international job market.

1.2   Globalisation and Its Politico-Economic Impact on Societies

The above shows that the term 'globalisation' is a complex construct and a convenient euphemism concealing contested meanings, ranging from Wallerstein's (1979, 1980, 1983, 1984, 1989, 1998) politico-economic 'world-systems' model, Giddens' (1990) notion of 'time-space distantiation' highlighting the 'disembeddedness' of social relations with their effective removal from the immediacies of local contexts. These meanings also include Castells' (1989) approaches to globalisation by way of networking, proposing that the power of flows of capital, technology and information, constitutes the fundamental morphology of an emerging 'network society', as well as a neo-liberal and bourgeois hegemony, which legitimates an 'exploitative system' (Petras, 2002). James Petras believes that leftist intellectuals are themselves perpetuating 'bourgeois hegemony' by using terms like 'globalisation' instead of 'imperialism', or 'structural adjustment' instead of 'monopolisation of wealth', while searching for 'bourgeois prestige, recognition, institutional affiliation, and certification'. He labels them provocatively 'cocktail left', who tend to ignore 'the ideological distortions' and inappropriate theoretical frameworks that are taught at prestigious colleges', and who, as they vent their 'inconsequential radical views' climb the academic ladder (*The Chronicle of Higher Education*, p. 3, from http://chronicle.com/chronicle).

From the macro-social perspective it can be argued that in the domains of language, policy, education and national identity, nation-states are likely to lose their power and capacity to affect their future directions, as the struggle for knowledge domination, production and dissemination becomes a new form of cultural domination, and a knowledge-driven social stratification. Globalisation weakens the idea of the nation-state. The global economy, argues Walters (1997), makes it more difficult for the nations affected to carry out social policy 'which is governed by national interests':

> The acceleration in globalization since the mid-1970s has nevertheless caused a loss of effectiveness of national policies in the sphere of welfare. (Walters, 1997, p. 19)

Furthermore, the evolving and constantly changing notions of national identity, language, border politics and citizenship, which are relevant to education policy need to be critiqued within the local–regional–national arena, which is also contested by globalisation. Current education policy research reflects a rapidly changing world, where citizens and consumers are experiencing a growing sense of uncertainty and alienation. Jarvis (2000) comments on the need to "rediscover" one's social identity in active citizenship:

> Democratic processes are being overturned and there is an increasing need to rediscover active citizenship in which men and women can work together for the common good, especially for those who are excluded as a result of the mechanisms of the global culture. (Jarvis, 2000, p. 295)

The above reflects both growing alienation and a Durkheimian sense of anomie in the world 'invaded' by forces of globalisation, cultural imperialism, and global hegemonies that dictate the new economic, political and social regimes of truth. These newly constructed imperatives in educational policy could well operate as global master narratives, playing a hegemonic role within the framework of economic, political and cultural hybrids of globalisation.

The transition from the nation-state and the 'national' economy to a 'liberal competition state' under the sign of ubiquitous globalism questions the relationship between the nation-state, democracy and freedom. The dominant ideologies of economic and political order, and the 'political correctness' in both developed and developing nations are likely to shape the nature and direction of comparative education research in the future. Globalisation, characterised and dictated by the market forces, economic and political determinism, volatile financial markets (e.g. September 2008 collapse of some major financial institutions in the USA), ethnic and racial inequality, instability and conflict, is likely to have a profound impact on education and social change. The dramatic consequences of globalisation on the world's economy are such that they change the meanings of our taken-for-granted assumptions about education, economy and society in the post-industrial age. The very idea of autonomous and independent national economies is becoming obsolete, as demonstrated by economic collapses during the 1990s in Argentina, Japan, South Korea, Indonesia, the Russian Federation and elsewhere, as well as the September 2008 sharemarket collapse of brand-name investment banks and other financial institutions in the USA, and possible future economic collapses elsewhere.

1.3   Globalisation, Marketisation and Quality/ Efficiency-Driven Reforms

Globalisation, marketisation and quality/efficiency-driven reforms around the world since the 1980s have resulted in structural and qualitative changes in education and policy, including an increasing focus on the 'lifelong learning for all', or a 'cradle-to-grave' vision of learning and the 'knowledge economy' in the global culture. Today, economic rationalism and neo-conservative ideology have become a dominant ideology, in which education is seen as a producer of goods and services that foster economic growth. Ideals of human rights, social justice, ethnic tolerance and collectivity are exchanged for key concepts from the discourse of global economy, including productivity, competitiveness, efficiency and maximisation of profit.

Governments, in their quest for excellence, quality and accountability in education, increasingly turn to international and comparative education data analysis. All agree that the major goal of education is to enhance the individual's social and economic prospects. This can only be achieved by providing quality education for *all*. Students' academic achievement is now regularly monitored and measured within the 'internationally agreed framework' of the OECD Programme for International Student Assessment (PISA). This was done in response to the growing demand for international comparisons of educational outcomes (OECD, 2001, 2008, 2006, p. 8). To measure levels of academic performance in the global culture, the OECD, in cooperation with UNESCO, is using *World Education Indicators* (WEI) programme, covering a broad range of comparative indicators, which report on the resource invested in education and their returns to individuals (OECD, 2001, 2006, 2007, p. 6).

Clearly, these new phenomena of globalisation have in different ways affected current developments in education and policy around the word. First, globalisation of policy, trade and finance has some profound implications for education and reform implementation. On the one hand, the periodic economic crises (e.g. the 1980s, September 2008), coupled with the prioritised policies of the IMF and the World Bank (e.g. Structural Adjustment Policies or SAPs), have seriously affected some developing nations and transitional economies in delivering basic education for all. The poor are unable to feed their children, let alone send them to school. This is particularly evident in sub-Saharan Africa, Latin America, Asia, Central Asian Republics (former member states of the USSR), South East Asia and elsewhere, where children, for instance (and girls in particular, as in the case of Afghanistan, Tajikistan and rural India, to name a few), are forced to stay at home, helping and working for their parents, and thus are unable to attend school. Second, the policies of the OECD, UNESCO, the World Trade Organization (WTO) and the General Agreement on Trade and Services (GATS) operate as powerful forces, which, as supranational organisations, shape and influence education and policy around the world. Third, it can be argued that in the domains of language, policy, education and national identity, nation-states are likely to lose their power and capacity to affect their future directions, as the struggle for knowledge domination, production and dissemination becomes a new form of knowledge and technology-driven social stratification.

I would like to stress that one of the central and unresolved problems in the process of globalisation within a modernist context is the unresolved tension, and ambivalence 'between cultural *homogenization* and cultural *heterogenization*' (Appadurai, 1990, p. 295, italics mine), or the ongoing dialectic between globalism and localism, between faith and reason, between tradition and modernity, and between totalitarianism and democracy.

1.4 Evaluating Globalisation and Competing Ideological Interpretations

Apart from the multifaceted nature of globalisation that invites contesting and competing *ideological* interpretations, numerous paradigms and theoretical models have been also used to explain the phenomenon of globalisation. These range from modernity to postmodernity. When, for instance, a writer or a seminar speaker uses the word 'globalisation' in a pedagogical and educational policy context, one wonders what assumptions, be they economic, political, social and ideological, have been taken for granted, and at their face value uncritically, and as a given, and in this case, as a *globocratic* (like technocratic) phenomenon. The politics of globalisation, particularly the hydra of ideologies, which are inscribed in the discourse of globalisation, need to be analysed critically, in order to avoid superficial and one-dimensional interpretation of the term.

If we define the global system (e.g. the global economy, the global markets, the global media, etc.) as referring to economic, political and social connections which cross-cut borders between countries and have a significant impact on 'the fate of those living within each of them' (Giddens, 1996, p. 520), then we are focusing on the culturally and economically interdependent 'global village'. The term 'culture' already includes all other dimensions and artefacts. In an attempt to explain the phenomenon of globalisation Giddens focuses on the 'increasing interdependence of world society' (Giddens, 1996, p. 520), whereas Korsgaard (1997) and others argue that globalisation reflects *social relations* that are also linked to the political, social, cultural and environmental spheres (Korsgaard, 1997, pp. 15–24). The globalisation process is characterised by the acceptance of 'unified global time', the increase in the number of international corporations and institutions, the ever-increasing global forms of communication, the development of global competitions, and, above all, the acceptance of global notions of citizenship, equality, human rights and justice (see also Featherstone, 1990, p. 6).

The above critique of globalisation, policy and education suggests new economic and political dimensions of cultural imperialism. Such hegemonic shifts in ideology and policy are likely to have significant economic and cultural implications for national education systems, reforms and policy implementations.

For instance, in view of GATS constraints, and the continuing domination of multinational educational corporations and organisations in a global marketplace, the 'basis of a national policy for knowledge production may be eroded in a free-market context of a knowledge-driven economy' (Robertson et al., 2002, p. 494). This erosion signifies the corresponding weakening of the traditional role of the university, being the pursuit of knowledge for its own sake, or an intrinsic, rather than extrinsic role:

> [T]he heart of the academic dogma is the pursuit of knowledge for its own sake. Knowledge and the processes of coming to know are good in themselves, and the university, above all institutions, is – or used to be – devoted to them. To investigate, to find out, to organise and contemplate knowledge, these are what the university is about. (Nisbet, 1971, p. vi)

In short, 'forces of globalisation' and have contributed to the ongoing globalisation of schooling and higher education curricula. This has involved together accompanying global standards of excellence, globalisation of academic assessment (OECD, PISA), global academic achievement syndrome (OECD, World Bank), and global academic elitism and league tables, or the positioning of distinction, privilege, excellence and exclusivity. Finally, global marketing of education in terms of excellence and quality in academic achievement and prestige has increased global competition for desirable students.

1.5 Globalisation, Policy and Comparative Research

In his opening chapter, 'Globalisation, Policy and Comparative Research', Joseph Zajda (Australian Catholic University) examines various major discourses of globalisation in comparative education. He argues that globalisation discourses demonstrate that globalisation is a multidimensional theoretical construct, which embraces political, economic, social, cultural and technological dimensions. He also believes there is sufficient evidence to suggest that globalisation and the forces of globalisation have contributed to a new dimension of socio-economic stratification, which will have implications for equity and equality of educational opportunities in decades to come. As Zajda and Gibbs (2008, p. 1) argue elsewhere: 'One of the most important engines of the evolving phenomenon of globalisation has been the rapid development of information and communications technologies' (Zajda and Gibbs, 2008). This has resulted in a new digital divide.

Lynn Davies (University of Birmingham), in 'Comparative Education in an Increasingly Globalised World', argues that in terms of economic growth, comparative education can help to critique the taken-for-granted assumption that neoliberalism, competition and markets are the only way to organise economic, social and educational institutions and life. She suggests that in terms of conflict research, comparative education can demonstrate that formal schooling contributes more to conflict and violence than it does to peace (Davis, 2005, 2008). In terms of education and social justice, Davies believes that there are pedagogical myths to be debunked about education necessarily contributing to tolerance, peace and harmony, to less ethnic division, to greater gender equity or to breaking down social and economic barriers between rich and poor (see also Zajda et al., 2008). The chapter also critiques some conflicting and ambivalent dimensions of globalisation, which include global economic markets, global transnational corporations, global competition and global reinvention of nationalism and identity politics. Similar ideas concerning globalisation and its negative effects are advanced by Patricia Kubow (2008), who believes that globalisation itself is a serious threat to South Africa's nation-building efforts. With its Western-driven and hegemonic dimensions, the economic and cultural forces of globalisation are likely to dislodge local culture and decontextualise pluralist democracy.

Crain Soudien (University of Cape Town), in 'Globalisation and its Malcontents: In Pursuit of the Promise of Education', draws our attention to both oppressive and liberational potential of globalisation and its impact on education and society. He argues that emancipatory pedagogy provides individuals and communities ways of both engaging with, and navigating a way through, the difficulties of globalisation. He examines two dominant critiques of globalisation, namely, 'the delinking' position, or standing 'outside' of globalisation, and the 'subverting' position, or staying 'inside', and reforming the structures from 'within'. He concludes that globalisation discourses and global pedagogies demonstrate what is at stake in the struggle for a different kind of schooling, which is both emancipatory and empowering.

David Wilson (OISE), in 'To Compare Is Human: Comparison as a Research Methodology', examines the phenomenon of comparison as such, and the historical development of comparative research methods. He examines methods used to structure comparative studies over millennia and the contemporary debate between *quantitative* and *qualitative* research methodologies related to comparative education research. He assesses the state of the field by Bereday's 'yardstick', which called for an advanced stage of *juxtaposition*, which, he argues, has not yet been attained.

Adeela Arshad-Ayaz (McGill University), in 'Globalisation and Marginalisation in Higher Education', argues that education cannot escape the process of globalisation, which is based on the principles of neo-liberal economic reform, a process that increases inequalities and marginalises already muted voices. She discusses the tensions between the market orientation of globalisation and the democratic function of higher education, and argues that globalisation can be a useful analytical category to examine contemporary problems of higher education, including such factors as funding, privatisation and academic freedom and autonomy. Similar concerns are raised by Rosamunde Becker (2008) in her 'States, Markets and Higher Education Reform: the Netherlands and England' (see below).

Letitia Williams (University of Maryland, College Park), in 'Globalisation of Education Policy: Its Effects on Developing Countries', suggests that the economic effects of globalisation on education policy are not uniform, and that the ability to resist adverse effects of globalisation is mainly a privilege of developed nations. Developing countries are more dominated and more susceptible to global forces. Like Tikly (2001) she argues about the inability of African states to resist globalisation, which she believes can be extended to developing countries in general.

In 'Globalisation and the Challenges for Education in Greece', Petroula Siminou (Institute of International Education, Stockholm University) explores the impact of globalisation on education in Greece and examines challenges emerging from this process. More specifically, the author examines and discusses the influence of globalisation on educational changes in Greece with reference to recent associated phenomena such as international sports–cultural manifestations, unemployment and the brain drain of scientists. The Europeanisation of Greece is evident in the constant educational changes since its accession to the European Union, especially after the 1997 educational reforms associated with the EU subsidies. Aspects of globalisation are reflected in education reforms and restructuring, attributed to the need for new skills in the 'knowledge society' of a competitive European and global market. It is concluded that in Greece, educational changes are attributed to globalisation, coupled with the Europeanisation process.

In 'Organizational Trends of Chinese Higher Education: The Influence of Strategy and Structure at Ten Case Study Universities', James Jacob (University of California, Los Angeles) offers both an overview of the way Chinese higher education institutions (HEIs) are adapting to dynamic local and global forces, and a critique of a transitional stage of Chinese HEIs and the way the system has established a unique organisational structural trend that combines the traditional divisional form with the more fluid network framework. He argues that the balance between the local and the global is an organisational dialectic that will need to be continually addressed among Chinese HEIs.

The final three chapters are concerned with globalisation, higher education and intellectual property, the global importance of local language contexts in teaching Mathematics (as a case study), and the relationships between the State, the market and higher education in the Netherlands and England. Armando Alcantara (National Autonomous University of Mexico) and Margaret M. Clements (Indiana University) focus on intellectual property and the cultural aspects of a collaboration in the global culture. They evaluate comparisons between Mexico and the USA concerning the complex issues surrounding university involvement in the production of intellectual property in the global culture. Philip C. Clarkson (Australian Catholic University), in 'Globalisation and Mathematics Teaching: The Global Importance of Local Language Contexts', argues that there has been little research on the issue of globalisation in relation to mathematics education. He discusses the global importance of local language contexts in mathematics pedagogy, and reviews the different contexts and situations that arise with language, mathematics and classroom pedagogy in the global culture. Rosamunde Becker explores aspects of higher education reform in the Netherlands and England, with a particular focus on market regulation. She argues that in order to survive in an increasingly competitive environment, higher education institutions are developing closer ties with business and industry, and move towards a 'user-pays' philosophy for most services. According to Becker, higher education institutions in a coordinated market economy tend to be more heavily funded by the government, which still believes to a degree in keeping tuition fees low enough to guarantee student access. She concludes that in the two countries there have not only been different policies of market framing and quality management, but also different resistances against them.

1.6   Conclusion

In evaluating current research on globalisation, policy and comparative research, it needs to be concluded that education and societies are under constant pressure from the forces of globalisation. It is a paradox that cultural globalisation is unleashing forces that tend to standardise lifestyles through commodities, and commodification of the self, information technology and the mass media. Consumer-based social identities are dependent on commodities and commodified forms of selfhood (Langman and Morris, 2002). Yet, at the same time, globalisation creates opportunities for cultural resistance by 'powerfully entrenched local cultures' (Smolicz, 2006, p. 118), where both the 'old' (traditional) and/or indigenous historical minorities, and the 'new' migrant communities, are growing as a result of economic globalisation and job mobility. One could argue that the state's very autonomy and its regulatory role have been eroded by forces of globalisation and decentralisation and privatisation in particular (Zajda, 2004; 2006). However, globalisation, with its seemingly ubiquitous dimension of cosmopolitanism, while it impacts on nation-states, does not necessarily transcend or supersede them (Smith, 1991, p. 175).

In selecting these chapters for inclusion in this volume (see also the previous volumes in *Globalisation, Comparative Education and Policy Research* 12-volume Book Series, Springer, 2008, http://www.springeronline.com/sgw/cda/frontpage), we have deliberately included scholarly research which is representative of diverse people, regions and institutions. Our contributors engaged in an informed critical discourse about the nature of the relationship between globalisation, comparative education discourses, pedagogy and social change globally. The task was not to present a hegemonic monolithic sense about *what is*, but to extend, inform and critique assumptions about the contested discourses of globalisation, comparative education and pedagogy, and their possible implications for global stratification. This can be done in terms of cultural capital, knowledge, ICTs and equality between nation-states in the future (Biraimah, 2005; Zajda, 2005; Clayton, 2006; Zajda et al., 2008a, b). The aim was to evaluate globalisation and education reforms, and their possible implications for a new global stratification along dimensions of knowledge, ideology and power.

Finally, there is no doubt that globalisation and competitive market forces have generated a massive growth in the knowledge industries that are having profound differential effects on educational institutions and nations in general. One of the effects of globalisation is that educational organisations, having modelled their goals and strategies on the entrepreneurial business model, are compelled to embrace the corporate ethos of the efficiency, accountability and profit-driven managerialism. Globalisation, with its evolving and increasingly complex social stratification of nations, technology and education systems, has a potential to generate further polarisation and socio-economic divisions in society that are likely to create discontent and social conflict.

References

Appadurai, A. (1990). Disjuncture and Difference in the Global Cultural Economy. *Theory Culture and Society*, 7, 295–310.

Apple M. (1995). *Education and Power*. New York: Routledge.

Apple, M. (2004). *Ideology and Curriculum* (3rd Edition). New York: Routledge Falmer.

Bahruth, R. (2005). Foreword. In P. McLaren and R. Farahmandpur, *Teaching against Global Capitalism and the New Imperialism*. Lanham: Rowman & Littlefield.

Baudrillard, J. (1986). *Simulacra and Simulation (Simulacres et Simulation)*. Ann Arbor: University of Michigan Press.

Biraimah, B. (2005). Achieving Equitable Outcomes or Reinforcing Social Inequalities? *Educational Practice and Theory*, 27(2), 25–34.

Bourdieu, P. (1986). The Forms of Capital. In J. G. Richardson (Ed.), *Handbook of Theory and Research for the Sociology of Education* (pp. 241–258). New York: Greenwood Press.

Castells, M. (1989). *The Informational City Information Technology, Economic Restructuring, and the Urban-Regional Process*. Oxford: Blackwell.

Chabbott, C. and Elliott, E. (Eds.) (2002). *Understanding Others, Educating Ourselves*. National Research Council. Washington DC: the National Academy Press.

Clayton, T. (2006). *Rethinking Hegemony*. Melbourne: James Nicholas Publishers.

Dahrendorf, R. (1959). *Class and Class Conflict in Industrial Society*. Stanford: Stanford University Press.

Dahrendorf, R. (1988). *The Modern Social Conflict*. Berkeley/Los Angeles: University of California Press.

Daun, H. (2005). Globalisation and the Governance of National Education Systems. In J. Zajda (Ed.), *International Handbook of Globalisation and Education Policy Research* (pp. 93–107). Dordrecht: Springer.

Delanty, G. (2001). Challenging Knowledge: the university in the knowledge society. Buckingham: Open University Press.

Giddens, A. (1990). *The Consequences of Modernity*. Stanford: Stanford University Press.

Giddens, A. (2000). *Runaway World: How Globalization is Reshaping our Lives*. New York: Routledge.

Kubow, P. (2008). Democracy, Identity, and Citizenship Education in South Africa: Defining a Nation in a Post Colonial and Global Era Patricia. In J. Zajda, H. Daun and L. Saha (Eds.), *Nation-Building, Identity and Citizenship Education: Cross-Cultural Perspectives*. Dordrecht: Springer.

Langman, L. and Morris, D. (2002). The Net and the Self: Cyberactive versus Ludic Identities. *Information, Technology, Education and Society*, 3(1&2), 23–46.

Marx, K. and Engels, F. (1848/1969). *Selected Works* (pp. 98–137). Volume One. Moscow: Progress Publishers.

McLaren, P. and Farahmandpur, R. (2005). *Theaching Against Global Capitalism and the New Imperialism*. Lanham: Rowman & Littlefield.

Nisbet, R. (1971). *The Degradation of the Academic Dogma*. London: Heinemann.

Nyberg, D. (1981). *Power over Power*. Ithaca/London: Cornell University Press.

OECD, (2001). *Education at a Glance. OECD Indicators*. Paris: OECD.

OECD, (2006). *Education Policy Analysis*: Focus on Higher Education. Paris: OECD.

OECD, (2007). *Education at a Glance. OECD Indicators*. Paris: OECD.

Petras, J. (2002). *The Chronicle of Higher Education*, p. 3, from http://chronicle.com/chronicle).

Sabour, M. (2005). The impact of globalisation on the mission of the university. In J. Zajda (Ed.), *The International Handbook of Globalisation and Education Policy Research* (pp. 189–205). Dordrecht: Springer.

Saha, L. (2005). Cultural and Social Capital in Global Perspective. In J. Zajda (Ed.), *International Handbook of Globalisation and Education Policy Research* (pp. 745–755). Dordrecht: Springer.

Secombe, M. and Zajda, J. (1999) (Eds.). *Education and Culture*. Melbourne: James Nicholas Publishers.

Smith, A. (1991). *National Identity*. London: Penguin Books.

Smolicz, J. (2006). Globalism, Nation-State and Local Cultures. In J. Zajda (Ed.), *Society and the Environment* (pp. 115–133). Melbourne: James Nicholas Publishers.

Stromquist, N. and Monkman, K. (2000) (Eds.) *Globalization and Education: Integration and Contestation Across Cultures*. New York: Rowmand & Littlefield.

Wallerstein, I. (1979). *The Capitalist World Economy*. Cambridge: Cambridge University Press.

Wallerstein, I. (1980). *The Modern World-System II: Mercantilism and the Consolidation of the European World Economy, 1600–1750*. New York: Academic Press.

Wallerstein, I. (1983). The three instances of hegemony in the history of the capitalist world-economy. *International Journal of Comparative Sociology*, 24, 100–108.

Wallerstein, I. (1984). *The politics of the world-economy: The states, the movements, and the civilizations*. Cambridge: Cambridge University Press.

Wallerstein, I. (1989). *The Modern World-System III: The Second Great Expansion of the Capitalist World-Economy*. New York: Academic Press.

Wallerstein, I. (1998). The rise and future demise of world-systems analysis. *Review*, 21, 103–112.

Waters, M. (1995). *Globalization*. London: Routledge.

World Development Indicators (2001). Washington, DC.: World Bank.

World Development Indicators (2008). Washington, DC.: World Bank.

Zajda, J. (2002). Education and Policy: Changing Paradigms and Issues. *International Review of Education*, 48(1&2), 67–91.

Zajda, J (2004). Decentralisation and Privatisation in Education—The Role of the State. *International Review of Education*, 50(3&4), 199–221.

Zajda, J. (2005). Globalisation, Education and Policy: Changing Paradigms. In J. Zajda (Ed.), *International Handbook on Globalisation, Education and Policy Research* (pp. 1–2). Dordrecht: Springer.

Zajda, J. Majhanovich, S. and Rust, V. (2006) (Eds.) *Education and Social Justice*. Dordrecht: Springer.

Zajda, J. (2006). *Decentralisation and Privatisation in Education*. Dordrecht: Springer.

Zajda, J. and Zajda, R. (2007). Marketing School quality and Effectiveness in a Global Culture. In J. Zajda, (Ed.). *Education and Society* (3rd edition) (pp. 97–108). Melbourne: James Nicholas Publishers.

Zajda, J., Davies, L. and Majhanovich, S. (2008). (Eds.). *Comparative and Global Pedagogies: Equity, Access and Democracy in Education*. Dordrecht: Springer.

Zajda, J. Biraimah, B. and Gaudelli, W. (2008). (Eds.). *Education and Social Inequality in the Global Culture*. Dordrecht: Springer.

Zajda, J. and Gibbs, D. (2008). Comparative Information Technology: Languages, Societies and the Internet. In Zajda, J. and Gibbs, D. (Eds.), *Comparative Information Technology: Languages, Societies and the Internet* (pp. 1–12). Dordrecht: Springer.

Chapter 2
Comparative Education in an Increasingly Globalised World

Lynn Davies

2.1 Introduction

In this chapter I would like to argue that comparative education in an increasingly globalised world has possibly never had such an important function than in this age of different globalisations. This chapter identifies two seemingly contradictory but eventually complementary roles for comparative education: firstly destroying myths and fighting simplistic or dangerous universalisms; and secondly extracting signs of hope which show how education – both within and regardless of culture – could contribute to a better world.

After defining what is meant by 'increasingly globalised', I prioritise three crucial types of relationships for scrutiny: the relations between education and economic growth or sustainability; between education and conflict; and between education and social justice. In each of these there are myths to be debunked and serious challenges to contemporary orthodoxy. The first task, to question generalisability, is not just saying that context matters – comparative education has always said this – but that spurious or romanicised claims for the benefits of education wherever found need to be challenged. Why doesn't education always promote economic growth? Why has education failed to prevent war? Why has education failed to promote social justice, whether across the globe or within a nation? In contemporary terms, how has globalisation further influenced these tenuous relationships? In my current work I use complexity theory to understand social phenomena, and would argue not only that trends are non-linear, but linked in highly complex ways (Davis, 2004, 2005, 2008). Small turbulences can make an impact. This is both depressing and exhilarating for educationists and for commentators on education.

Much writing is demonstrating the effect of globalisation *on* education – but it is less easy to look at the reverse, the effect of education on new and old global

L. Davies
School of Education, University of Birmingham, Birmingham, B15 2TT, UK
e-mail: L.Davis@bham.ac.uk

J. Zajda and V. Rust (eds.), *Globalisation, Policy and Comparative Research*,
DOI: 10.1007/978-1-4020-9547-4_2, © Springer Science + Bussiness Media B.V. 2009

realities. Academic writing about globalisation is often written by 'us' about 'them': Luke and Luke (2000) argue instead for a cultural politics of the local, to show the complexity of the multidirectional traffic of 'flows'. We should avoid the globalisation of the discourses of globalisation.....Or the irony of a sign that was spotted at the World Trade Conference: 'Join The World Wide Movement against globalisation'. I would agree with Anthony Sweeting (1999) therefore, that comparative education can usefully be done in one country, using comparisons of time and history. I like his claim that 'non-linear, almost random, outcomes of educational practices seem almost daily occurrences' (Sweeting, , p. 278).

The second of the important tasks is not just to reveal realities, but to build a profile of how comparative education has actually influenced policy. Reynolds and Farrell (1996) have had this influence in UK, it seems, through their highlighting of the supposedly superior performance of Pacific Rim countries in international surveys of educational achievement. Their study of Taiwan however significantly omitted reference to the largely homogenous nature of Taiwanese society, the common language and the role of the family in supporting education, as Watson (1999) pointed out. But we should be looking at not just the bilateral transferability of policy and practice (the 'what works' syndrome), but broader political questions about what education is for, and whom it benefits. Broadfoot (1999, p. 25) defines comparative education as 'centred on the more general project of explaining and exploring the nature of social life and conceptualising this in a way that provides both insight and guidance concerning how learning may best be facilitated and provided for in a particular time and place'. But does this go far enough? Learning about what? Learning to do what? Do we want to facilitate learning in a terrorist training camp? Who decides what constitutes useful learning? Are these decisions becoming globalised?

2.2   Types of Globalisation

We need a brief review of the different types of globalisations that are occurring. The usual types cited are:

- The spread of common world culture, or the homogenisation of culture and even language
- The ascendancy of a particular form of capitalism, championed in North America and parts of western Europe as the attainment of ideals of free trade liberalism
- Knowledge transfer and increased ICT
- More personal mobility
- The spread of democracy, human rights and environmental concerns

Jones (2000) in fact distinguishes globalisation and internationalism – the former the emergence of a world economy and the latter the development of global solidarity through democracy and peace. But typical concerns have been expressed, such as:

> …..strong Americanization which threatens to overwhelm all forms of identity that are not minor variations of global themes (Marginson & Mollis, quoted in Stromquist, 2002).

> Globalisation and dehumanisation are two faces of today's capitalism, which is more productive than ever (Monge, 1998).

> … the euphoric marketing rhetoric of the global village, an incredible place where tribespeople in remotest rain forests tap away on laptop computers, Sicilian grandmothers conduct E-business and 'global teens' share, to borrow a phrase from a Levi's Web site, 'a world-wide style culture'. Everyone from Coke to Macdonald's to Motorola has tailored their marketing strategy around this post-national vision, but it is IBM's long-running 'solutions for a Small Planet' campaign that most eloquently capture the equalizing promise of the logo-linked globe. (Klein, 2001, p. xvii)

> Definitions of globalisation have varied from one author to another. Some have described it as a process, while others a condition, a system, a force or an age…Economic globalisation is a historical process, the result of human innovation and technological progress. It refers to the increasing integration of economies around the world, particularly through trade and financial flows. The term sometimes also refers to the movement of people (labour) and knowledge (technology) across international borders…Globalisation has come to be associated with exacerbating social inequality, exemplified in the proverbial race to the bottom. (Zajda et al., 2008, pp. xvii–xix)

Globalisation is seen as not decentred, but as having definite points of origin – initiated by advanced industrial countries (Stromquist, 2002). Today's globalisation seeks the union of science and industry; the apoliticisation of unions; the organisational fragmentation in the production process; the globalisation of cultural, information and business networks; and the unification and standardisation of pleasure and consumption.

Globalisation is felt in education largely through the uncontested adoption of initiatives in developed countries along such lines as decentralisation, privatisation, the assessment of student performance and the development of tighter connections between education and the business sector (Stromquist, 2002). We should also not ignore the power of regional blocs: NAFTA left out explicit references to education, which meant it could be defined as 'any other tradeable good or service'. Schugurensky and Davidson-Harden (2003) examine the educational dimension of the General Agreement on Trade and Services (GATS) of the World Trade Organisation (WTO), which is a strategy to transform education into a tradeable commodity, with a free educational market. They argue that Latin American countries can be adversely affected by this in terms of their sovereignty on cultural policy, the quality and accessibility of their public education systems, the training of scientists and researchers oriented towards national development, and the contribution of their education systems to the common good and to equalisation (see also Schugurensky & Davidson-Harden, 2005).

The EU on the other hand sought the creation of a European identity, operated through benchmarks and performance indicators as a means of bringing together different national goals and aspirations for education in a more coherent way at European level. APEC wanted Information Technology as a 'core competency in

education', with lots of networking, and links between education and business
(Dale & Robertson, 2002). Burbules and Torres (2000) also identify three trends in
educational writing and analysis:

- Policy buzz words such as privatisation, choice, decentralisation; research agendas
  based on rational organisations and management theories
- The role of national and international organisations in education, including
  teacher unions, parent organisations and social movements
- New scholarship on race, class, gender and the state in education – multiculturalism,
  identity, critical race theory, feminism, postcolonialism, diasporic communities
  and new social movements

It is worth at this point examining the ideology of markets, as one of Burbules and
Torres' 'policy buzz words'. The market does not have behaviour attributes and
does not make political commands. It is institutions and decision-makers who are
market makers and not merely market takers. Petras (1999) includes individual
level actors in this – such as professionals and consultants, who shape the economic
programmes of developing countries to maximise the global interests of multinationals and receive lucrative fees.

There are some interesting studies which demonstrate the dodgy effects of
economic rationalist approaches, as those prototyped in UK and then exported.
Luke and Luke (2000) examined the Rajabhat Institutes in Thailand which have
been enabled to set their own fee levels and establish businesses. So-called reforms
meant funding cuts of 25–30%. The tendency across Asia has been for central
governments to attempt to emulate Western systems' responses to decreased funding, to new curriculum demands, and to changing student populations. As consultants,
Luke and Luke had difficulties in contributing to such educational change, as they
knew that (1) such reforms had not generated the kinds of productive results promised
in Australian contexts and (2) local and regional impacts of globalisation are best
addressed by locally driven curriculum development, innovation and institutional
reorganisation. Is this an irony, that globalisation is best dealt with locally? When
you translate the steering from a distance of Thatcherite Britain (quality assurance,
performance indicators, corporate systems of accountability) it tends to get hybrid-
ised and indigenised – and not work.

James Porter (1999) comments on the way that a deeply flawed market ideology
has been uncritically accepted in education, as elsewhere. He examines the key ideas
of market economics and 'competitive equilibrium' and the assumptions behind
them – that all human conduct can be related to a ranking of economic choices and
weighing up costs and benefits, and that the various transactions are optimal and
balance out for everybody. It is an astonishing influence. But the theory does not
explain actual behaviour of real people in uncertain conditions and without the information and computational capacity to make 'rational' choices. Again, this is a linear
approach applied to complex, non-linear situations and actors. He quotes Ormerod:

> The promotion of the concept that the untrammelled, self sufficient, competitive individual will
> maximise human welfare, damages deeply the possibility of ever creating a truly affluent cohe-
> sive society in which everyone can participate. (1994, p. 211)

Yet free market economics provide a powerful legitimising framework for the continued existence of privileges, or unrestricted individualism. Industries and services have to be privatised and the market deregulated, with the state not interfering. This means a reduction in state services and in democratic concerns about welfare, justice and security. But is democracy also being spread globally, to counter such tendencies? Perhaps only particular versions are. It has been argued by western lenders (and endorsed through various conditionalities) that democracy is needed as the life support of globalisation, as a free market requires massive information to be circulated and unfettered initiative to materialise. Yet we see that international agreements can be achieved without necessarily engaging in respect for human rights or equity. Only a particular and narrow version of democracy is adhered to. It was interesting that an adman for *Our Master's Voice* said in 1934:

> A democratic system of education....is one of the surest ways of creating and greatly extending markets for goods of all kinds and especially those goods in which fashion may play a part.

Let us turn then to the evidence base for the positioning of education in all these movements – or stagnations.

2.3 Education and Economic Growth or Sustainability

In spite of frequent questioning, the link between education and economic growth remains one of the underpinnings of education and aid policy internationally. So what is new with the advent of globalisation in terms of policy analysis? Not a lot, it would seem. The World Bank clings to a human capital theory approach. This is not surprising – it is a bank, and banks survive on investment. How we ever let a bank decide educational policy will be a puzzle for educational anthropologists of the future. It is the equivalent of NatWest deciding the curriculum, or the Hong Kong and Shanghai Bank telling us the length of the school holidays. The Bank's *Education Sector Strategy* reveals no new thinking, no mention of education as a basic human right.

Crossley and Watson (2003) point out that the World Bank largely ignores educational research undertaken by non-Bank staff; it is still predicated on human capital theory which sees education solely as a means of economic expansion; it ignores local analyses and knowledge; and ignores the interdependency of education, health, rural development, the environment and economy (and I would add the political and stability context); and the fact that education cannot be treated as a sector isolated from society as a whole. It ignores the causes of global poverty and ignores the academic critiques of the Bank's role in actually extending poverty.

Economists such as Stiglitz (2002) make a fundamental criticism of IMF/ Washington consensus approach – it does not acknowledge that development requires a transformation of society. Uganda understood this in its elimination of school fees, against the advice of economists. Stiglitz criticises the new 'trickle-down plus' – the new version of the idea that growth will automatically help the poor, and structural adjustment will in the end somehow benefit education. In Latin America, growth has *not* been accompanied by a reduction in inequality, and in some cases poverty has increased. In fact it was land reform which preceded several of the most successful instances of development, such as in Korea and Taiwan – not on the Bank's agenda. Access to education *may* alleviate poverty, but we need the studies which tell us in conjunction with what other factors. Similarly, we need to know about the role of education in conjunction with what might protect against economic collapse, as can be seen in parts of Russia or Eastern Europe.

Stiglitz' argument is that government can play an essential role in mitigating market failures, slumps, recessions or depressions that lead to massive unemployment. In USA and East Asia, governments have done this reasonably well. They have provided a high quality education to all and furnished much of the infrastructure – the legal system, regulation of financial sector, safety nets for the poor. He admits the debates – how concerned should we be about the environment if we can have higher GDP, how concerned should we be about the poor, how concerned should we be about democracy and rights – but he argues for government intervention to compensate for market failures. The Asia financial crisis was brought on by a lack of adequate regulation of the financial sector, and Mafia capitalism in Russia by a failure to enforce the basics of law and order.

But all the linkages can be ignored in educational research. As James Porter argues, there has been unprecedented attention to education. Since success in the global economy has come to be seen as vital for national survival, the economic purposes of the school have come to dominate the political agenda. Education reform is seen as crucial to economic progress. The World Bank insists that aid and loans are tied to the use of education for competitive participation in the global economy.

> As signs of global alienation and insecurity multiply, the growing pressure to control and limit education threatens to rob societies of a vital resource for sustaining democracy and for developing the creative and varied responses that will be called for in an increasingly uncertain future. (Porter, 1999, p. 7)

Yet Jurgen Schriewer (1999) in his chapter 'Coping with complexity in comparative methodology' examines the findings produced by international comparative education research on the connections between education, modernisation and development. What links there are between education, economic growth and employment, for example, are highly complex, indirect and certainly not linear, nor do they produce the same effects in different societies. 'Instead they are as a rule not very pronounced, only partially effective, basically dysfunctional, or simply counter-productive' (p. 40). This relates to the old and obvious point about education being simultaneously a producer of social mobility and an agent for reproduction of the social order. Hence the failure of grand theory, of the grand narratives. Comparative education research tends to produce falsifications; but does anyone listen? Complexity is not popular. Simple solutions and lines of rationality are preferred.

One example of complexity is the impact of vocational education. Schriewer (1999) reports on the increasingly extensive body of comparative research dealing with the interconnections between vocational education and training, qualification structures of the labour force, and work organisation in large-scale manufacturing units. He writes:

> Such studies have taught us to thoroughly distrust the thesis – posited by industrial sociology and the economics of education – stating that qualification-requirements and educational structures are largely determined by technological change, economic development, and the exigencies of a universal rationality purportedly intrinsic to industrialism. (Schriewer, 1999, p. 39)

Instead, the studies have insistently shown us that vocational education and training is to a large extent determined by social and cultural factors. Strangely, educational systems appear relatively autonomous in this regard.

A recent study reported on the ID21 website (2004) asked whether investing in education reduced poverty, and provided evidence from Ghana, Uganda and Malawi. Some curious facts emerged:

1. Almost universally, education is found to lift people out of poverty
2. But when compared with other forms of investment, the returns on investing in education are on average lower
3. Thirdly, the returns in terms of increment in income are much higher for those with higher levels of education
4. Macro evidence does not support the view that investing in education has an impact on underlying productivity growth
5. The returns to education are lower in the rural than in the urban sectors – with the result that one of the effects of education is to encourage a shift to the urban sector
6. Greater electoral competition leads to greater expenditure on primary education

Walter McMahon (a World Bank economist) in some ways tackles complexity in distinguishing direct impact and indirect impact, as education operates through other variables such as the wider diffusion of technology, as well as private and social goods (2003). One additional year's schooling is associated with about 30% higher GDP per capita – but which came first? Education affects health – but is this indirect in terms of being able to buy better health care? There is nonetheless the claim that education contributes to a larger and stronger middle class, to civic institutions and hence to greater political stability. In spite of a lot of overstatements of governments to UNESCO and other holders of statistics about enrolment rates and their country's investment in education, 'pure externalities' include lower population growth, strengthening the rule of law, more community involvement and greater dissemination of knowledge. Interestingly, education is associated with less water pollution but more air pollution. However, what McMahon does not acknowledge is that all these positive effects are *internal* to a country, and ignore the effects on *other* countries of one country's growth or political stability. An 'educated' population does not necessarily challenge aggression towards another country, nor the source of their own economic prosperity through certain sorts of trade or imperialism. This is a vital omission in cost–benefit analysis of educational effects – and one where comparative education could have a crucial role.

There are interesting points too about democracy. Essentially all countries in the world with per capita incomes below about $600 are authoritarian. The one exception is India. Military expenditure has a negative relation to democratisation. It could be that democracies spend less on the military and more on education. McMahon suggests that rising income contributes to democratisation. Some regimes hang on longer with large military expenditure (North Korea?) but the eventual change over to fragile democracies from military dictatorships has been remarkable in the last 40 years in Latin America. The impact of secondary education is largest when there is a control for larger military expenditure, since the latter appears to contribute to rural poverty.

The problem with the above analysis is however those effects are *very* long term. Human rights increase by 8% in Africa on the average *40 years* after education investment is increased by 2% of GDP. Most impacts are long delayed. This is a problem for comparative education.

2.4   Academic Achievement and School Effectiveness

But let me look at some of the relatively quick falsifications that we can engage in. Comparative education can destroy the myths about the relationship between test scores and economic growth, for example. In US and elsewhere, there is a culture of blaming schools for contributing to a less competitive global economy, less productivity, losing jobs to other nations. The false connection between test scores and economic growth then leads to calls for privatisation, a longer school year, more testing and more technical skills (Cuban, 2001). Porter (1999, p. 82) quotes what Charles Handy has described as the 'MacNamara fallacy':

> The first step is to measure what can be easily measured….the second step is to disregard that which can't be easily measured or to give it an arbitrary quantitative value. This is artificial and misleading. The third step is to presume that what can't be measured isn't really important. This is blindness. The fourth step is to say that what can't be easily measured doesn't exist. This is suicide.

He also quotes me and others in the anti-school effectiveness movement, arguing fiercely how school effectiveness research dehumanises pupils – and teachers – by reducing them to 'intake variables'; there is a cultural deficit, a stereotypical approach which appears to sympathise with the 'underachieving school' for the 'poor quality' of its intake. Alexander (2000) did challenge some of the simplistic 'border crossings' of school effectiveness studies (arguing for Pacific Rim practices of desks in rows for example) by his contextualised and cultural studies of five countries. But much more is needed – particularly about comparing educational goals, not just processes. Carney (2003) argues that global managerialist tendencies in education such as those represented by school effectiveness research actually *distort* the possibilities for schooling to contribute to societal development:

> Evidence suggests that a focus on the technology of school effectiveness encourages narrow definitions of good schools and, in the process, enables powerful groups to unduly distort education for their own purposes. (Carney, 2003, p. 91)

The role of formal schooling in the production of broadly educated, competent and democratic citizens is thus compromised. The Basic and Primary Education project in Nepal shifted from inputs such as curriculum and books to 'processes and outcomes', especially managerial efficiency and improved exam pass rates. This particular approach to 'quality' created space for donor-funded achievement studies that shifted attention away from the Government's overall policy objective of democratic and inclusive schools, towards the technical and managerial inputs required to enhance pupils' cognitive development. And this adds to inequality, to new forms of privilege.

In research terms, Carney asks for breaking of the tight coupling between educational research, policy and international comparison that characterises the SE tradition, and to engage in forms of inquiry that locate issues of social inequality within considerations about schooling. We need *critical ethnography* – how stakeholders interpret various acts that constitute formal schooling. Are families actually colluding with policy makers about credentialism? Perhaps only the middle class are; for rural people, it is a respite from oppression – or they are unaware of the benefits it might bestow.

2.4.1 Testing and Assessment in Education

This leads to the problem of testing and assessment. Business norms are being applied to education through:

(a) 'Efficiency' in the transmission of knowledge (coverage, impact at lowest cost)
(b) 'Equity' in the shape of high standards for all, the competitive 'world-class schools' syndrome

Another irony is that globalisation and the spread of neoliberalism seem to lead to a greater emphasis on *national* level measures of economic growth and sustainability, instead of regional ones. But this blames failure on the schools themselves. Accountability is operationalised on testing, and is standardised, particularly in 'high stakes' testing (those used for major decisions such as graduation). But even economists admit that current achievement tests are not strong predictors of economic success. Ninety-six percent of variance in earnings in the USA are not explained; only 6% of supervisory ratings correlate with education (Levin, 2000). Now, this isn't comparative education: but why is this not replicated in lots of countries? In the developing world, testing has also become a major practice. Before 1991, only four countries in Latin America (Chile, Colombia, Mexico and Costa Rica) practiced nationwide evaluations of basic education. By 2000, almost every country in the region was attempting to test student performance. In the adoption of the testing policy, UNESCO has played a role, so has IDB, World Bank, the Organisation of Iberoamerican States in Spain and USAID – all investing in assessment.

As can be seen, testing is not about diagnosis, but about *competition*: as Stromquist points out, public/state schools are seen as essentially deficient because they operate under monopolistic conditions (with no incentives to perform well). Therefore there are prevailing voices for privatisation and/or competition to increase standards, improve efficiency and reduce costs, together with the ideologies of parental choice and vouchers. We need to look at the implications of the state shifting from a provider of goods and services (schools, teaching, credentials) to a buyer of goods and services produced in the private sector. This means comparative analysis. Our own European study of pupil democracy found countries like Sweden and Denmark (economically successful, very peaceful, with a low income distribution gap) had features such as children not starting school until 7 years old, bans on competitive publication of results and encouragement of democratic participation in schools, with pupil consultation and real choice on curriculum (Davies and Kirkpatrick, 2000). Yet the UK does not look at this. Instead, it wants testing and national curriculum brought down to nursery level, i.e. longer surveillance and narrower curriculum, and even more emphasis on standards and measurable results.

2.4.2 Literacy and Global Standards

Crossley and Watson (2003) examine the perennial debate over the relationship between literacy and economic growth. The UNESCO major report *World Illiteracy* in 19572000 had three principles: that the best way of eradicating illiteracy is through primary education (a view which continues right up to Jomtien); that the higher the levels of literacy, the greater the level of economic development; and the greater the diffusion of literacy throughout the society, the greater the likelihood of industrial and economic development. At the time, there was little research evidence to support these assertions, but they have never really been challenged. These powerful messages, coming from such an august international body, profoundly shaped the thinking and actions of many governments. There has been much analysis subsequently about thresholds (that you need 40% to begin economic development) – but in fact India only claims to have reached 50% during the last few years of the 1990s. There is no agreed definition of literacy; and the global agendas have ignored the many different 'literacies' in a culture, and how language is used culturally in daily discourse in different settings. Has the emphasis on supporting international languages hampered educational development, destroyed local textbook production in indigenous languages and weakened local cultures? (see Brock-Utne's, scathing critique of 'recolonizing the African mind'). Similarly, Anne Hickling-Hudson (2002) launches in, criticising the World Bank's assertion, that advances in literacy may have done more to improve the human condition than any other public policy as dangerous and simplistic:

> The way literacy has been used to solidify the social hierarchy, empower elites and ensure that people lower in the hierarchy accept the values, norms and beliefs of the elites, even when it is not in their best interests to do so. (Hickling-Hudson, 2002, p. 568)

Computer literacy should be not just about technical skills, but social/political analysis. The spread of communications (and increased mobility of peoples, and tourism) has also led to increase or globalisation of prostitution, child abuse or pornography (see Stromquist, 2002). The internet gives crime an extraordinary facility to engage in drugs and the arms trade, and to launder earnings through immediate investment in stocks. Learners need a critical analysis of this. I would argue not against literacy, but for different definitions of functional literacy which, simultaneously with basic decoding, begins from political literacy and health literacy. It is an irony that while economic models of schooling predominate, few schools would have economics education as the top compulsory subject.

2.5   Education and Conflict

I turn now to the second main area of impact of education. Despite the lack of a demonstrable cause and effect relationship between poverty and conflict, nonetheless out of the 34 countries furthest away from the international development goals, some 20 are in conflict or emerging from conflict. Conflict has a self-sustaining nature: the state has often lost the monopoly over decision-making and there is large scale availability of arms. The diminishing economic power of the nation state links to consolidation of mass unemployment in most developing countries and the rapid growth of similar conditions of enforced idleness in the industrial nations. Hence the regional trading blocs and a growth in protectionism; and, more sinister, an extension of military power. Where is education in this? While increased access to schooling can be shown to help political stability within a country, comparative analysis can question the myth that universal formal education also automatically creates international harmony.

In my recent book *Conflict and Education: Complexity and Chaos* (2004) I have examined the complex relationship between education and conflict (see also Davies, 2005, 2008). There is the more obvious effect of conflict on education itself – disruption, loss of physical and human resources, hardening of attitudes to the enemy, to the outgroup; but there is the perhaps less obvious impact of education on conflict. I firstly trace three sorts of contributions to the roots of conflict: social inequality or polarisation; dominant forms of competitive and macho masculinity and militarism; and hardening of ethnic or religious identifications rather than the encouragement of hybrid identities. Globalisation brings permeable borders, increasing diversity and awareness of diversity, but sometimes leading to a hardening of identities, as I saw in Bosnia and Kosovo. I then look at specific actions in schools: curriculum, physical and symbolic violence and forms of retribution, cadet forces and individualistic competition rather than collaboration – not helped by the league tables and the competition between schools and between countries mentioned earlier. I do look also at the possibilities for citizenship education – which is in itself increasingly globalised, as are concerns about 'global citizenship', where we have a research project and examine various sorts of peace education. But schools are far geared to preparation for war than preparation for peace. As Porter (1999) so eloquently comments:

> The efforts to ameliorate the steadily growing divisions in the world are marginal and are failing to stem the dangerous and ultimately disastrous descent into a world that is so split that many will assume that violence is the only available way to seize wealth or power…it is the

pervading hopelessness and cynicism of the economically abandoned that may prove to be
the most dangerous and ultimately destructive element…support for terrorism has its roots in
the desperation of the reviled, the poor, the ignored and those that have no opportunity for a
decent life or for influence or power in the existing situation. (Porter, 1999, p. 39)

It is interesting that an economist like Amyrta Sen, talking at the Commonwealth
Ministers conference in 2003, homed in on issues such as fundamentalist religious
schools and the 'narrowing of horizons, especially of children, that illiberal and
intolerant education can produce'. To define people just in terms of religion-based
classification of civilisations can itself contribute to political insecurity and cultural
segregation and stratification – people belonging to 'the Muslim world' or 'the
Western world' or 'the Hindu world'. He (and I) believe the UK government made
a mistake in expanding rather than reducing faith-based state schools, 'especially
when the new religious schools leave children very little opportunity to cultivate
reasoned choice and decide how the various components of their identities…should
receive attention'. In the schooling of children, we have to make sure that we do not
have smallness (not greatness) thrust upon the young.

A major concern in post-conflict societies is not to reproduce the education
structure that may have contributed to the conflict in the first place (Davies, 2004,
2005, 2008). We do have a lot to learn from some of the humanitarian education
post-conflict, as it is based on principles of building confidence, giving skills, building
collaboration, providing dialogue and encounters, and rebuilding political and public
cultures. It is not about testing.

How does the globalisation of culture fit into this? It has been argued that
MacDonalds did play a role in apartheid South Africa, where they provided the
only place where different races could share public space on an equal basis. Yet the
sponsorship issue paints a different picture. After a few years of Pepsi-sponsored
papal visits, or Nike after school basketball programmes, everything from small
community events to large religious gatherings are believed to 'need a sponsor' to
get off the ground. 'We become collectively convinced not that corporations are
hitching a ride on our cultural and communal activities, but that creativity and
congregation would be impossible without their generosity' (Klein, 2002, p. 35).
UNESCO selling out to Daimler-Chrysler in their Mondialogo project is another
example. Brand managers are envisioning themselves as sensitive culture makers,
and culture makers are adopting the hard-nosed business tactics of brand builders.

So now there is the tension in culture between the ways that globalisation brings
more standardisation and cultural homogeneity while also more fragmentation
through the rise of locally oriented movements. Barber characterised this dichotomy
in the title of his book *Jihad vs McWorld*. Burbules and Torres (2000) argue a third
possibility of cultural homogeneity and cultural heterogeneity appearing simultaneously – the 'glocal'. But how you research this I don't know. We do now have a
pressure towards global citizenship, with exhortations to feel part of the greater
collectivity. Yet local community is the real cultural space, rather than virtual ones
created by electronic communication and networks of flows of goods and services.
Here, identity politics coheres around memories of conflict, failure, domination or
nostalgia for a past age.

Citizenship education studies are seeing an increased number of comparative studies. But these tend to compare the curriculum or evaluation processes of various countries (Torney-Purta et al., 1999; Kerr, 2000) and demonstrate how citizenship education is gaining prominence worldwide; but it is difficult to go deep into either the social and political context or into social impact. Torres (1998) argues that one of the problems of citizenship education research is contextualisation, and that in order to grasp the tension inherent in citizenship education between inclusion and exclusion, we need to look at the specific relationship between the state, citizenship as political identity and citizenship education. We need to draw on theories of democracy and multiculturalism, especially in diverse societies. One interesting IIEP study for example demonstrated that a code of conduct for teachers diminishes unethical behaviour. Teachers are the highest cause of spending in post-conflict societies, therefore it is worthwhile to implement a form of social control which is effective, such as a code of conduct (UNESCO, 2004).

I would say that two positive aspects of globalisation have been an agreement on human rights and the spread of democracy, however interpreted. There has been a spread of environmental concerns. As Sen has pointed out, no democratic country has ever had a famine. In terms of enabling schools to counter negative conflict, my book develops the idea of 'interruptive democracy', which uses the ideas of dialogue, encounter and challenge in order to promote positive conflict in educational institutions.

2.6   Education and Social Justice

In my third area for exploration, we are talking about two sorts of inequality: between countries and within countries. Jared Diamond (1998) argues for history as a science (his book is about why some nations or regions have the 'cargo'; and why some groupings formed political systems while others remained in bands or tribes). He has interesting hypotheses which bring together ecological or geographical determinism with historical accidents and individuals – hence the resonances with complexity theory. There are historical 'wild cards' or 'frozen accidents' – the QWERTY keyboard, or the 24-hour clock and the 60-minute hour based on the Sumerian counting system of 12 rather than the Meso American 20. Why did complex Andean civilisations not develop writing? How did the abundance of homophones in Chinese language, and therefore the need for thousands of signs in traditional Chinese, influence literacy? Was there anything in India's environment predisposing to rigid socio-economic castes, with grave consequences for the development of technology? Why was a proselytising religion (Christianity and Islam) a driving force for colonization and conquest among Europeans and West Asians but not among Chinese?

We do know that the world is becoming more unequal. The top 20% is a more exclusive First World Club in 1999 than it had been in 1965. Income differentials are widening, according to UNDP. In 1913, individuals in rich countries earned 11 times those in poor countries. In 1960 this was 30 to 1, in 1997, 60 to 1 and in 1997 it was 71 to 1. Immense wealth is being created, accompanied by an increasing share of workers without contracts. Nike opposed the work of the Worker Rights Consortium, cutting funds to the universities which supported this.

> On the whole, TNCs aim at making the world less risky and expensive for commercial investment rather than seeking democratic or humanitarian objectives. As a whole, TNCs have been gaining so many rights before the state that they are becoming the new citizens of the 21st century. (Stromquist, 2001, p. 99)

There are 'manic renditions of globalisation' (Klein, 2002) but 'we in the west have been catching glimpses of another kind of global village, where the economic divide is widening and cultural choices narrowing'. MNCs, far from levelling the playing field with jobs and technology for all, are in the process of mining the planet's poorest black country for unimaginable profits.

> This is the village where Bill Gates lives, amassing a fortune of $55 billion while a third of his workforce is classified as temporary workers, and where competitors are either incorporated into the Microsoft monolith or made obsolete by the latest feat in software bundling....On the outskirts of Manila...I met a 17 year old girl who assembles CD-ROM drives for IBM. I told her I was impressed that someone so young could do such high-tech work. 'We make computers', she told me, 'but we don't know how to operate computers'. Ours, it would seem, is not such a small place after all.

MNCs and global companies are of course claiming that they are great equalizers, promoters of diversity in images or race; and that they brought down the Berlin wall single-handed. Murdoch told the world that satellite broadcasting made it possible for information-hungry residents of many closed societies to bypass state-controlled television. Crossley and Watson (2003) point out that often under government auspices, the wealthy classes and TNCs are seeking to expand private schooling in the belief that this will open up opportunities at a global or international level. The curriculum emphasises international languages, computer skills, information sciences, mathematics, analytical skills, etc. Yet this all leads to greater divisiveness.

If we now look *within* countries, Crossley and Watson argue that the signing of the UN Declaration of Human Rights in 1948 which identified education as a basic human right has had a 'profound influence on the shape of educational development throughout the world', and can be seen to have influenced many of the newly independent countries' constitutions and plans. I am less sure. How much is lip-service, and how much acknowledgement of human capital theory's promise of economic growth and modernisation? Diamond for example asks, why do people support kleptocrats? (leaders who keep most of the 'tribute' for self-enrichment). He cites a mix of four devices that kleptocrats use:

(a) Disarm the populace and arm the elite
(b) Make the masses happy by redistributing taxes/tribute
(c) Promote happiness by maintaining public order and curbing violence
(d) Construct an ideology or religion justifying kleptocracy

Bands and tribes did have supernatural beliefs, but these did not necessarily justify centralised authority or transfer of wealth or maintain peace between unrelated individuals. When supernatural beliefs gained these functions and became institutionalised, they were transformed into what we call a religion. Chiefs would assert divinity, or a line to God, claiming to intercede; or would support a separate group of kleptocrats (priests) whose function is to provide ideological support for the chief. Hence the collecting of tributes for the construction of temples, the centres of official religion. Religion solves the problem of how unrelated individuals are to live together without killing each other – by providing them with a bond not based on kinship. It gives people a motive for sacrificing lives on behalf of others. At the cost of a few society members who die in battle as soldiers, the whole society becomes much more effective at conquering other societies or resisting attacks.

Has globalisation in terms of markets become the new religion? Or in fact education? Why is there not more resistance to elites? Is this the legitimisation function of education, now an international phenomenon? Knowledge is perhaps the new religion – and has doubtful effects on equity. Concentration on knowledge is depoliticising, drawing attention away from conflict and controversy in economic, political and social terms (Stromquist, 2002). A key feature of 'knowledge management systems' (KMS) is to reduce large amounts of text to short summaries. Policy makers apparently have not the time or inclination to read long studies. The APQC and other consulting firms promoting KMS argue that there exist such things as 'just-in-time knowledge' and 'just enough knowledge'. Are information and knowledge conflated? The World Bank calls knowledge gaps 'information problems', that is, they are nothing to do with critical or humanistic evaluation. Even social or political conflicts of interest about dams or forestry projects are reinterpreted by the World Bank as 'lack of complete knowledge'.

2.6.1 Quality Higher Education for All

In spite of the rhetoric about higher education for all, between 40% and 50% of jobs in the new economy will not require university training, but some type of work-based technical or trade credentials. There is a decrease in critical thinking in universities. Stromquist (2002) argues that with the growth of English comes the growth of Anglo-American functionalist modes of thought, framing of problems as technical rather than political. Ironically, universities do become more global in terms of students and marketing interests, but at the same time, their concerns focus on material interests. There is a decline of sociology (especially in teacher education), although I think not in Japan or Europe so much. Stromquist cites (anecdotal) evidence of the impact of competition among students, indicating that young university students in US tend to be more individualistic and less likely to be concerned with social issues. We see the emergence of the 'organization kid' who rarely questions authority and who readily accepts his or her elite position as part of the natural order of life. In UK, we have the insistence on 'evidence-based research', concerned with developing and disseminating 'good practice', that is focussing on micro-task efficiency and disembedded from wider contexts (Tikly & Crossley, 2001).

The question of knowledge of context is an interesting one. Many (all?) comparative educators argue strongly for contextualised data: Broadfoot (1999) comments on the OECD indicators of provision, process, effectiveness and so on as enormously complex, yet its model is almost entirely detached from culture. We need more than just economic cultures, but cultures of conflict, peace and stability; and more importantly, what these schools are trying to **do** with their process variables. What is the effect of EFA targets, except to drive poor district education officers to falsify their figures in order to gain brownie points, or conversely for governments to play down their figures in order to get more aid?

Higher education is increasingly dependent on business for survival, creating a new business norm in universities (Mok, 2000). In Singapore, serving industry is not enough: 'universities must take on the new role of fostering an entrepreneurial climate'. Multinationals themselves are establishing private universities, or their own programmes within universities, particularly in instrumental fields – commerce, business or engineering. Which way will comparative and international education go? This is of greater importance with the flow of students. Both altruistic and self-serving reasons will operate. There is a perceived need to foster social justice and sustainable development; yet also the need to become more competitive, so universities must learn what others are doing. Stromquist argues that a desirable direction for comparative and international education is to deal with problems that go beyond the nation-state, such as AIDS, ethnic conflict, gender asymmetries and environmental impact. I would add – or preface – conflict and peace to this list. Williams (2000) notes that the concept of 'global security' is being redefined from ensuring safety through military means alone to understanding threats to human well-being from development, environment and violence.

2.7   Gender, Sexual Identities and Education in the Global Culture

Gender justice is a significant example or indicator of social justice in general. Here we have a mixed bag of change – there are more opportunities, but a weakening of the welfare responsibilities of the state and a depoliticization of culture. We still need to examine the rhetoric from international agencies about the importance of education for women – for the next generation, the family, the community – that is, not as a human right, only as a sort of multiplier effect. Evidence would in fact seem to show an even stronger human capital investment than for men. So economic and neoliberal perspectives prevail – that the integration of workers of both sexes into the international capitalist economy will eliminate poverty, as poverty is simply under-utilised labour. Poverty has the problem for capitalists of evincing low consumption levels. Over-consumption by others, and offering low wages, is of course not seen as a cause of poverty.

Global magazines are promoting apolitical and sexual identities, 'delusory subjectivity' in young women, causing them to think of themselves as already free and equal to men. They do not see the need for political activity. But studies of successful businesswomen in Asia find global modern discourses coexisting with traditional practices, such as deference to males or acceptance of domestic tasks. In certain Asian countries (Singapore, Malaysia, Hong Kong) women constitute the majority of university graduates, so one would expect to find a large number in high positions, yet this is not the case (Luke, 2000). There are gains in school enrolment (access but not success). The use of quotas is very iffy, and needs much comparative research. Perhaps quotas work best in public office rather than in school or higher education enrolment. But if you still need quotas in work, then how effective is education? There has been a growth of women's studies and gender studies – but for how long?

Ilon (quoted in Crossley & Watson, 2003) claims that globalisation is having a new impact on female enrolments in schools over and above any local cultural constraints. She demonstrates that as TNCs seek cheap labour, the demand for a modestly educated workforce rises. Since female labour is usually cheaper, more compliant and more willing to accept lower wages, the demand for more female education will also rise. Is this a mixed blessing? Resistance comes from transnational feminist alliances – although there are continued debates about the presentation of Third World women, and of clashes of interests between rich and poor women. One interesting new global economic coalition is the Women's Global Alliance for Development Alternatives, setting an agenda for global economic issues from the perspective of the women's movement.

2.8 What is the Resistance to Globalisation and Monopolisation of Minds?

This brings us on to resistance in general – an important study for comparativists. Schools are not only concerned with preparing students as producers, but also as consumers, shaping consumer attitudes and practices, encouraged by the corporate sponsorship of educational institutions and products (Burbules & Torres, 2000). Writers such as Klein (2001) and others are concerned with the unquestioning acceptance of advertising in schools. Increasing technology means poorer state schools turning to the private sector to finance technology purchases. Channel One in USA and Youth News Network in Canada are the best-known examples of in-school branding. Channel One gives current affairs programmes in exchange for 2 min advertising a day. Teachers get the A/V equipment but are unable to adjust the volume during the broadcast, so that there is no 'audience erosion'. There is an in-school computer network 'ZapMe' which monitors students' paths as they surf the Net, providing valuable market research. It sets little research tasks for them, so students are asked to create a new advertising campaign. The Cover Concepts company sells slick ads that wrap around books to 30,000 US schools, where teachers use them instead of plastic as protective jackets. Pepsi brands entire schools: 'Pepsi – Official Soft Drink of Cayuga secondary school' is giant sign beside the road.

Klein (2001) asks 'where is the opposition?' Unlike the furores over sex education or prayer in schools, the move to allow advertising in education did not take the form of one sweeping decision, but rather thousands of little ones. Parents and teachers could not see a problem – they thought kids were bombarded by advertising anyway, and it was more important to get funding. Is there no unbranded space left? China of course is a huge market, with parents and grandparents spending on 'the little Emperor'. Klein talks ruefully of her feminist days – was this focussing on the wrong thing? On representation, rather than ownership? 'We were too busy analysing the pictures being projected on the wall to notice that the wall itself had been sold.'(Klein, 2001, p. 124). Yet there is evidence of resistance to current market ideology. Proposition 38 in California focused on school vouchers and would have permitted parents to send their children to private or religious schools by granting them vouchers for $4,000 a year. This raised £31 million from supporters but generated $32 from oppositional forces and did not pass (Stromquist, 2002).

The major adversaries of globalisation in the poor countries have been the peasant movements, particularly in Latin America, parts of Asia, and to a lesser degree, Africa. Most opposition by NGOs has been to defend existing rights and interests threatened by global ruling classes (Petras, 1999). Klein believes that as more people discover the brand-name secrets of the global logo web, their outrage will fuel the next big political movement, a vast wave of opposition squarely targeting transnational companies, particularly those with very high name-brand recognition.

Campus politics are broadening therefore from race, discrimination etc. to corporate power, labour rights etc. (although she acknowledges this is not the majority of the demographic group). Klein asks what the forces are that push more people to be enraged at MNCs, particularly young people?

September 11 and the attack on US capitalism did make people talk about the global haves and have-nots. But free trade is being rebranded as the war on terrorism. To criticise the US government is to be on the side of the terrorists. A strong public realm is needed, otherwise Osama fills the gaps – the extreme Islamic seminaries in Pakistan that indoctrinated so many Taliban leaders thrive precisely because they fill a huge social welfare gap. The country spends 90% of its budget on military and on debt, but a pittance on education: the madrassas offer not just education but food and shelter. Post September 11, clinging to *laissez faire* free-market solutions, despite overwhelming evidence of their failings, looks a lot like blind faith, and as irrational as any belief system clung to by religious leaders fighting a suicidal jihad.

The rise of popular education movements in protest against globalisation is therefore significant. The 1995 International Forum on Globalisation held the first Global Teach-in in New York, bringing together leading scientists, activists and researchers to examine the impact of the single, unfettered world market on democracy, human rights, labour and the environment. There were seminars on NAFTA, APEC, IMF, World Bank and structural adjustment. The internet is a decisive weapon here. Protesters managed to get the Multilateral Agreement on Investment taken off the OECD agenda in 1998. An interesting comparative study would be the educational background of those who join resistance and protest movements. The emerging anti-globalisation movement is a diverse set of groups, with different levels of sophistication – unions, intellectuals, anarchists, cyber-activitists as well as small farmers and indigenous groups. Lipman 2000 (quoted in Stromquist, 2002) reports resistance against neo-liberal policies at all levels of educational system in her study of Chicago. NGOs do press for greater support of education; but are not really 'oppositional':

> Most resistance is not aimed at changes in the educational arena, despite the enormous consequences that formal education has on a society's ideology and the social stratification being created by globalisation. There is a desperate need for more critical examination by educators of current developments related to globalisation. (Stromquist, 2002, p. 173).

2.9 Agenda for Comparative Education Research

From all the above, I suggest a menu of ten priorities for comparative education research in this era of globalisation:

1. Stopping doing achievement studies based on maths achievement and conventional literacy indicators, i.e. the old school effectiveness indicators, and starting doing more comparative studies based on indicators of 'achievement' in political literacy, agency, democracy, peace education and human rights education.
2. Case studies of where education actually does contribute to a decrease in poverty (Durston argued this for Malawi, but what actually happened was that some of the money went to the community to build the schools, therefore helping the local economy; but it was not the actual education that contributed).
3. A new agenda for what in education contributes to economic and political sustainability *across* nations (including environmental sustainability).
4. Studies of where education has actually contributed to a general health improvement (not just that bought by bigger earnings) and a decline in the spread of HIV/AIDS.
5. Studies of the impact of citizenship education or other types of education that have contributed to peace or conflict. (Question one for exam paper: critically evaluate either the American/UK invasion of Iraq *or* World Bank education strategy, *or* both). This might include critical media education and consumer education.
6. The study of resistances to the negative impact of globalisation, markets, aA advertising, branding in education.
7. The study of resistance to testing and assessment regimes.
8. The study of resistances to gendered practices and disparities, and of the impact of alliances.

And for comparative education impact itself:

9. The collection of examples about where comparative education research has actually made a difference to policy, how and for how long.
10. The collection of successful strategies for influence on major agencies and opinion formers – UNESCO, World Bank etc., where they have taken account of comparative education research done outside their remit.

2.10   Conclusion

As demonstrated above, in terms of economic growth, comparative education can help mount the challenge to the taken-for-granted assumption that neo-liberalism, competition and markets are the only way to organise economic and hence educational life. In terms of conflict, comparative education can reveal the sad reality that formal schooling contributes more to conflict and violence than it does to peace (Davis, 2005, 2008). In terms of social justice, there are myths to be debunked about education necessarily contributing to less ethnic division, to greater gender equity or to breaking down divides between rich and poor (Zajdaet al., 2008). The chapter critiques three types of highly linked relationships against some conflicting features of contemporary globalisation. These include markets, transnational corporations, competition, revivals of nationalism and identity politics, knowledge management control and life-style consumerism/culture, but also – more positively – the spread of democracy and human rights and the growth of international protest.

References

Alexander, R. (2000). *Culture and Pedagogy: International Comparisons in Primary Education.* Oxford: Blackwell.

Appleton, S., et al. (2004). Does investing in education reduce poverty? Evidence from Ghana, Uganda and South Africa. (accessible at: http://www.id21.org/education/s5bft1g1.html).

Bray, M. (1996). *Counting the Full Cost: Parental and Community Financing of Education in East Asia.* Washington DC: World Bank.

Brock-Utne, B. (2000). Whose Education for All?The Recolonization of the African Mind. New York: Falmer Press.

Broadfoot, P. (1999). Not so much a context, more a way of life: comparative education in the 1990s. In R. Alexander, P. Broadfoot, & D. Phillips (Eds.), Learning from Comparing: New Directions in Comparative Educational Research. Oxford: Symposium.

Burbules, N. & Torres, C. (Eds.) (2000). *Globalisation and Education: Critical Perspectives.* London: Routledge.

Carney, S. (2003). Globalisation, Neo-liberalism and the limitations of school effectiveness research in developing countries: the case of Nepal'. *Globalisation, Societies and Education, 1,* 1, 2003.

Crossley, M. & Watson, K. (2003). *Comparative and International Research in Education. London: RoutledgeFalmer.*

Cuban, L. (2001). 'The Convenient Fallacy of Education'. San Jose Mercury News January 7, pp1C, 3C.

Dale, R. & Robertson, S. (2002). The Varying Effects of Regional Organisations as Subjects of Globalisation of Education. *Comparative Education Review,* 46(1), 10–36.

Davies, L. (1996). The management and mismanagement of school effectiveness. In J. Turner (Ed.), The State and the School. London: Falmer.

Davies, L. (2004). Conflict and Education: Complexity and Chaos. London: RoutledgeFalmer.

Davies, L. (2005). The Edge of Chaos: Explorations in Education and Conflict. In J. Zajda, (Ed.), The International Handbook of Globalisation and Education Policy Research (pp. 631–642). Dordrecht: Springer.

Davies, L. (2008). Interruptive Democracy in Education. In J. Zajda, L. Davies, & S. Majhanovich (Eds.), Comparative and Global Pedagogies: Equity, Access and Democracy in Education (pp. 15–31). Dordrecht: Springer.

Davies, L. & Kirkpatrick, G. (2000). *The Euridem Project: A Review of Pupil Democracy in Europe*. London: Children's Rights Alliance.

Diamond, J. (1998). *Guns, Germs and Steel: A Short History of Everybody for the last 13,000 Years*. London: Vintage.

Fox, R. (1995). Manipulated Kids: Teens tell how ads influence them. Educational Leadership, September, 77.

Harber, C. & Davies, L. (1998/2002). *School Management and Effectiveness in Developing Countries*. London: Cassell.

Hickling-Hudson, A. (2002). Re-visioning from the inside: getting under the skin of the World Bank's Education Sector Strategy. International Journal of Educational Development, 22(6).

Held, D., McGrew, A., Goldblatt, D., & Perraton, J. (1999). *Global Transformations, Politics, Economics and Culture*. Cambridge: Polity Press.

Jones, P. (2000). Globalisation and Internationalism: Democratic Prospects for World Education. In N. Stromquist & K. Monkman (Eds.), *Globalisation and Education: Integration and Contestation across Cultures*. Boulder: Rowman & Littlefield.

Kerr, D. (2000). Citizenship Education: An International comparison. In D. Lawton, J. Cairns, & R. Gardner (Eds.), *Education for Citizenship*. London: Continuum.

Klein, N. (2001). No Logo. London: Flamingo.

Levin, H. (2000). Economic Consequences of High-Stakes Testing. Paper presented at AERA New Orleans, April 24–28.

Luke, A. & Luke, C. (2000). A situated perspective on cultural globalisation. In N. Burbules & C. Torres (Eds.), *Globalisation and Education: Critical Perspectives*. London: Routledge.

Luke, C. (2000). Globalisation and Women in Higher Education Management in South East Asia. Paper presented at AREA, New Orleans, April 24–28.

McMahon, W. (2003). Shorter and Longer Impacts of Education on Development Goals. Paper presented at OXCON conference, September.

Mok, K. (2000). Impact of Globalisation: A Study of Quality Assurance Systems in Higher Education in Hong Kong and Singapore. *Comparative Education Review*, 44(20), 148–74.

Monge, P. (1998). 1998 ICA Presidential Address: Communication Structures and Processes in Globalization. *Journal of Communication*, Volume 48 (accessible at: www.questia.com/PM. qst?a=o&se=gglsc&d=96424779).

Ormerod, P. (1994). The Death of Economics. London: Faber & Faber.

Petras, J. (1999). *Globalization: A Critical Analysis. Journal of Contemporary Asia*, 29(1), 3–37.

Porter, J. (1999). Reschooling and the Global Future. Oxford: Symposium.

Reynolds, D. & Farrell, S. (1996). Worlds Apart? A Review of International Surveys of Educational Achievement including England. London: HMSO.

Schriewer, J. (1999). *Coping with Complexity in Comparative Methodology: issues of social causation and processes of macro-historical globalisation*. In R. Alexander, P. Broadfoot, & D. Phillips (Eds.), Learning from Comparing: New Directions in Comparative Educational Research. Oxford: Symposium.

Schugurensky, D. & Davidson-Harden, A. (2003). From Cordoba to Washington: WTO/GATS and Latin American Education. *Globalisation, Societies and Education*, 1(3), 321–357.

Schugurensky, D. & Davidson-Harden, A. (2005). The GATS and Trade in Educational Services: Issues for Canada in the Pan-American Context. In Zajda, J. (2005) (Ed.). *International Handbook on Globalisation, Education and Policy Policy Research* (pp. 457–479). Dordrecht: Springer.

Stiglitz, J. (2002). *Globalization and its Discontents*. London: Penguin.

Stromquist, N. (2002). *Education in a Globalised World*. Oxford: Rowman & Littlefield.

Sweeting, A. (1999). *Doing Comparative Historical Educational Research: problems and issues from and about Hong Kong. Compare*, 29(3), 269–286.

Tikly, L. & Crossley, M. (2001). Teaching Comparative and International Education: Separation, Integration or Transformation? *Comparative Education Review*, 45(4), 561–80.

Torney-Purta, J., Schwill, J., & Amadeo, J. (1999). Civic Education across Countries: Twenty-four national case studies from the IEA civic education project. Amsterdam: IEA.

Torres, C. (1998). *Democracy, Education and Multiculturalism: Dilemmas of citizenship in a global world*. Lanham: Rowman & Littlefield.

Watson, K. (1999). *Comparative Educational Research: the need for reconceptualisation and fresh insights. Compare*, 29(30), 233–248.

Williams, C. (2000). Education and Human Survival: the Relevance of the Global Security Framework for International Education. *International Review of Education*, 46(3&4), 183–203.

Zajda, J. (Ed.) (2005). *The International Handbook of Globalisation and Education Policy Research*. Dordrecht: Springer.

Zajda, J., Davies, L., & Majhanovich, S. (Eds.) (2008). *Comparative and Global Pedagogies: Equity, Access and Democracy in Education*. Dordrecht: Springer.

Zajda, J., Biraimah, B., & Gaudelli, W. (Eds.) (2008). *Education and Social Inequality in the Global Culture*. Dordrecht: Springer.

Chapter 3
Globalisation and Its Malcontents: In Pursuit of the Promise of Education

Crain Soudien

3.1 Globalisation Discourses: Introduction

The nature of the debate around globalisation has in recent years taken on a much more sophisticated tone. In its infancy the debate was essentially engaged as a conflict between starry-eyed romantics seeing the dawn of a glorious age of anxiety-free social development, on the one hand, and dour pessimists who saw only the advance of a new rapacious imperialism on the other. We are now witnessing, in a range of fields of knowledge, much finer analyses of the significance of globalisation (see Dimmock and Walker, 2000; Soudien, 2005; Zajda, 2005; Zajda et al., 2008; Amin 2001; Chatterjee 1997, 1998; Archibugi 2003; McGrew 1992; Meyer & Ramirez 1999; Nandy 2002; Rust 2000; Touraine 2000; Zajda 2008b) that are alert to both its oppressive and liberatory potential. Similar possibilities, it is argued here, exist for discussions of globalisation and education. In terms of this, the purpose of this chapter is to make the argument that education – as a space in which processes of self-reflection are possible – provides individuals and communities ways of both engaging with and navigating a way through the difficulties of globalisation. The argument is made in two stages. First it explores two dominant critiques of globalisation, namely, 'the delinking' position, that is, standing 'outside' of globalisation and its educational cultures and apparatuses, and the 'subverting' position, which essentially calls for staying 'inside' and reforming the structures from 'within'. Secondly, it attempts to show that an alternative position to globalisation already exists in the practice of individuals and groups around the world that is premised on a critical synthesis of the insights of the 'delinkers' and the 'subverters', and that this practice, in its recognition of the limitations of language to deal with the complexity of social identity and social issues, encapsulates

C. Soudien
Professor, Room 5.03.3, School of Education
University of Cape Town
Private Bag, Rondebosch 7701, Republic of South Africa
e-mail: Crain. Soudien@uct. ac. za

J. Zajda and V. Rust (eds.), *Globalisation, Policy and Comparative Research,*
DOI: 10.1007/978-1-4020-9547-4_3, © Springer Science + Bussiness Media B.V. 2009

the 'promise' of education. Central to the synthesis is what 'delinkers' and 'sub-verters' bring to a new and alternative pedagogical practice. 'Delinkers' bring a scepticism rooted in alternative understandings and knowledges of the world, while 'subverters' bring a conviction that dominant forms of social practice, and their pedagogical forms, can be overhauled. It is in the interaction of these two core elements of the delinking and subverting perspectives that new pedagogical practices can be envisaged that have the potential to resist those forms of globalisation that are only about standardisation, homogenisation and universalisation. How this interaction is managed as an educational act is the primary objective of the chapter.

Towards developing a working understanding of globalisation, a useful stepping-off point for this discussion is to signal the difference between the approach taken here and that of Joseph Stiglitz's (2002) similarly styled *Globalization and its Discontents*. In introducing his work and setting up his argument, Stiglitz asks why, when it has brought so much good, globalisation has become so controversial. He explains that those who vilify globalisation too often overlook its benefits (Stiglitz, 2002, p. 5). In this respect his argument anticipates the hermeneutic suggested by Held and McGrew (1991), partly on which this essay itself will draw. The significance of this line of thinking is its refusal to make globalisation a totalising discourse which ineluctably pulls the world in a single direction only and so conditions and determines the fate of all who come within its compass. This position is suggested by some of globalisation's malcontents, such as Amin (1997), Wallerstein (1983), and even, in some ways, in the much more nuanced work of Castells (1996).

Making the point, however, that globalisation has its 'pros' and its 'cons', and to argue, as Stiglitz's (2002) does, that blame can be apportioned to both the developed and the developing world for the problems that surround globalisation (such as either erecting trade barriers or not taking advantage of economic opportunity) is understanding the concept almost entirely in economic terms. While the centrality of the economy is accepted, there is a need to remain aware also of the cultural and social messages and frameworks that operate within it. Market forces – such as investment and entrepreneurial decisions and money flows – function, it is argued in this essay, within the constraints of the new information order. Central to these constraints is the re-articulation of the local and the global into a new relationship defined by the disembedding and re-embedding of actual time and space. This argument – time-space compression – is well-known now.

It is in the context of these globalised developments that the question of education has assumed much greater significance (see Giddens, 1991, p. 4). It has become much more difficult for both individuals and groups to make their way through the intricate puzzles of modern life with its competing claims on their loyalties, particularly with respect to events that are culturally and socially distant and remote from them. The moral, political and ideological marshland in which many in the world find themselves today is marked by, on the one hand, the oppositional logics of 'blood' – nation, culture, race or their supposed common history – and on the other, morality and justice – that which they think is *right*. Where, in the last hundred years or so, a concern with these issues may have been the preserve of the intellectual classes (see Sanders, 2002, p. 4), talking of the intellectual after the Dreyfus affair in France in 1898), or as Giddens (1991, p. 86) says, the 'affluent strata', it is increasingly so that they have become general social questions. People are having to think their way through profoundly difficult moral questions which, just a generation ago, assertions of their identity as Africans, Indians, Europeans, Chinese and so on – thinking with their 'skins' – would have resolved.

What, however, can education offer? What promise does education have for developing the ability of young men and women to think their way through these challenges? What *kind* of education will equip people, wherever they might find themselves, to deal with these issues? The answers to these questions are many and varied and are being approached differently by different groups of thinkers in different places and different social, cultural and intellectual spaces. The approach taken in this essay, following Held, McGrew, Goldblatt and Perraton's work (1999), which essentially seeks to understand globalisation, is to argue for a way engaging globalisation. Such a way, it is suggested, is by bringing the scepticism of what is called the 'outsiders' into a conversation with the optimism of those referred to as the 'subverters'.

Who the 'outsiders' and the 'subverters' are and what they stand for is the focus of the next section of the discussion. In sketching the outlines of 'outsider' and 'insider' positions it is recognised that what is being attempted here is not a full and final account of the complexity and contradictions of the postures taken by the respective theorists and the schools of thought to which they belong, but a recognition of those elements of their arguments that speak to the condition of globalisation and its derivative meanings such as universalism, standardisation, homogeneity and uniformity. In accepting that the theorists referred to are not all *strictly* addressing the question of globalisation, it is important, nonetheless, to recognise how much they are talking about the *substance* of globalisation, such as universalisation, homogenisation, integration, uniformity and standardisation. It is this that makes the 'delinkers' and the 'subverters' necessary objects of scrutiny. They help to inform what a politics of engagement with globalisation might look like.

3.2 The 'Outsiders' Within Globalisation Discourses

The work of the 'outsiders' is varied and complex, and ranges from culturalist perspectives to political economy approaches. The immediate focus of their analysis is hegemony – that of 'white' masculinity, as in the case of Lorde and Hooks, and of imperialism, as defined by Amin. They all, however, operate with a globalising conception of hegemony. While they do not consistently use the term globalisation, it is the assimilative and controlling characteristics of globalisation that they seek to reject. Occupying a significant position in the grouping of 'outsiders' are black feminists such as Audre Lorde and Bell Hooks. Seeking to end the burden the 'oppressed' carry of 'teach(ing) the oppressors their mistakes…', because 'there is a constant drain of energy which might be better used in redefining ourselves and devising realistic scenarios for altering the past and constructing the future', their imperative is to look towards what one might call a new cultural imagination. In 'Zami: A New Spelling of my Name' Lorde (1982) writes in what Lewis-Qualls (2000) calls 'a self-defined, self-created genre, emphasizing the multiplicity inherent in her knowledges/experiences, and refocusing, reshaping, and challenging traditional epistemic concepts'. Lorde is unhappy with the way in which traditional, 'objective' knowledge obscures biases, excludes viewpoints, and creates absences. To deal with these difficulties she argues for a way of understanding that embodies complexity, multiplicity, contradiction and change. She insists upon being fully herself, making the comment (see also Schneir, 1994, p. 169):

> It's easier to deal with a poet, certainly a black woman poet…when you categorize her, narrow her so she can fulfil your expectations… I am not one piece of myself. I cannot be simply a Black person, and not be a woman, too, nor can I be a woman without being a lesbian.

Based on a body of writing that has become iconic, particularly but not only in Feminist circles, epitomised by the line 'the Master's tools will never dismantle the Master's House' (Hooks, 1994, p. 96), Lorde's work has provided malcontents with interesting critiques of dominance. Significant, however, about this posture is its unspecified level of traction for developing an approach to education. While there is much commentary on the state of education and knowledge about self and 'other', how one begins the process of developing alternative forms of education is unstated. There is, in the end, contrary to what Lewis-Qualls (2000) argues, epistemic critique, but no epistemic break. Left behind, however, and this is possibly Lorde's great contribution, is 'the realisation that knowledge, reality, and categories can be questioned but there is a gap language cannot express—she lacks a language to communicate what she knows about multiplicity' (Lewis-Qualls, 2000). It is this notion of the gap that will be returned to later.

Briefly, Bell Hooks (1997), also writing from a black Feminist perspective, finds herself taking a similar position to that of Lorde. She explains:

> It was disturbing to me that intellectual radicals who speak about transforming society, ending the domination of race, sex, class, cannot break with behaviour patterns that reinforce and perpetuate domination, or *continue to use as their sole reference point* (her emphasis) how we might be or are perceived by those, whether or not we gain their acceptance and approval. (Hooks, 1997, p. 129).

Evident in these arguments is an intense desire to 'escape' from the embrace of the globalised mainstream but little elaboration of *how* this might be done. Similar difficulties are evident in particular versions of Afrocentric, indigenous-knowledge and other religiously centred philosophies. An example of the first is what Adams (1997) describes as the self-determination school of thought in the United States. This view emerged out of frustration with the mainstream establishment and sought to separate black people physically and socially from the majority society and to create an independent 'environment such as a state in which blacks can implement their survival strategies' (Adams, 1997, p. 441). This frustration is also seen in the work of

Aboriginal educators in Australia. Brady (1997, p. 421), for example, says that her ancestors had in place systems of education and social cohesion 'which sustained them for 40,000 years... I believe that it is time we empowered ourselves to take back our education so that we can move with pride into the next 40,000 years'. Another example is found on the African continent itself and is promoted by Banteyerga (1994) who argued that '"modern education" is not satisfactorily addressing the problems of Africa to meet the needs and aspirations of the African people.' Supporting Banteyerga, Nekhwevha (1999) makes the point that Africans need to move away from 'their long academic sojourn' in the Western imagination and should struggle 'to make African culture and experience the primary constituent of our world view'. For Nekhwevha this approach would be integrative, empowering and liberatory. Central to all these critiques is a very specific construction of the forms of hegemony against which they are fighting as predatory globalising movements which have no respect for local culture and local knowledges. In globalising the local, they instantly relegate non-Western forms of understanding and knowledge to the margin.

What these challenges lose sight of, however, without wishing to diminish the importance of their critique of mainstream education, is how Africanisation or indigenous knowledge systems are *already* engaged in articulation with the global world. It is true, as Seepe (1998) and others imply that intense processes of cultural alienation have taken place within African communities. What, however, an appeal for reviving a *displaced* Africa underestimates is the extent to which African people continue to hold on to their own cultural practices, are taking these practices into modernity – the dominance of institutions and practices defined by ideas of rationality such as humanism, individualism, democracy, parliament, systems of justice, education and so on that emerged in Europe in the eighteenth century – and, are, in the process, redefining modernity, and, indeed, their own traditions. Globalisation in this situation is not a one-way process. A similar point could be made about particular forms of Islamic education, and indeed other religiously based forms of education that seek to extract young people from the commitments and entanglements they already have with the existing modern global world in which they find themselves. Unilateral declarations of epistemic independence are hardly possible and any attempt to police the boundaries of the knowledge-making experience and to insist on 'protecting' it from globalisation is, as Sardar (2004) argues in his *Desperately Seeking Paradise,* fraught with the dangers of authoritarianism and intolerance.

A somewhat different line of thought is evident in the political economy debate where scholars such as Samir Amin have sought to argue for the delinking of the local sphere from that of the global. Amin (1997) argues that the global hierarchy has used what he calls five monopolies to assert its precedence politically and economically. These are technological monopoly, financial control of worldwide markets, monopolistic access to the planet's natural resources, media and communication monopolies and monopolies over weapons of mass destruction. He argues that the national level, 'which in my view remains the crucial link simply because of the existence of a political organization that we will be experiencing for a long time yet, what I call delinking ... is unavoidable' (Amin, 1997, p. 40). Instead of the world generating solutions to problems through international agencies, nations and regions must define their own solutions. The point of the argument is not to avoid globalisation but to redefine the terms of its development. Solutions in this view emerge from the bottom up. Nations work with their own political dynamics and then take these to the next regional level from which positions are then distilled in the global arena.

Evident in the variety of these outsider approaches to globalisation, it needs to be said, is a serious and sustained critique of the hierarchalising and ranking, the dividing, and indeed the 'othering' proclivities of globalisation. The problems pointed to are deep but, unfortunately, the critiques fail to engage the complexity of dominance. On the one hand, the culturalist approach of the black feminists and the religious and political fundamentalists fails to provide the basis for a real alternative episteme (to retain the claims made with respect to Lorde). While the literary outsiders and some of the African-centred philosophies, such as Lorde's, assert combativeness, the effect of their work is to produce a set of dispositions and behaviours which, in the end, turns them into critical 'insiders'. The delinking economists, in their turn, fail to engage with the politics of the conjuncture and to deal with the existing conditions of connectedness. Absent in their approach is a recognition of the already-connected world and the ways in which institutions and individuals are, everywhere, articulated into processes and protocols which cannot, it is suggested, be conducted on the basis of a national or regional independence. While authors such as Amin (1997) say that the economic and cultural system they are arguing for is not an autarchy, it is exactly the autarchic principle of economic autonomy, and by implication, cultural autonomy that underpins their approach. As Ramirez (1999) argues, there is an explicit world order which is in operation which provides the world with models for it to copy and to standardise and which increasingly makes it difficult, if not impossible, for even the remotest parts of the globe, to seek independent lines of development.

3.3   The 'Insiders' within Globalisation

As opposed to 'outsider' positions, classic insider arguments begin from a deep commitment to engagement with the mainstream and with globalisation. Examples of such 'insider' engagements include the contributions of particular radical constructivists (Harding, 1993), post-Fordists (King and McGrath, 2002), multiculturalists and a range of Marxists. Again, as was explained in the introduction, the way in which the perspectives are worked with here are not intended to represent the broad schools of thought out of which they come but those elements of the perspectives that bear on globalisation.

Two interesting approaches that currently enjoy a great deal of support and are worthy of consideration are found in specific approaches to social constructivism and post-Fordism. Constructivism takes some of its roots from scholars such as Dewey who were deeply concerned about developing knowing citizens who were actors rather than spectators in social life. The essential argument it makes is that knowledge and knowledge claims are sociologically founded (see Phillips and

Burbules, 2000, p. 33). A leading radical proponent of the position, Harding (1993, p. 54), for example, argues that in societies organised hierarchically 'by race, ethnicity, class... or some other such politics... (elites) both organise and set limits on what persons who perform such activities can understand about themselves and the world around them.' What is needed, instead, she argues, is an approach which works epistemologically with the positions of the people 'upon whom limits are set' because these people are able to generate more critical questions and so provide a more inclusive framework for working with a diversity of knowledge bases. The relevance of this position for developing an inclusive rather than marginalising form of globalisation is great.

Some post-Fordists (King and McGrath, 2002, p. 33), aware of this marginalisation, argue that globalisation has the potential to further marginalise "already economically peripheral individuals, communities and economies. Their interest is in turning globalisation, through education, into marginalised people's favour:

> Post-Fordism emphasises ... the need to extend both quality and quantity in a drive towards a high skill economy,... to greater worker autonomy and the need for a new combination of knowledge and skills. The rapid nature of technological change under post-Fordism highlights the need to foster skills and attitudes for lifelong learning and highlights the impossibility of once-and-for-all training at the beginning of a career path.

Interesting as the radical constructivist positions and the post-Fordist positions are, particularly in so far as they appeal for the need for higher-order thinking, they do not obviously engage with the central question of power. In different ways, they essentially accord an agency to the individual and the group which underplays the extent to which social structures (the social structures of dominance in globalisation) shape the conditions of their participation in society. Critics (Prawat, 1995, p. 14) of social constructivism have pointed to an 'excess of individuality' in its approach, while post-Fordists have been slated for taking the politics out of knowledge production. A riposte to these complaints can be found in Marxist and neo-Marxist positions.

Marxism and neo-Marxism, in the wake of the retreat of the socialist project with the collapse of the Soviet Union, have found their basic sociological moorings seriously threatened by new and rival epistemological readings of society. The most critical reading of Marxism has come from post-Colonialism which has accused Marxism, and indeed Marx himself, of being reductionist, essentialist and totalising, and, swingeingly, of being complicit with a Eurocentric project: 'complicit with imperialism in its contemporary guise as globalization' (see Bartolovich, 2002, p. 1). In reply, Bartolovich complains that a disavowal of the economic has taken place in postcolonial studies exemplified by a deliberate abstraction of the semiotic from the economic. Referring to a recent editorial in *Postcolonial Studies* in which a Benetton exhibition is reviewed, she comments, 'Does it never really occur to (the editors) that these material forces (the economy) might have something to do with Benetton's "semiotic" success?' Prakash 1996; Bartolovich (2002, p. 11) carries on to make the point that the 'dizzying disequilibria' of power and resources in the contemporary world system are 'literally *irreducible* without closing the gaps in *material* inequalities among peoples' (emphasis in the original). Significantly, for contemporary Marxists, the preoccupation of Post-Colonialists with the 'contest of cultures' (and education) misreads the imbalances within the global political economy and the very material ways in which the imbalances produce intellectual and cultural effects: 'Radical metropolitan intellectuals must recognise that it will only be possible to "think globally" as a matter of course when the current global asymmetries... have been eliminated' (Bartolovich, 2002, p. 14).

This line of thought has been taken up explicitly in education in the work of McLaren (1995) and McLaren and Farahmandpur (2003, 2005) who make the comment that the 'globalization of capital and its profane partnership with neo-liberal politics pose unique and urgent challenges to today's progressive educators'. These challenges, they argue, can be addressed through the 'advance of contemporary Marxist scholarship.' At the heart of McLaren and Farahmandpur's argument is the thesis that education is necessary to the direct production of labour power – the one commodity that generates the entire social universe of capital. Educators constitute the guardians of capital's most potent resource – labour power – and can either reproduce or subvert it 'by inserting *principles antagonistic* (emphasis in the original) to the social domination of capital' (ibid). The principles referred to include social justice, equity and solidarity for progressive change and are materialised through the process of explicitly teaching students how knowledge is related historically, culturally and institutionally to the process of production and consumption. The role of a critical pedagogy is to help people live humanely and to live as humans and to enable people to realise their powers and capacities. Unlike liberal education which is focused on the individual, critical pedagogy is social, 'revolutionary critical pedagogy attempts to help individuals liberate themselves *through* the social, through challenging, resisting and transforming commonly held discourses and practices... the creation of a society in which each person participates according to his or her abilities for the benefit of his or her needs' (McLaren and Farahmandpur, 2003, p. 72). Elements of this line of thinking are evident in Grossberg's (1994) praxical pedagogy in terms of which people are offered the skills that would enable them to understand and intervene in their own history.

McLaren and Farahmandpur's and Grossberg's contributions are important for the purposes of this discussion. However, there remains a difficulty with the approach they suggest. Tired as they are (see Bartolovich, 2002, p. 15) of the debate, the problem remains that the nature of the world as they conceive it is configured around a 'Western' version of modernity. This modernity provides the temporal framework for understanding and locating all meaning. Presented this way, sensitive as they might be to difference (see Bartolovich, 2002, p. 15), this perspective decentres and in some ways delegitimates experiences outside of the struggle for what it means to be a modern subject.

What this critique of the insiders suggests, is that one is confronted with social constructivists who accord too much freedom to the individual and with Marxists who continue to operate inside a structural hermeneutic framed by an over-determinative economic analysis. What this over-determinance produces is what Wagner (see Le Grange, 2004, p. 73) has very usefully referred to as a blind-spot. A blind-spot is what scientists don't know enough about or care about. Try as the Marxists do to take the 'non-Western' other – the colonial, or the 'non-European' – they cannot help themselves but to see the humanity of this subject against a future Western version of this modern humanity, and it is only until this version of modernity is attained that the subject might attain full humanity.

3.4 Working Across the 'Outside' and the 'Inside'

While there is a great deal that can be said about the hegemony of Western forms of cultural capital (see for example Tomlinson, 2003, p. 225 and Soudien, 2005), important about it for this discussion is the impact that it has had on educational practice around the world and especially the choices that have been made in educational policy. Critically, inclusive as educational policy has attempted to be in most countries, it has come to settle around normative markers – literacy and competence in the global economy – that advantage English-speaking middle-class groupings and disadvantage others who do not fit this profile or who struggle to obtain the attributes of English-speaking and middle-class behaviour. There is a disjunction between preferred pedagogical cultures almost everywhere and the daily lives that people live. Characteristic of these daily lives, it is argued, are dispositions and forms of deportment that are rooted in everyday knowledge (constituting what Muller (2000, p. 79) would call the 'profane'), that have insufficient purchase in the world of achievement. Confronting modern education in all of its complexity, young marginalised people, and sometimes their teachers, operate in a world signposted by people other than themselves and with what describes as "the imposition of high culture on society." The effect of this, as says, is that young people and their teachers have to work, with a "discourse… which, even as it challenged the colonial claim to political domination, it also accepted the intellectual premises of 'modernity' *on which colonial domination was based.*" This, it is suggested, constitutes the central paradox for globalisation and education for many countries around the world. The paradox, for a country amounts to the abidingly complex puzzle of how it might engage with this 'high' road and still remain alert to the challenges of including all its people. Even in countries such as Japan, Taiwan and South Korea, which stand as examples of alternative but successful forms of modernity, where it has been argued that Confucianism and systems of trust were powerfully influential in fostering economic development (see Amartya Sen, 2000), the paradox continued as Japan wrestled with the question of how to bring up its children and to deal with new social problems such as youth crime (see Numata, 2003, p. 261; Kamijo, 2000, p. 183).

It is against this backdrop that working with the 'outsider' and 'insider' positions of our malcontents we are left with two interrelated problems; with respect to the first it is about dealing with the contradictions that come with their own 'insider' locations. The second, for the avowed 'insiders', is managing their bewilderment, and often ineptness, with respect to the totalizing discourse that globalisation stands for. I made the argument in an earlier (see Soudien, forthcoming) critique that 'engaged' forms of pedagogy rhetorically proclaim a position but seldom manage to demonstrate what such a position consists of. Towards developing such a position, I suggest that critical engagements with globalisation *already* exist in practice and that instead of having to invent new ways of explaining how individuals and societies might mitigate, overcome and even transform the corrosive and exclusionary standardisation and homogenisation of globalisation, the challenge of contemporary education is how to make explicit pedagogical processes surrounding practices that already exist. Efforts in this direction have also been made by people such as Gough (2000), drawing on an argument about performativity, says, 'if knowledge is recognised as both representational and performative it will be possible to create a space in which knowledge traditions can be performed together' – a third interstitial space between the local and the global.

Significant in understanding this practice as it is *already-there* is its locatedness in what Gough and others, including Lorde, Grossberg, have termed the third space or the gap. This third space is neither inside nor outside but pivots across the difference of between being inside and outside. Central about this third-space, it is argued here, is the fact that it already is a deep feature of everyday life in many societies. It is already present, for example, as young Chinese people encounter the similarities and differences of the old cultures their parents remember and cherish with the Western world presented to them in film, song, text and social practice. Towards understanding the pedagogical character of this pivotal point and to see how it might be made explicit and so, therefore, inform practice, it is necessary to turn to literary theory and the work of scholars of difference and the interpretation of difference such as Homi Bhabha (1994). Referring to interpretation and the challenge of understanding, he makes the comment that 'the linguistic difference that informs any cultural performance [and here it is important to include "education" too] is dramatised in the common semiotic account of the difference between the subject of a proposition [the "you"] and the subject of enunciation [the 'I']'. The drama of the moment is captured in the act of interpretation where the 'I' *cannot* address its history in its own words and is not conscious – because of the general conditions of language and discourse – of the strategies that are mobilised in the moment of enunciation. This difficulty of expression is important to grasp. It points to an ambivalence, or better, an instability, deep in the heart of the moment of enunciation. How am I to speak? How might I represent this object? *This* is the moment of possibility. It is at this moment that the enunciator experiences an episode of crisis. What he or she is representing is not a mirror of anything but, as Bhabha (1994, p. 37) says, an 'open, expanding code' framed by the possibility of language. Language, in itself, is never sufficient to encompass or consume the object of representation. It is always grasping. Trinh T. Minh-Ha (1996, p. 5), referring to exactly this difficulty, speaks of 'language only communicates itself in itself... (and) constitutes a material reality of its own. How one renders this reality is another matter'. This opens up the way for the enunciator (the educator) to begin to question his or her relationship with the object of his or her enunciation. If he or she cannot find all the words to contain that object, can it ever be fully understood? At its most complex, but also its powerful, this is the most critical moment in any learning process. It demonstrates to the learner and the teacher the hubris of any form of totalisation. Knowledge is never capable of being faithfully and completely reproduced. It is always in a state of interpretation. Looking at it in this way, all knowledge is therefore provisional and vulnerable. No knowledge is absolute. Globalisation as universalism, homogeneity and standardization as a new form of totalisation are therefore problematic. Knowledge itself must therefore be made the object of inspection and not simply accepted or rejected because of where it comes from. What is its history, its objective and its scope?

Following this line of thought any pretension of the *inherent* originality and purity, and therefore superiority, of one knowledge form over another is untenable. As Bhabha says, '[this moment], though unrepresentable in itself, constitutes the discursive conditions of enunciation and ensure[s] that the meanings and symbols of culture have no primordial unity or fixity; that the same signs can be appropriated, translated, rehistoricised and read anew'. It is only a sustained process of education as the skill of deep historicisation and deep interpretation (and it is true that different forms of education as Appiah (2002) and Wright (2002), talking of Ashante and Yoruba history, argue can achieve the same effects) that can make this appropriation possible. Subjecting all forms of knowledge to the test of not only what it proposes but also where it comes from, and how it is constructed is opening it up to a scrutiny that reveals its constructedness. It is then that one can really work with it. These approaches are inherently the approaches of the sceptical 'outsider', always alert to how he or she is positioned in relation to the dominant knowledge forms (am I included in it or not), and the determined 'subverter' seeking to include himself or herself on absolutely equal grounds in terms of it.

Importantly, however, it needs to be understood, that this is the promise only and not, *ipso facto*, the fulfillment. While historicisation and crises of interpretation always produce something new, it is *possible* that the attempt to mediate, translate and interpret the 'other' often produces 'an assimilation of contraries' which either domesticates the object or ruptures the continuity that binds it to the enunciator. This assimilation of contraries produces what Gough (2000) has spoken of as 'perturbation' or Bhabha (1994, p. 38), quoting Fanon, described as 'that occult instability which presages powerful cultural changes'. That those changes could be perverse as far as the 'other' is concerned is important to recognise.

3.5   Conclusion

The above analysis of globalisation discourses and global pedagogies demonstrates what is at stake in the struggle for a different kind of education. To the standardised forms that are taking root everywhere, minimally, we ought to be insisting on the development of deep forms of engagement with the *range* of knowledges that people have access to. Said (2002, p. 46), refers to the 'critical sense that can only come from a sustained encounter with the actualities of reading and interpretation'. This reading, I want to suggest, need not only be textual. It must be that largely, but not only. It needs to include the oral, the visual and other forms of knowledge acquired in other kinds of ways. While this deep form of engagement does not guarantee that the young people who emerge from an encounter with it are, of necessity, better people, the chances that they will be able to deal with the complexity of globalisation more assuredly and with a sense of themselves in relation to the world must certainly be greater.

References

Adams, R. (1997). Epistemology, Afrocentricity, and Ideology. In P. Logan (Ed), *A Howard Reader: An Intellectual and Cultural Quilt of the African-American Experience*. Boston, MA: Houghton Mifflin Custom Publishing.

Amin, S. (1997). *Capitalism in the Age of Globalization*. Zed Books: London.

Amin, S. (2001). Imperialism and Globalization. In *Monthly Review*, 53(2) (electronic version), HYPERLINK Http://www.monthlyreview.org/0601amin.htm.

Appiah, K. (2002). Citizens of the World. In *Biblio: A Review of Books*, Special Issue, March–April, 6–10.

Banteyerga, H. (1994). An Alternative Model in Teacher Education: The Classroom in Focus. A Paper presented at the Pan-African Colloquium: Educational Innovation in Post-colonial Africa. University of Cape Town, Rondebosch.

Bartolovich, C. (2002). *Introduction: Marxism, Modernity and Postcolonial Studies*. In C. Batolovich & N. Lazarus (Eds), *Marxism, Modernity and Postcolonial Studies*. Cambridge: Cambridge University Press.

Bhabha, H. (1994). *The Location of Culture*. New York: Routledge.

Bourdieu, P. (1993). *The Field of Cultural Production*. Cambridge: Polity Press.

Brady, W. (1997). Indigenous Australian Education and Globalization. In V. Masemann & A. Welch (Eds), *Tradition, Modernity and Post-Modernity in Comparative Education*. Dordrecht: Kluwer.

Castells, M. (1996). *The Information Age: Economy, Society and Culture, Volume 1: The Rise of the Network Society*. Oxford: Blackwell.

Chatterjee, P. (1997). 'Our Modernity', a lecture published by the South-South Exchange Programme for Research on the History of development (SEPHIS) and the Council for the development of Social Science Research in Africa, Rotterdam/Dakar, 1997.

Chatterjee, P. (1998). Beyond the Nation? Or Within? *Social Text*, 16(3), 57–69.

Dimmock, C. & Walker, A. (2000). *Globalisation and Societal Culture: Redefining Schooling and School Leadership in the Twenty-First Century. Compare*, 30(3), 303–312.

Giddens, A. (1991). *Modernity and Self-Identity: Self and Society in the Late Modern Age*. Stanford, CA: Stanford University Press.

Gough, N. (2000). Globalization and Curriculum Enquiry: Locating, Representing and Performing a Transnational Imaginary. In N. Stromquist & K. Monkman (Eds), *Globalization and Education: Integration and Contestation Across Cultures*. Lanham, MD: Rowman & Littlefield.

Grossberg, L. (1994). Introduction: Bringin' it All Back Home – Pedagogy and Cultural Studies. In H. Giroux & P. McLaren (Eds), *Between Borders: Pedagogy and the Politics of Cultural Studies*. New York: Routledge.

Harding, S. (1993). Rethinking Standpoint Epistemology: "What is Strong Objectivity?" In L. Alcoff & E. Potter (Eds), *Feminist Epistemologies* (pp. 49–82). New York: Routledge.

Held, D., McGrew, H., Goldblatt, D., & Perraton, J. (1999). *Global Transformations: Politics, Economics and Culture*. Cambridge: Polity Press.

Hooks, B. (1994). *Outlaw Culture: Resisting Representations*. New York: Routledge.

Hooks, B. (1997). Keeping Close to Home: Class and education. In V. Cyrus. (Ed), *Experiencing Race, Class, and Gender in the United States*. Mountain View, CA: Mayfield Publishing.

Kamijo, M. (2000). Education in the 'Melting Society': New Challenges Facing Japanese Schools and Society. In K. Mazurek, M. Winzer, & C. Majorek (Eds), *Education in a Global Society: A Comparative Perspective*. Boston: Allyn & Bacon.

King, K. & McGrath, S. (2002). Globalisation, Enterprise and Knowledge: Education, Training and Development in Africa. Oxford: Symposium Books.

Koenig, Archibugi, M. (2003). Introduction: Globalization and the Challenge to Governance. In D. Held & M. Koenig-Archibugi (Eds), *Taming Globalization: Frontiers of Governance*. Cambridge: Polity Press.

Le Grange, L. (2004). Ignorance, Trust and Educational Research. *Journal of Education*, 33, 69–84.

Lewis-Qualls, C. (2000). To learn that knowing was not enough: Epistemic Refocusing in Audre Lorde's Zami: A New Spelling of My Name (Retrieved July 14, 2004, from http://users.ev1.net/~aquila/chandra/audrelorde.html.

Lorde, A. (1982). *Zami: A New Spelling of my Name*. Freedom, CA: Crossing.

McGrew, T. (1992). A Global Society. In S. Hall, D. Held, & T. McGrew (Eds), *Modernity and its Futures*. Cambridge: Polity Press in Association with the Open University.

McLaren, P. (1995). *Critical Pedagogy and Predatory Culture*. New York: Routledge.

McLaren, P. & Farahmandpur, R. (2003). The Globalization of Capitalism and the New Imperialism: Notes Towards a Revolutionary Critical Pedagogy. In G. Dimitriadis & D. Carlson (Eds), *Promises to Keep: Cultural Studies, Democratic Education and Public Life*. New York: RoutledgeFalmer.

McLaren, P. & Farahmandpur, R. (2005). *Teaching against Global Capitalism and the New Imperialism*. Lanham: Rowman & Littlefield.

Meyer, J. & Ramirez, F. (1999). The Globalization of Education. Unpublished Mimeo.

Minh-ha, T. (1996). Trinh T. Minh-ha in Conversation with Annamaria Morelli. In I. Chambers & L. Curti (Eds), *The Post-Colonial Question: Common Skies Divided Horizons*. London/New York: Routledge.

Nandy, A. (2002). *Time Warps: The Insistent Politics of Silent and Evasive Pasts*. Delhi: Permanent Black.

Nekhwevha, F. (1999). No Matter How Long the Night, the Day is Sure to Come: Culture and Educational Transformation in Post-Colonial Namibia and Post-Apartheid South Africa. In C. Soudien & P. Kallaway (Eds), *Education, Equity and Transformation*. Dordrecht: Kluwer.

Numata, H. (2003). What Children Have Lost by the Modernisation of Education: A Comparison of Experiences in Western Europe and eastern Asia. In M. Bray (Ed), *Comparative Education: Continuing Traditions, New Challenges, and New Paradigms*. Dordrecht: Kluwer.

Phillips, D. & Burbules, N. (2000). *Postpositivism and Educational Research*. Lanham, MD: Rowman & Littlefield.

Prakash, G. (1996). Who's Afraid of Postcoloniality? In *Social Text* 14(4), Winter, 186–203.

Prawat, R. (1995). Misreading Dewey: Reform, Projects, and the Language Game. *Educational Researcher*, 24(7),13–22.

Rust, V. (2000). Educational Reform: Who are the Radicals? In N.Stromquist & K. Monkman (Eds), *Globalization and Education: Integration and Contestation Across Cultures*. Lanham, MD: Rowman & Littlefield.

Said, E. (2002). The Book, Critical Performance and Education's Future. In K. Asmal & W. James (Eds), *Spirit of the Nation: Reflections on South Africa's Educational Ethos*. Claremont, Cape Town: New Africa Education.

Sanders, M. (2002). *Complicities: The Intellectual and Apartheid*. Pietermaritzburg: University of Natal Press.

Sardar, P. (2004). *Desperately Seeking Paradise*. London: Granta.

Schneir, M. (Ed). (1994). *Feminisms in our Time*. New York: Vintage Books.

Seepe, S. (1998). Towards an Afrocentric Understanding. In S. Seepe (Ed.), *Black Perspectives on Tertiary Institutional Transformation*. Johannesburg: Vivlia Publishers.

Sen, A. (2000). Culture and Development. Talk at World Bank Meeting, 13 Dec 2000. Mimeo.
Soudien, C. (2005). Inside but Below: The Puzzle of Education in the Global Order. In J. Zajda
    (Ed), *International Handbook on Globalisation, Education and Policy Research: Global
    Pedagogies and Policies* (pp. 501–516). Dordrecht: Springer.
Stiglitz, J. (2002). *Globalization and its Discontents*. London: Penguin.
Tomlinson, S. (2003). Globalization, Race and Education. *Journal of Educational Change*, 4(3),
    213–230.
Touraine,A. (2000). Can We Live Together? Cambridge: Polity Press.
Wallerstein, E. (1983). *Historical Capitalism*. London: Verso.
Wright, H. (2002). Editorial: Notes on the (Im)Possibility of Articulating Continental African
    Identity. *Critical Arts*, 16(2), 1–18.
Zajda, J. (2005) (Ed). *The International Handbook of Globalisation and Education Policy
    Research*. Dordrecht: Springer.
Zajda, J., Davies, L., & Majhanovich, S. (Eds). (2008a). Comparative and Global Pedagogies:
    Equity, Access and Democracy in Education. Dordrecht: Springer.
Zajda, J., Biraimah, B., & Gaudelli, W. (Eds). (2008b). *Education and Social Inequality in the
    Global Culture*. Dordrecht: Springer.

Chapter 4
To Compare Is Human:
Comparison as a Research Methodology

David Wilson

4.1 Comparative Education as a Methodology: Introduction

Comparison may be an integral aspect of all cultures, as humans have compared phenomena since well before the beginning of recorded history. The ability of most traditional peoples to compare their observations about the weather, game, crops, human behaviour and everything else of importance to their daily lives, with their recollections of previous years, may well be at the core of culture. Such comparisons were important to their survival and differentiated humans from other species, because humans are the only species capable of 'creating' its own culture. In modern societies, Ragin asserts that 'thinking without comparison is unthinkable' (Burns &Welch (1992); Fraser (1962); Hall, 1990; Hans (1958); Kandel (1955); King (1968); Schriewer & Holmes (1998); van Daele, 1993; Ragin, 1987, p. 1). With the beginnings of recorded history, there are accounts of comparisons of education in various localities. For example, Plato compared education in Athens and Sparta. Similarly, Thucydides compared Athenian civilisation and *paidea* with other Greek city states and Xenophon wrote about Persian laws and education. One of this writer's fellow doctoral students in the 1960s, John Holland, even asserted on his comprehensive examination that the biblical Joseph (of the 'coat of many colours') may have been the first comparative educator. In this respect, our field of Comparative Education can also be noted to span millennia.

In view of its prehistorical origins, comparison antedates the development of 'research' methodology. Moreover, in modern times the integration of the *reportorial-descriptive* 'method' common to the 'travellers' tales' period of comparative education, with the more *quantitative* orientation involving the use of statistics, beginning with Marc-Antoine Jullien in 1817, prompts the conclusion that

D.Wilson
Comparative, International and Development Education Centre, Ontario Institute for Studies in Education, University of Toronto, 252 Bloor Street West, Toronto, Ontario M5S 1V6
CANADA

J. Zajda and V. Rust (eds.), *Globalisation, Policy and Comparative Research,*   49
DOI: 10.1007/978-1-4020-9547-4_4, © Springer Science + Bussiness Media B.V. 2009

Comparative Education may well have been the first social science to blend *qualitative* and *quantitative* research methods. However, in terms of 'pure' research methodology, the first modern qualitative research known to have been published was Znanecki and Thomas', *The Polish Peasant* (1919). The chapter examines the development of comparative research methods. The transition from the use of, largely, historical methods to the increasing employment of methods and approaches from the social sciences, during the previous century, will be the major focus of this chapter. The chapter will conclude with an examination of some of the contemporary research methods utilised by Comparative Educators. Noah and Eckstein (1969) wrote that:

> The purpose of reviewing the development of comparative education is ... to search out in the predecessors of modern comparative education those elements of their thought pertinent to understanding their motives for undertaking comparative work, the types of data they used, the ways they handled the data, and their interpretations of them. (Noah & Eckstein, 1969, p. 3).

4.2 Methods Used in Classic Historical Comparative Studies

The first two centuries of Comparative Education were characterised by a 'poverty of method', according to Brickman (1960). This comment was likely not meant to imply that there was no comparative methodology used, but rather that comparative methods were either rudimentary, or haphazard, or lacking in rigour and coherence. Throughout recorded history, itinerant social commentators have described education in other countries. The designation of a *classical*, or prehistoric, phase of comparative education by this writer was prompted by Brickman's 'pre-history' article that placed 'the roots of comparative education [as lying] deeper in history'. He cited Herodotus (484–525 BC), Xenophon (430–355 BC), Cicero (106–43 BC), Scipio Africanus (AD 185–129) and Tacitus (AD 70) from ancient Greece and Rome (Brickman, 1966). The *methodology* used in such early classical comparative studies was, at best, expository or philosophical, and these works were decidedly rhetorical. This period was followed by a period, which Noah and Eckstein labelled as 'travellers' tales', which they characterised as producing 'subjective' and 'unsystematic' 'reports on foreign education'. The methods used were largely descriptive and occasionally explanatory, but still anecdotal in nature. Some of these itinerant comparativists included Rabbi Benjamin of Tudela (1165–1173) from pre-Inquisition Spain, who travelled as far as India, Niccolò and Maffeo Polo writing about China (AD 1254–1324), Abd-al-Rahman Ibn Khaldun (1332–1406) of Tunisia and others 'who journeyed from medieval Europe to Asia and Africa, or from one Islamic centre to others'. (Brickman, 1966).

During the seventeenth and eighteenth centuries, a shift is evident from writings of a philosophical nature to studies relating the observations of travellers and describing observed educational practices and institutions. The *use* of comparative information also evolved from a mere description towards the facilitation of *borrowing* and *adaptation* of the educational practices and structures studied. In these works, the method was still more descriptive than analytical, but some attention was paid to the systematic ordering of these descriptions. Kazamias (1961) noted that 'in some primordial sense comparative education may be considered as an ancient phenomenon'. However, he asserted that 'it was not until the nineteenth century... that attempts were made at a more systematic approach to comparative education' (Kazamias, 1961, p. 90).

One more systematic form of comparative study resulted from diplomatic and academic missions sent by one country to another. Kobayashi wrote about a mission sent to China in AD 607 by Prince Shokotu of Japan, 'which resulted in the establishment of Japan's first national system of education, modelled on the Chinese' (Kobayashi, 1990, p. 202). A subsequent Japanese mission, was led by Prince Tomomi Iwakura, who led a mission to study European and US education 4 years after the Meiji Restoration in 1872 (Brickman, 1960, p. 10). Such commissioned 'voyages of discovery' included Domingo Fausto Sarmiento, described by Brickman as 'the famous statesman-educator of Argentina and Chile', whose *De la educación popular* described and analysed education in France, Prussia, Holland and the US state of Massachusetts (Brickman, 1960, p. 9). Brickman also mentions the writings of Russian Count Leo Tolstoi on education in Germany, France, Switzerland and England (1857–1861) and Bereday includes Konstantin D. Ushinsky as a second nineteenth century Russian comparativist (Brickman, 1960, p. 9; Bereday, 1964, p. 7).

To this grouping one might add Victor Cousin (1831) who studied Prussian education and adapted aspects to French education, and John Griscom (1774–1852) from New Jersey, Calvin Stowe from Ohio (1802–1886) Horace Mann (1796–1859) from Massachusetts and Henry Barnard (1811–1900) from Connecticut, who studied European education and adapted aspects to education in the US (Noah & Eckstein, 1969, pp. 16–25). In Great Britain, Sir Michael Sadler was a member of the Bruce Commission on Secondary Education and then an official at the Board of Education in London. Noah and Eckstein wrote that 'Sadler drew upon a wide range of authors in England and abroad to analyze trends in educational developments all over Europe, while in his own contributions he employed sociological as well as historical data to explain the interaction of education and society' (1969, p. 45). In the Canadian context, Edgerton Ryerson (1868) was identified by Nicholas Hans as the founder of a 'non-denominational public school system', rather than separate denominational schools. Wilson explains an interest in borrowing innovative pedagogies from around the world:

> Like Cousin and Jullien in France, Barnard in the U.S., Sarmiento in Argentina and Chile, and Sadler in the U.K., Ryerson was a public official interested in borrowing innovative educational models, structures and practices. (Wilson, 1994a, p. 455)

4.3 'Modern' Comparative Education

There is consensus among most authors that 'modern' comparative education dates from the nearly-parallel writings of César Auguste Basset in 1808 and Marc-Antoine Jullien in 1817. Jullien was the first writer to use the term 'comparative education', but the term was continually reinvented during the late 1800s and early 1900s, as evidenced by Brickman's comment that 'Peter Sandiford (the first Canadian comparativist), editor of the volume *Comparative Education* (1918), states in his preface that 'comparative education is a phrase recently invented in the United States ...' (Brickman, 1960, p. 12). Jullien developed a taxonomy of data necessary to describe an educational system, but never made use of his approach to study any educational system. Noah and Eckstein described his methodology, as follows:

> Jullien, though unable to realize any of his sophisticated comparative projects, insisted on the prime necessity of structured inquiry. His work in comparative education rested on four practical bases. The first was a proposal for an international commission on education with a permanent staff of international civil servants. The second was a questionnaire to be administered to a number of countries that would provide the information on which the international commission could make its recommendations. Third, there was to be a net-work of normal schools to train teachers in the most up-to-date methods. Finally, there would be a multi-lingual journal of education to disseminate information about innovations in education to all interested. (Noah & Eckstein, 1969, p. 27)

Bereday acknowledged that Jullien was the 'first scientifically minded comparative educator', but asserted that Sir Michael Sadler 'interposed a preparatory process before permitting transplantation' of the aspects of the educational systems that were studied in other nations (Bereday, 1964, pp. 8–10). Kazamias further noted that 'from the methodological standpoint it was not until the appearance of I. L. Kandel's monumental *Comparative Education* in 1933 that the foundations of a truly scientific study of comparative education were laid' (Kazamias, 1961, p. 90). The focus on methodology in the field of Comparative Education was most likely enhanced by the establishment of university courses – and later programmes – in North America and Europe, and later elsewhere. The first regular course in Comparative Education was offered at Teachers' College, Columbia University by James E. Russell in the 1899–1900 academic year, making our presence in academia a century old (Wilson, 2000, p. 13).

One problem with categorising developments into discrete periods is that these 'neat' periods usually overlap. For instance, although Julien (1817) is recognised as the founder of the scientific study of comparative education, and Sadler (1901) is recognised as the first scientific comparativist, and Kandel (1933) is recognised as the first modern methodologist, other authors studied, wrote and published throughout this period, using comparative methodologies which a clear-cut period approach suggests should have been discredited and displaced; while in actual fact they were not. History is *never* neat and clear-cut.

From the perspective of comparative method, Bereday divided the 'history' of comparative education into three phases. The first phase included Jullien and was labelled the *period of borrowing*. The second phase was labelled as the *period of prediction* and focused upon Sadler. His third phase was called the *period of analysis* and was attributed to Friedrich Schneider, Isaac Kandel and Robert Ulich (Bereday, 1964, pp. 7–8). While all three began their careers in Germany, Kandel and Ulich migrated to the USA, to Columbia and Harvard Universities, respectively, to escape Nazism, while the Nazis terminated Schneider's employment at the University of Cologne and the Bonn Academy of Pedagogics (Wilson, 1994a, p. 475). Bereday further differentiated the field into *area studies*, 'concerned with one country or region', and *comparative studies* 'concerned with many countries or regions at a time' (1964, pp. 8–10). To some extent, this writer is a 'product' of an area studies programme (at Syracuse University) and is a proponent of this methodological approach to the study – and practice – of comparative education.

This writer has added a *social science methodology phase* to Bereday's classificatory phases, which began after World War II. The most prominent contributors have been C. Arnold Anderson (of The University of Chicago), Brian Holmes (of The University of London) and Harold Noah and Max Eckstein (of Columbia University and Brooklyn College) (Wilson, 2000, p. 9). The 'blossoming' and experimentation that fostered this climate was noted to be 'directly related to the expansion of the field from one with a small number of adherents to a worldwide field with hundreds of faculty and thousands of graduate students at hundreds of universities' (Wilson, 2000, p. 9). Crossley and Broadfoot added Philip Foster (Chicago) and Edmund King (London) to this group of prominent comparativists (Crossley & Broadfoot, 1992, p. 103). Finally, this writer also asserted that the 1970s and 1980s could be called a *phase of theoretical contention* (Wilson, 2000, p. 10) with 'methodological and ideological diversity' that 'led to vigorous and at times acrimonious debate over methodological rigor and explanatory power' (Altbach & Tan, 1995, p. xi). Altbach and Tan also noted that 'another important development since the late 1980s has been the growing recognition that there is no single orthodox method of research within comparative education' (Altbach & Tan, 1995, p. xiii).

4.4   Comparative Methodology

What does appear to transcend the methodological and theoretical 'divide' is the common commitment to the comparative method. However, definitions of the comparative method appear to vary widely. Bereday (1964) wrote that comparative education attempted to look for similarities and differences in the world:

> Comparative education seeks to make sense out of the similarities and differences among educational systems. It catalogues educational methods across national frontiers; and in this catalogue each country appears as one variant of the total store of mankind's (sic) educational experience. (Bereday, 1964, p. 5)

At the same time, Noah and Eckstein asserted that comparative education was a synthesis of various disciplines and approaches:

> The field of comparative education is best defined as an intersection of the social sciences, education, and cross-national study. (Noah & Eckstein, 1969, p. 121)

and in that regard, Noah and Eckstein (1969) noted the significance of cross-national research in comparative education:

> Comparative education in its most recent phase emerges as the attempt to use cross-national data to test propositions about the relationship between education and society and between teaching practices and learning outcomes. (Noah & Eckstein, 1969, p. 114)

Brian Holmes and Jürgen Schriewer traced the social science antecedents of comparative education. Schriewer attributed the 'transference of a successful research approach from the life-sciences to the social sciences and humanities' to Wilhelm von Humboldt, who originated Comparative Anthropology, and Emile Durkheim, who 'showed the comparative method to be the substitute – peculiarly suited to the social sciences – for macro-social experiments' (Schriewer, 1997, pp. 7 and 11). Holmes cast an even wider 'net' and drew from John 'Dewey's reflective thinking (or problem-solving) approach' and Karl Popper's 'hypothetico-deductive method of scientific enquiry and his critical dualism (conventionalism)' (Holmes, 1981, p. 14). In doing so, he rejected the inductive method of John Stuart Mill and Karl Mannheim's 'social reconstructionist' perspective favoured by Geoge Bereday and Edmund King. Holmes wrote that:

> Both Dewey and Popper regard hypotheses as tentative solutions to identified problems and consider that in order to test hypotheses the circumstances (specific initial conditions) should be identified and described. Testing involves comparing outcomes predicted from general hypothetical statements under specified conditions with observable events. If events confirm prediction for Dewey the problem has been solved and the hypothesis verified. Verification is consequently an important feature of problem-solving. Popper, on the other hand, has stressed the need for scientists to try to refute or falsify hypotheses. (Holmes, 1981, p. 10)

Writing from the general perspective of 'the comparative method', and 'comparative social science', Ragin (1987) addresses 'meta theoretical differences between approaches generally called *qualitative* (or case-oriented) and *quantitative* (or variable-oriented) – primarily in terms of their different orientations toward the analysis and interpretation of data' (Ragin, 1987, p. xi). He asserts that 'the essential characteristics of the qualitative/quantitative split in the social sciences are clearly visible in comparative social science' and that 'in contrast to other subdisciplines, this field has a long tradition of qualitative work that is stronger and richer than its quantitative counterpart'. He further indicates that 'case-oriented studies, by their nature, are sensitive to complexity and historical specificity'. In addition, he notes that 'case-oriented methods are holistic – they treat cases as whole entities and not as collections of parts or as collections of scores on variables' (Ragin, 1987, pp. ix and x). This writer has often drawn both theoretical and methodological guidance from the various comparative social sciences; such as, comparative sociology, comparative ethnography, comparative politics and comparative law. This writer asserts that variables need not necessarily be only quantitative in nature, since one can also develop and use variables that are qualitative in nature.

This writer finds Ragin's perspective to be quite useful – and comfortable – because it validates the blend of qualitative and quantitative methods that this writer both uses to undertake comparative studies and to teach comparative education method-ologies. The reader will recall the assertion in the Introduction to this chapter that comparative education may have been the first social science to blend these oft-perceived to be contradictory – but in actual fact, complementary – research perspectives. It is the 'different orientations towards the analysis and interpretation of data' which, in this writer's judgement, constitute the complementarity of the quantitative and qualitative approaches.

Although educated in the *quantitative* genre of comparative education research, and having used a quantitative, variable-rich, methodology in thesis and other research, this writer underwent a 'conversion' to the *qualitative* mode in the 1970s. After the sudden death of a colleague, this writer was asked to join a Ph.D. committee for a thesis that had just been completed by a Thai graduate student. This writer was asked to write the internal appraisal and concluded that, even if the student had surveyed 1,000 international students by questionnaire, he could not have obtained as 'rich' data as he had obtained by the intensive, in-depth, interviewing of nine international students. This writer, subsequently, adopted a qualitative approach and – in programme evaluation – found that a blend of a qualitative method provided a comprehensive understanding of the dynamics of the programme, which then facilitated the construction of a better quantitative survey instrument for the second phase of an evaluation. This approach has become an integral part of this writer's graduate courses on programme, project and institutional evaluation and is also employed in graduate courses on comparative methodologies.

Ragin (1987) asserts that the "qualitative tradition is dominant" in comparative social science, which he notes is 'the opposite of the situation in most other fields' (Ragin, 1987, p. 2). As one trained in geography, this writer recalls the assertion that geography was the 'mother discipline' of the social sciences. The focus upon description and analysis, and upon studying geographic areas as 'cases,' may have contributed to the qualitative 'tradition' in the social sciences. This writer believes that the qualitative tradition in comparative education is a likely artefact of both the case-specific nature of the field, i.e., dealing with one, two, and occasionally more, nations and the descriptive nature of most comparative education studies. Our experimentation with quantitative studies has, often, led us to inconclusive findings that may have biased our policy advice. In particular, this writer was appalled at policy advice given to Indonesia in the late 1980s to reduce investment in technical-vocational education, on the basis of one rate-of-return study (Wilson, 1990). It is interesting that the highly quantitative transnational data-rich studies that were 'born and died' during the 1960s, due largely to the poor quality of available cross-national data, have recently again become in vogue.

Regardless of whether one utilises a qualitative or a quantitative method in compara-tive education research, the *mechanics* of comparison are likely to be the same, or simi-lar. This writer's preference in structuring comparisons is to follow Bereday's advocacy of the use of *juxtaposition*, which is the process of ordering materials for comparison. Juxtaposition identifies the *similarities* and *differences* between data sets and enables identification of the systematic variations that permit the construction of typologies and the formulation of research questions and/or hypotheses (Holmes, 1981, p. 62).

4.4.1   One Approach to Comparative Methodologies

As the 'product' of two Area Studies programmes (Latin American Geography at the M.Sc. Level and African Studies in conjunction with doctoral studies in Comparative Education and Educational Planning), this writer was prone to give favourable consideration to Bereday's assertion that the field of comparative education comprised two elements: '*area studies*, concerned with one country or region, and the *comparative studies,* concerned with many countries or regions at the same time' (1964, p. 9). Bereday further divided these two aspects of the field into a '*descriptive phase*, or geography of education, the collection of purely pedagogical data, and ... the *explanatory phase,* or social analysis, the application of methods of other social sciences to interpret the pedagogical data thus assembled' (1964, p. 9). However, at the young age of a doctoral student, this writer was also somewhat appalled when Bereday intimated that only senior comparativists should 'turn to total analysis'. However, after 3 decades the wisdom of his intimation has become clearer (1964, p. 25). Bereday was also prescient in asserting that comparativists should develop both a multilingual capability and have a multidisciplinary orientation.

This writer has found ample validation for these assertions during his long and varied career, which has encompassed all continents (with the exception of Antartica). The ability to interact with counterparts in various nations in local and/ or regional languages, and the ability to undertake limited translation of primary documentary materials, enhances the effectiveness – and accuracy – of comparative educators. This writer asserted – in his welcoming address to the VII World Congress of Comparative Education in Montréal – that learning another language is the key to understanding another culture. Moreover, it has been this writer's experience that, even if one does not speak the language well, the mere fact that one is trying is appreciated by one's international colleagues. One can only admire the 'polyglot' comparativists, such as Brickman, Bereday and Schriewer. The ability to utilise 'tools' from various social sciences to analyse the nations being compared has also proven to be an asset. Finally, the long-term benefit of an area studies approach is that, having learned how to study *one* area, the comparative educator is well-prepared to undertake the study of new geographic areas. He/she has learned how to learn.

Now, *how* can comparative educators best *educate* future generations of comparativists? This issue was addressed at an early stage in this writer's academic career with the development of two basic graduate courses in Comparative Education at The Ontario Institute for Studies in Education. The introductory course (*Comparative Education: Third World Development*) required students to prepare an *Educational Profile* of one country of their choice in the first course assignment. The original profile was modelled upon profiles developed for UNESCO by John Chesswas in the 1960s, which this writer subsequently modified for use on UNESCO and World Bank Project Preparation Missions, and later for The Asian Development Bank.

The premise of the course assignment was that students of comparative education should learn how to study *all* aspects of one country; from geography to demography, to economy, to labour market, to political system, and of course, its educational system. A taxonomy, somewhat similar to that originally designed by Jullien, facilitates the holistic study of that country. The effectiveness of this learning experience has been validated time and time again by former students, whose country studies undertaken *after* taking this course are significantly more comprehensive than those undertaken *prior* to taking the course. In fact, last year one former student who had just begun teaching comparative education and international development education requested this writer's profile materials in order to give her students the same preparation that she had found to be invaluable.

The advanced course, *Methodologies for Comparing Educational Systems*, regrettably appears to be the only discrete comparative methodology course taught at any Canadian university. This lacuna was the topic of this writer's Presidential Address to the Comparative and International Education Society of Canada in 1990 (Wilson, 1994b). While there are many courses in research methods, there are few-to-none in comparative research methods. It was concluded that one possible reason for the dearth (or lack) of comparative methodology courses in Canada (Wilson, 1994b), and also in the USA, as reiterated in this writer's CIES Presidential Address in 1994, is that Comparative Education is *not required* for teacher certification (Wilson, 1994a, p. 464). Therefore, comparative courses – and comparative educators – are targets for cutbacks when budgetary retrenchment becomes necessary. In these instances, the multidisciplinary orientation of comparative educators often equips them to teach other courses in education. Students are encouraged to use the *Educational Profiles* prepared in the basic course to make comparisons in three or four other countries. These comparisons are structured in the first course exercise, which requires them to define and exemplify two educational and two non-educational variables. These four variables are then used in the final course chapter to compare three or four countries (or sub-national jurisdictions). The course title, *Methodologies for Comparing Educational Systems,* indicates this writer's belief that there is no single method (or no favoured method) for making comparisons; therefore, a variety of available comparative methods are examined.

4.5 The State of Comparative Methodologies

Wilson (1994) examined 'The Evolution of Comparative TVE Studies' in the *International Encyclopedia of Education* entry on 'Technical-Vocational Education: Comparative and International Studies' (Wilson, 1994c, p. 6261, 2005b). With regard to the *types* of comparative studies, it was noted that:

> The majority of available studies, unfortunately, examine TVE in single countries, with few binational or multinational comparative studies. Bereday (1964, p. 22) labels national studies "area studies," but also considers them comparative since they facilitate comparisons "in the mind of the reader" with his or her own system. (p. 6261)

and that:

> A related development appears to be the proliferation of education sector and policy studies undertaken by most bilateral (country-to-country) and multilateral (international organization) donor agencies and development banks. Individual national sector studies have been

undertaken to describe the status and role of education and to identify future developmental options. Such studies do not purport to be comparative but, as noted above, do facilitate comparisons with those educational systems with which they are familiar.

and finally:

There is a significantly smaller number of between-country studies comparing themes or TVE developments, than within-country studies.... From a methodological perspective, the single-country studies comparing TVE subsystems and the two-country comparative studies facilitate *actual* comparisons, rather than what Bereday (1964) called comparisons "in the mind of the reader." (p. 6263)

The small number of transnational comparative studies were categorised in *International Encyclopedia of Education* article according to the social science perspectives that they employed, including those which focused upon economics, pedagogical concerns, sociology and political perspectives (p. 6263). It was then noted that questions concerning the 'factors and features [that] make studies in TVE comparative' and how should 'valid comparisons of TVE systems and structures be made', as well as how 'TVE comparisons [should] be structured' were 'not readily addressed in the literature on comparative methodologies' (p. 6264). Potential future trends in comparative TVE methodologies were noted to include 'large-scale cross-national statistical studies intended to explore developmental similarities and differences... since TVE systems appear to amass greater volumes of quantitative data than most other education subsectors', and 'a transnational study similar to the International Association for the Evaluation of Educational Achievement (IEA) studies ... [might] ... be undertaken in connection with one or more aspects of TVE', possibly focussing upon 'the relationships between upgrading mathematics and science content in TVE curricula and attributes of economic and/or social development'. Other types of TVE comparative studies advocated included 'comparisons of countries with TVE enrolment over 50 percent' at the secondary education level, and 'empirical studies to assess the internal and external efficiency of TVE', as well as 'micro level comparative case studies *within* single nations' (p. 6264). This writer has often observed that Canada is the comparative educator's 'dream,' because it has 13 educational systems – ten provincial and three territorial.

4.6   Conclusion

Although Bereday (1964) claimed that Comparative Education was entering a 'more advanced *stage of juxtaposition*', in which he claimed that studies were 'no longer monographs dealing with a single situation, but works grouping side-by-side several studies of a common problem observed in different countries or regions', studies of methodologies used to date suggest that this advanced stage has not yet been attained. This comment on the state of the field from the perspective of comparative methodology usage may be an appropriate point to conclude our discussion of comparison as a research methodology. This is because the comment indicates just how far the field has yet to evolve in the future (Wilson, 2005a).

References

Altbach, P. & Eng Thye Jason Tan. (1995). *Programs and Centers in Comparative and International Education: A Global Inventory.* Buffalo, NY: SUNY Buffalo.

Basset, C. (1808). *Essais sur l'organisation de quelques parties d'instruction publique.* Paris (reprinted by The International Bureau for Education, Geneva, 1962, IBE No. 243).

Bereday, G. (1964). *Comparative Method in Education.* New York: Holt, Rinehart & Winston.

Brickman, W. (1960). A Historical Introduction to Comparative Education. *Comparative Education Review,* 3(3), 6–13.

Brickman, W. (1966). Prehistory of Comparative Education to the End of the Eighteenth Century. *Comparative Education Review,* 10(1), 31–35.

Burns, R. & Welch, A. (Eds.) (1992). *Contemporary Perspectives in Comparative Education.* New York: Garland.

Crossley, M. &Broadfoot, P. (1992). Comparative and International Research in Education: Scope, Problems and Potential. *British Journal of Educational Research,* 18(2), 99–112.

Fraser, S. (1962). *Jullien's Plan for Comparative Education: 1816–1817.* Nashville, TN: George Peabody College.

Halls, W.D. (Ed.) (1990). *Comparative Education: Contemporary Issues and Trends.* Paris: UNESCO/ Jessica Kingsley Publishers.

Hans, N. (1958). *Comparative Education.* London: Routledge & Kegan Paul.

Holmes, B. (1965). *Problems in Education: A Comparative Approach.* London: Routledge & Kegan Paul.

Holmes, B. (1981). *Comparative Education: Some Considerations of Method.* London: George Allen & Unwin.

Jullien, M.-A. (1817). *L'Esquisse et vue préliminaire d'un ouvrage sur l'éducation comparée.* Paris (reprinted by The International Bureau for Education, Geneva, 1962, IBE No. 243).

Kandel, I. (1955). *The New Era in Education: A Comparative Study.* Cambridge, MA: Houghton Mifflin.

Kazamias, A. (1961). Some Old and New Approaches to Methodology in Comparative Education. *Comparative Education Review,* 5(2), 90–96.

King, E. (1968). *Comparative Studies and Educational Decision.* London: Methuen.

Kobayashi, T. (1990). China, India, Japan and Korea. In W. D. Halls (Ed.), *Comparative Education: Contemporary Issues and Trends* (pp. 200–226). Paris: UNESCO.

Noah, H. & Eckstein, M. (1969). *Towards a Science of Comparative Education.* New York: Macmillan.

Ragin, C. (1987). *The Comparative Method: Moving Beyond Qualitative and Quantitative Strategies.* Berkeley, CA: University of California Press.

Schriewer, J. (1997). *World System and Interrelationship Networks: The Internationalization of Education and the Role of Comparative Inquiry.* Berlin: Humboldt University Research Papers, No. 2.

Schriewer, J. & B. Holmes (Eds.) (1998). *Theories and Methods in Comparative Education.* Frankfurt-am-Main: Peter Lang.

van Daele, H. (1993). *Que sais je? L'éducation Comparée.* Paris: Presses Universitaires de France.

Wilson, D. (1990). The Deleterious Impact of Rate-of-Return Studies on LDC Education Policies: An Indonesian Case. *Canadian and International Education,* 19(1), 32–49.

Wilson, D. (1994a). Comparative and International Education: Fraternal or Siamese Twins? A Preliminary Genealogy of Our Twin Fields. *Comparative Education Review,* 38(4), 449–486.

Wilson, D. (1994b). On Teaching the Methodology of Comparative Education: Why are There So Few Courses in Canada? *Canadian and International Education,* 23(1), 13–24.

Wilson, D. (1994c). Technical – Vocational Education: Comparative and International Studies. In T. Husén & N. Posthethwaite (Eds.), *International Encyclopedia of Education* (Second Edition) (Volume 11, pp. 6261–6266). Oxford: Pergamon Press.

Wilson, D. (2005a). A Prosopographic and Institutional History of Comparative Eduaction. In J. Schriewer (Ed.), *Discourse Formation in Comparative Education*. Frankfurt: Peter Lang, Comparative Studies Series.

Wilson, D. (2005b). The Education and Training of Knowledge Workers. In J. Zajda (Ed.), *The International Handbook of Globalisation and Education Policy Research*. Dordrecht: Springer.

Chapter 5
Globalisation and Marginalisation in Higher Education

Adeela Arshad-Ayaz

5.1 Introduction

Education cannot escape being influenced by the process of globalisation based on the principles of neo-liberal economic reform, a process that increases inequalities and marginalises already muted voices. The neo-liberal economic rationality of globalisation has framed the restructuring of education in such a manner that its function has changed from the production of knowledge to the production and management of wealth. As such, the interplay of market forces in higher education has undermined a vision of democratic society due to the superordinate influence of economic and political globalisation (Zajda 2008a and Zajda 2008b). As a result of accepting the dominant discourse of the neo-liberal, globalisation agenda without much critical analysis or debate regarding its consequences, education has forfeited its basic function of producing democratic citizens (see also Zajda, 2005; Zajda et al., 2008).

Globalisation is a popular and multidimensional concept. Political, economic, social and cultural dynamics of the contemporary world are subsumed within globalisation. In its political manifestation, globalisation refers to the dual phenomena of post-Cold War United States unipolarity, demonstrated by political and military hegemony. In its economic dimension, globalisation signifies, on the one hand, the neo-liberal economic agenda (also referred to as *McDonaldisation*) that is sweeping the world and, on the other, growing regional economic configurations. In the domain of culture, globalisation has come to signify both increased cultural contact (mainly but not exclusively through information and communication technologies; or ICTs) and cultural fragmentation manifested in the resurgence of micro, local and national cultural identities. Globalisation as a phenomenon is thus not a monolith, as it is often portrayed. It subsumes contradictory tendencies and forces, signifying tensions of cohesion on a scale hitherto unknown while

A. Arshad-Ayaz
Department of Integrated Studies in Education, McGill University, 3700 McTavish Street, Montreal, Quebec, H3A 1Y2, Canada

J. Zajda and V. Rust (eds.), *Globalisation, Policy and Comparative Research*,
DOI: 10.1007/978-1-4020-9547-4_5, © Springer Science + Bussiness Media B.V. 2009

suggesting the fragmentation of political, cultural and social identities at all levels (Zajda et al., 2006). To say that this process has affected almost all walks of life in one way or another would not be an exaggeration. The degree, level, and intensity of the impact vary from one society to another and from one institution to the next, depending on the space these societies occupy, their relative power, levels of their embeddedness in world economics and politics and the relative lead or lag they have with respect to information and technology integration. Education, like any other social institution, cannot escape the influence of globalisation, and these influences have varied from one educational system to another depending on their contact and interaction with the larger world (see also Lyotard, 1984; Zajda, 2005; Zajda et al. 2008a).

5.1.1 Economic Globalisation and Schools

Economic globalisation can be seen as the methodical growth of corporate capitalism within and across national borders in continuous search of markets, raw materials and low-cost labour. This is made possible by the latest developments in technology, which in turn permits the mobility of capital aided by increasingly open trade, communications and information-sharing. Neo-liberal economic rationality, a core dimension of contemporary globalisation, is grounded in beliefs about the fundamental fairness and justice of market forces. The assumption is that markets will distribute resources efficiently and justly to all those who make an effort. It is precisely this conception of market ideology that has given momentum to the political economy of globalisation. Under such a concept, the world is seen as a competitive marketplace and students primarily perceived as human capital. This view has led to a shift in the focus of education from social justice, inclusion, empowerment, equality and production of democratic citizens to managerialism, accountability, efficiency, privatisation and profit-making. Apple (1998) succinctly describes this shift as follows:

> Neo-liberals…are guided by a vision of the weak state. Thus, what is private is necessarily good and what is public is necessarily bad. Public institutions such as schools are 'black holes' into which money is poured—and then seemingly disappears…For neo-liberals, there is one from of rationality that is more powerful than any other—economic rationality. Efficiency and an 'ethic' of cost-benefit analysis are the dominant norms. (p. 81)

The neo-liberal ideology in education is reflected in a variety of ways in different contexts. The reasons used by neo-liberals for the introduction of market principles into education are numerous, but they mainly contend that education is best delivered by the private sector as opposed to government schools. They point to the overcrowding of public schools and mounting budget deficits therein, along with the dissatisfaction of parents about both the quality and cost of public education. Neo-liberals propose a solution to these problems through increasing the role of market forces in the system of education, itself to be achieved through either contracting out education to the private sector, introducing user fees or excising from the curriculum those areas of study, such as history, social sciences, extra-curricular activities other than sports, and the arts, which they view as either irrelevant to the needs of the market or an anathema to this corporate ethos.

A variety of suggestions, including tax deductions for tuition expenses and compensatory tuition vouchers to low-income families are offered as an alternative to public education. But above all the proponents of the market model argue that people value the freedom to choose as a basic right. The core justifications of neo-liberals are based on the principles of *choice* and *democracy*. Proponents of neo-liberalism argue that democracy can only be granted by the freedom to exercise choice and as such parents should have a choice in sending their children wherever they prefer (Bast, 2002; Ebeling, 2000; Belz, 1998). Critics of neo-liberalism, however, point out that such a proposition tends to transform a political concept into an economic concept and disguises the race, class and gender dimensions of individuals − as customers (Ball, 1994; Apple, 1996). The popular slogans used by the pro-market advocates are all variations of the theme of education for employment (Chubb & Moe, 1990). These and other such slogans are based on the argument that schools should be able to produce a highly skilled advanced workforce for a technically advanced world market. Apple is nevertheless critical of such a misleading conception. According to him,

> The paid labor market will increasingly be dominated by low-paying, repetitive work in retail, trade, and service sector. This is made strikingly clear by one fact. There will be more cashier jobs created by the year 2005 than jobs for computer scientists, system analysts, physical therapists, operations analysts, and radiologic technicians *combined*. In fact it is the service sector where 95% of all new positions will be found. (p. 85)

Thus, what is being created is not a knowledge economy but a service economy.

5.1.2   *Democratic Education*

There is a consensus among scholars that, like democracy, democratic education is also a social construct. Dewey (1916/1985) argued that the qualities needed for democratic education must be socially created through appropriate education (p. 93). Democratic education aims to help students in gaining the knowledge, attitudes and skills needed to participate in a just and democratic society by guiding them to think beyond narrow self-interests, thereby challenging racism, religious intolerance, sexism, classism and other socially undermining prejudices. Democratic education provides students with an opportunity to see the world as it is, while giving them an opportunity to imagine a world in terms of how it might be, so to transform the unjust and mundane into the just and beautiful. According to Parker (2003), democratic education for 'advanced democracy' requires at least five qualities:

- A sense of the 'inescapable network of mutuality' and 'inter-being'
- Practical judgment (everyday, situated intelligence)

- A shared fund of civic knowledge (e.g. knowing the conditions that have undermined democracies in the past)
- A shared fund of civic know-how (e.g. deliberation skills and the disposition to use them)
- A thirst for justice for others and for oneself (p. 23)

Seen from this point of view the purpose of education is to encourage critical thinking that leads to the creation and dissemination of knowledge for social, moral and just purposes rather than the commercialisation of education for profit generation.

5.2 Higher Education, Globalisation and Democracy

The interplay of market forces in higher education has led to changes in educational policy and culture, which in turn have affected how education is defined, whom it serves, and how it is assessed. Given these broader trends, the following questions deserve attention: (1) How has the neo-liberal agenda shaped teaching and curriculum in higher education? (2) How has the neo-liberal agenda affected research and scholarship in higher education? (3) How has the neo-liberal agenda transformed the democratic mission of education? In this analysis, scholarship about the direction of higher education is examined, supplemented with examples from the developed world. This analysis seeks to address the interplay of market forces in higher education that have led to changes in educational policy which ultimately contravene the democratic purposes of schools, including higher education.

5.2.1 Aims of Neo-Liberal Agenda in Higher Education

Marketisation refers to the impact of globalisation on the organising, administration and policy principles of education in the global era. Commodification refers to the transformation of education into a commodity that can be bought and sold in accordance with the principles of supply and demand and on which other economic and market principles such as diminishing marginal utility, optimal value and satisfaction apply. With the economic, political and cultural processes of globalisation very much in place, there are visible tensions between the demands of global capital (the neo-liberal economic agenda) and the imperatives of education as a means of imparting civic and democratic values. The supremacy of economic logic and interests has, among other things, shifted the focus of education from producing democratic citizens to producing a flexible and adaptable work force for the new economy. Educational institutions are now expected to produce workers and not citizens. Coupled with this is an accompanying belief that schools and other educational institutions can be more effectively run as businesses (Osborne, 2001).

5.2.2 Affect of Neo-Liberal Agenda on Teaching and Curriculum

Corporate principles and practices of management are being introduced into the educational system by means of policy reforms. The underlying belief is that if corporations can be run successfully using these principles then so can schools and universities. Privatisation, reduced government spending, the elevation of tuition fees and introduction of user charges and the financing of only *profitable* and *market-oriented* fields of study seems to be the driving force in resource allocation not only in developing countries facing fiscal difficulties but also in more highly developed countries (Dei & Karumanchery, 2001).

Empirical evidence from the UK illustrates this pattern. Changes in higher education policy in the wake of Thatcherism were rapid and systemic (Gamble, 1989). In the mid-1980s, British business leaders worked with the Thatcher government to build an *enterprise* culture in tertiary education. In 1985, the Jarret Committee which was chaired by a leading industrialist, called for higher education to adopt more efficient managerial styles and structures. Similarly, the Council for Industry and Higher Education, an independent body, also aimed to encourage industry and higher education to work together. It called for 'access to and more variety in higher education, as well as a shift toward science and technology provision' (Pratt, 1992, p. 38). It is not surprising that the council was composed of 32 heads of large corporations and 12 heads of higher education institutions as the policy directions and values were closely aligned with neo-liberal principles.

In contrast to the rapid and systematic changes introduced in the higher education system in Britain, changes in the USA occurred over a longer period of time and through a variety of government bodies and agencies. The idea of market forces in higher education was introduced in the 1970s by the Nixon administration working with groups like the Committee for Economic Development and the Carnegie Foundation for the Advancement of Teaching. One of the outcomes of this marketisation of higher education was that the government shifted its aid focus from institutions (primarily universities) to individual students. This made students *consumers* of tertiary education. At the same time institutions started competing with each other to attract students and their grants (McPherson & Schapiro, 1993).

Research policies in the USA were also shaped by leaders of large corporations along with the heads of universities and political leaders, similar to what transpired in the UK. Organisations such as the Business-Higher Education Forum (1983, 1986) and Government-University-Industry Research Roundtable (1992) were responsible for crafting a policy of competitiveness that emphasised the role that high-technology research played in national economic development. The landmark act that encouraged *academic capitalism* was the Bayh-Dole Act of 1980. This allowed universities and small businesses to retain title to inventions developed with federal research and development monies. According to the Act, 'it is the policy and objective of the Congress...to promote collaboration between commercial concerns and non-profit organisations, *including universities*'

(Bayh-Dole Act, 1980). Although there was little formal national level policy for curricula and training between the 1980s and 1990s, the federal grant and contract monies for techno-science increased while monies for the humanities and social sciences decreased dramatically.

Scholars have noted the growing influence of corporate ideas and integration in higher education. Taylor (2001) argues that this increase is manifested in and through partnerships and multi-stakeholder collaboration. This tendency, according to Taylor, is produced by and in turn reproduces the discourse of 'education for economic prosperity' (Taylor, 2001, p. 176). This discourse has met with very little resistance from educators. This passivity, according to Taylor, is due to three main reasons:

> First, the futurist tone of *knowledge economy discourse* makes it difficult to challenge, and the promise of jobs in high performing, democratic workplaces is attractive to all stakeholders. Second, given youth unemployment rates and economic uncertainty, the discourse of progressive vocationalism… is seductive for parents, students, and teachers who are concerned about the life chances of non-college bound youth. Finally, the pragmatic realities of decreased educational funding make the idea of increased external support through partnerships attractive to educators. (Taylor, 2001, p. 176)

The increased private sector–government collaboration in higher education comes at a cost, however. While it does make available larger blocks of funding, it limits the focus of education from its democratic purpose. This translates, in practice, into shifting resources and attention away from liberal arts, humanities and social sciences to subjects that are more market-oriented. On the administrative side such collaborations result in a smaller work force of instructors and staff, increased workloads for teachers, arbitrary hiring and firing, and the renting out of educational space to corporate advertisements. It also compels national, state and provincial governments to push for market reforms in educational institutions.

These reforms do not take into consideration the variable and unequal impact of the resultant policies in terms of race, class and gender. Dei and Karumanchery (2001) build on Hatcher's (1998) study of educational reforms in Britain to argue that,

> these [neo-liberal] types of reforms display four main characteristics: an abstract universalism that downplays the specificities of local school situations; a decontextualization that devalues the importance of students' experiences, histories, cultures, and identities as they relate to the learning process; a consensualism that avoids dealing with conflict and controversy; and a managerialism that privileges a top-down approach to the administration of schooling. (p. 191)

McLaren (2003) refers to this as the 'corporatisation and businessification of education' (p. 43). The hallmarks of this phenomenon are trends such as standardised testing. Such testing financially benefits the large publishing houses and is used by the capitalist class as a mode of social control (pp. 43–45). Citing Gluckman (2002), McLaren states that:

> Today the creation and scoring of K-12 tests is a multimillion dollar industry. Businesses are predictably emphasizing "output" in their workers, and business based management techniques are increasingly being adopted in schools. The business model that drives the U.S. classroom requires frequent and efficient testing. The K-12 standardized testing industry generates sales of about 1.5 billion dollars a year. (p. 43)

5.2.3 Neo-Liberal Agenda Affect on Culture of Research and Scholarship in Higher Education

The corporate assault on education is not confined to K-12 education alone, as it is equally apparent in higher education as well (McLaren, 2003). Entrepreneurial practices have already permeated and become normalised in institutions of higher education. Salient among these practices are:

- The criteria employed in businesses for efficiency and production have been extended to educational institutions in an inappropriate fashion.
- The focus has shifted from citizen-centred, academic research-based curriculum to economy-centred vocational training.
- Education has lost ground as a public good and is increasingly becoming a marketable commodity.
- Teachers' autonomy, independence and control over their work has been reduced and placed in the hands of administrators.
- An increased trend towards privatisation and decentralisation has emerged.
- As a result of the above-mentioned factors, higher education is being linked more to the market and less to the pursuit of truth.

As Stromquist and Monkman (2000) aptly note:

> Guided by a climate of knowledge as production, the university may become hostile or indifferent to the subjects dealing with ethics, social justice, critical studies, and gender studies. Life in the university will likely change under globalisation. Intellectuals...will become less the guardians of the search for truth, and administrators will assume a dominant role. In this regard, norms that have traditionally been part of university life may come under questioning. One such norm is tenure. (p. 14)

Universities are increasingly being assessed and measured by performance indicators that are more quantitative than qualitative; more market-oriented than academic. Closer links between the universities and industry have led to a cross-commercialisation of research. As empirical evidence from the UK shows, the interest of British politicians and industrialists was clearly reflected in the Education Act of 1988, which began to transform the intentions of corporate leaders into laws. It lessened differences between universities and polytechnics and abolished the University Grants Committee (UGC) that used to act as a buffer between the state and the institutions of higher learning along with the polytechnic board, replacing them with smaller boards dominated by business leaders (Fulton, 1991). This resulted in the curtailing of academic autonomy and the end of an era of an independent academic culture (Shattock, 1994). By this time the British government had also declared that 'state expenditures on higher education should be regarded as payments for services provided rather than as block grants to institutions' (Johnes, 1992, p. 173). In 1992, the binary system was abolished by the Department of Education and Science (DES). As a result of this, teaching and research, once considered a single function in university funding, were differentiated and each allocated to institutions on a separate bidding system.

This was done under the rubric of liberalisation of the economy. This resulted in a significant shift towards career training with an emphasis on science and technology in both research and numbers of students. National research policies moved away from basic or *pure* research to state initiatives aimed at increasing industrial competitiveness. Due to the major changes in governance structures mentioned above, the education system lost its autonomy and professors lost many of their prerogatives with regard to control over their work:

Academic capitalism in the U.K. also resonated in the U.S... Slaughter (1998) notes,

Overall, in the 1980s and 1990s, U.S. policy at the federal level shifted so that colleges and universities were able to engage in academic capitalism. Professors were discouraged from pursuing pure research and encouraged to engage in more practical matters. (p. 64)

These trends are also apparent in other English speaking countries, such as Canada. Recent policy documents express a strong need to establish closer ties with the labour market and '[To adapt] education to the real requirements of the labour market...making it more relevant, and...easing the transition into the workplace' (Gouvernement du Quebec, 1996, p. 54).

A number of far-reaching implications of globalisation on higher education can be pinpointed. First, the funds available for post-secondary education have significantly shrunk. Second, techno-science and fields closely involved with markets, particularly international markets, are acquiring a growing importance in universities. Third, there is a tighter relationship between multinational corporations and state agencies concerned with product development. And fourth, there is an increased focus on global intellectual property strategies. All this has led to a substantial change in the culture of higher education over the past few decades. Universities have become more commercial and entrepreneurial while the 'civilising mission' of higher education, the weight that used to be given to the aesthetic and ethical ideals of liberal culture, seems to have been overshadowed by the new emphasis placed on techno-science. Accountability instead of quality seems to be the buzz word of higher education policy. Hecht (1994), in his study of contemporary college teachers, quotes a University of California at Los Angeles (UCLA) administrator as stating, 'Can a university be run like a business? You bet it can.... Most universities can do a significant job of cutting costs through the same re-engineering of processes and work that have characterized the best for-profit corporations' (p. 6).

The concept of *user pays* has spread to almost all universities, even inside universities, with each individual or department having to pay for services from other sections, such as interdepartmental payments for services like library usage, postage costs, media application, graphic services and utility costs which used to be centrally budgeted. As a result of economies of scale some sections of universities, such as small philosophy departments, are affected more than other sections. Increasingly more part-time staff are being hired, supplementing a small core of academics who receive higher pay and benefits.

In its 1994 report on higher education, the World Bank (1994) urged countries to shift from dependence on just one source of funding – the state – toward multiple sources, with more money coming from student fees, consultancies and donations. This message was quickly taken up by many Anglo-American countries. In Australia, for instance, a report released in November 1995 by the Economic Planning Advisory Commission stated that, 'micro-economic reforms embracing "market incentives" should be extended to the education and training sector' (Armitage, 1996, p. 8). This shift in higher education from ethical values, high ideals and the pursuit of pure knowledge in order to address civic needs is not only the result of influence from international financiers and supranational bodies like the World Bank and Organization for economic Cooperation and Development (OECD), but also the product of regional trade organisations. Buchbindar and Rajagopal (1996), writing about the impact of free trade and globalisation on Canadian universities, identify the specific chapters of North America Free Trade Agreement (NAFTA) – particularly Cross Border Trade and Services, Telecommunications, and Investment Services and Related Matters – that affect education. They also believe that the past 20 years of changes have 'softened up' Canadian universities and left them 'both vulnerable and to a great degree, acquiescent to the wide ranging influences of globalisation' (pp. 289–290).

In general the effects of such agreements and policies have led universities in Australia, Canada, the UK and the USA to respond in a similar manner, i.e. to rely less and less on the state and concentrate on market forces. Such trends have caused many academics to grow worried about the state of education. Aitkin (1996) records the concerns voiced by one university vice-chancellor:

> It sometimes seems that we are speeding towards a national system of post secondary credentialing, rather than a national system of education which produces self-confident altruistic adult citizens, capable of accepting responsibility for their own learning through life, and of making the hard decisions that build good societies. (p. 82)

Jessop (1993) and Mowery (1994) illustrate a trend towards advocacy of supply-side economic policies and a shift in public interest resources from social welfare programmes to economic development efforts in Australia, the UK, Canada, and the USA between the 1980s and the 1990s (see also Great Britain White Paper, 1993). Post-secondary education was to be directed towards national wealth creation and away from its traditional concern with the liberal education of undergraduates. Recently, due to global competition, there has been much emphasis on techno-science, but the problem with techno-science, as Aronowitz and Di Fazio (1994) point out, is that it makes impossible the separation of science and technology, basic and applied research, discovery and innovation. Such scholarship is at once science and product, thus collapsing the distinction between knowledge and commodity. Such emphasis on techno-science, as Aronowitz and Di Fazio point out, endangers the very idea of pure or disinterested shared knowledge or research. 'Funds increasingly are allocated on the criterion of applicability of results of inquiry to practical—that is, industrial—uses' (p. 66).

State and business leaders have joined forces to establish programmes to stimulate innovation, usually through industry–government–academic partnerships, led by industry, held together by government, and serviced by universities on the

techno-science side (Buchbindar & Newson 1990). With the progress of globalisation, more and more agreements like the European Community (EC), NAFTA, and the Trade-Related Aspects of Intellectual Property Rights (TRIPS) agreement established the protection of intellectual property resulting from techno-science. Although the TRIPS was initially aimed at reducing competition from states with low labour costs and rising educational attainment, it has nevertheless led to considerable pressure on higher education. As a result, universities have increasingly become a source that corporations and governments look to for discoveries that will yield intellectual property.

5.2.4   Impacts of Neo-Liberal Agenda on Democratic Function

The paradigm shift in education manifested in dual and self-reinforcing phenomena: increasing marketisation and the commodification of education. A net result of this interaction is the overshadowing of the democratic purposes of education. As Taylor (2001) notes, the market model of education moves away from

> Dewey's notion that the purpose of work education is not to adapt workers to an existing industrial regime but rather to alter the existing industrial system and ultimately transform it by developing capacities that allow workers greater control over their fates. (p. 182)

The results of failing to attend to the democratic goals of public education have resulted in more societies demonstrating the worrisome presence of a *democratic deficit*. The presence of this deficit shows that the dynamics of capitalism have an upper hand in this struggle and that more and more people seem to be giving up their demands for inclusive citizenship (Osborne, 2001, p. 37). Though, according to Osborne, education cannot fix this structural problem, it has an important role to play in informing students about its existence and about the various alternative ways of 'conceptualizing and organizing democracy to make it more socially just and inclusively participatory' (p. 38).

Pragmatists such as Dewey (1916/1985) and Parker (2003) have forcefully argued for a utilitarian notion of knowledge as against knowledge for the sake of knowing. Knowledge production in this democratic vein is a dialectical process embedded in a dialectical relationship between knowledge for its own sake and knowledge for productivity. To argue for one at the exclusion of the other will not only be naïve but also counterproductive. In what have come to be known as knowledge economies, knowledge or education that is not productive will be a detriment for both the recipients of such knowledge, as well as for the overall social and economic well-being of the society. Conversely if the ultimate goal of knowledge production is creation of wealth, it will give rise to a society where individualism replaces social responsibility and justice. As much as this might sound like a hen-and-egg dilemma, it is not. Knowledge has to be reoriented so that it fosters what Freire (1970) terms *consciencisation*. *Consciencisation* anticipates education as a powerful instrument for social change towards a just and equitable society. It is a process that leads to people's ability to analyze and connect knowledge to actual life situations and plan action, it demands critical understanding of ideology which is never free of social and historical forces. Any effort leading to consciencisation demands continued action and reflection in education. Such knowledge is not inimical to productive activity but puts the emphasis on social responsibility before productivity. This does not mean that by putting productivity second, however, that activities geared towards wealth generation suffer in any way. Knowledge based on the doctrine of democratic education not only produces better citizens but also produces better workers and a society where justice, tolerance, equity and inclusiveness prevail.

5.3 Evaluation

Global trends in higher education (in both the developed and developing worlds) have given rise to the 'entrepreneurial' or 'market university'. Such institutions are characterised by closer university – business partnership and greater faculty responsibility for accessing external resources for funding and managerialism. In short, the role of the university becomes more like that of any market-related organisation. Slaughter and Leslie (1997) term this 'academic capitalism'. As a result research is judged by its ability to produce new products. Teaching is assessed in terms of the marketable skills it develops. Universities are downsized and their 'peripheral' activities eliminated in the name of cost efficiency. Under such conditions knowledge is being reconceptualised so as to value entrepreneurial research, with emphasis being given to science, technology and innovation that are more marketable than such non-marketable forms of knowledge such as the social sciences and liberal arts.

This places the conventional role of education as the producer and guarantor of academic freedom, critical reflection, dialogue and exchange of ideas in tension with income-generating market-oriented activities. The above-mentioned educational policies have admittedly, yielded some positive financial results – most of which have accrued to the developed and some newly developing economies. On the other hand, these policies, heavily armed with and invested in techno-science, have led in part to the marginalisation of the 'other' and have deepened the already existing digital, economic, cultural and social divide between the rich and poor.

Let me return to the notion of democratic education that I explicated in the beginning of the chapter. Democratic education aims at creating a knowledge base which fosters a more inclusive society. It does not call for knowledge for the sake of knowing. It is also not against production of knowledge that will bring economic growth and progress to the society. What it calls for is caution and reflexive thinking on the dialectical relationship between democracy and the market. It calls for a balance between the forces of production and the demands for inclusion (political, economic, social, racial and cultural) and social justice. In practical terms it foregrounds and emphasises teaching of those subjects that foster democratic and inclusive values. This involves teaching such subjects from a paradigm that recognises difference, celebrates diversity and places democracy ahead of wealth generation and individualism. It is my conviction that democratic values will further and not negatively affect productivity in a knowledge-based-society.

In terms of educational policy reforms the developing countries have been brought into the process of globalisation through the finance-driven policy reforms. Finance for these reforms comes largely from the World Bank and other intergovernmental lending agencies and has strings attached to it. A net result of these finance-driven economically motivated reforms is adoption of educational policies that bear little or no relevance to the local political, social and cultural ethos. These policies focus more on teaching of subjects that would produce workers for a globalised economy. As in the West, subjects that teach or have the potential of imparting civic and democratic values are cut down in favour of market-oriented subjects. These policy reforms thus create a democratic deficit.

While the general thrust of globalised discourse is to operate in a homogenised and universalised world, or the global, it has to be kept in mind that local conditions have their own dynamics and that often there is a complex dialogue between the globalised and the local which may create new alliances or divides. It thus becomes very important for those who advocate the paradigm of globalisation to understand that there is a multitude of tendencies and trends operating within this framework, and that there is a continuing presence of a variety of discourses limiting the capacity of a homogenised globe.

There has also been growing concern over the lack of transnational imagination in curriculum both in developed and in developing societies, although the process of globalisation and its major themes themselves are very much the result of the success of transnational social movements. There is a continual worldwide convergence of educational systems and curricula. Not only is there an increased emphasis on subjects such as mathematics and science but even the number of classroom hours devoted to each is almost identical across nation states. There is also concern over the tendency of such progress to reinforce sameness by bringing the US community college education model to people around the world.

To conclude, having established that there are tensions between the market forces characterised by the neo-liberal economic agenda and the traditional vocation of higher education and that these tensions serve to undermine the democratic function of education and consequently a democratic society itself, the question that needs to be addressed is: Is there a way out of the situation? How can the tensions between the market forces and the demands for a democratic society be addressed? Who are the key players who need to discuss, debate and negotiate the checks and balances that should to be instituted so that the corporate agenda does not steamroll the democratic function of higher education? Finally, what are the main issues that need to be fore-grounded?

It would not be an exaggeration to say that the restructuring of higher education in the wake of the neo-liberal economic agenda has been rather one-sided. Even left of centre governments (these include socially liberal but fiscally conservative liberal governments in Canada, the labour government in Britain and Democratic governments in the USA) have brought about changes such as drastic cuts to education financing that have left universities with no choice but to look towards the private sector for help. The decisions in this respect were made without the participation or input of important stake-holders such as teachers, parents and most importantly the students themselves. There is a need to think of ways in which an inter-stakeholder dialogue might be initiated so that the demands of the market and the demands of a civil and democratic society can be accommodated.

5.4 Conclusion

While I have pinpointed some of the ways in which the tensions between the market-orientation of the process of globalisation and democratic function of higher education are being played out, there are a number of issues that need to be at the forefront of research on globalisation and higher education. First, I have argued that globalisation is a useful analytical category to examine the problems of higher education. There is however a need for further conceptualisation and theorisation on issues related to globalisation and education. Furthermore, issues related to the relationship between corporate/private sector funding and academic freedom need to be fore-grounded. Further research is needed on questions such as: How can checks and balances be created to avoid the transformation of universities from educational institutions into corporate bodies? To what extent are universities surrendering autonomy in order to get private funding and what measures can be taken to make them more autonomous? Finally, what measures are needed to ensure that the social sciences, liberal arts and humanities are assigned equal importance in the higher education system?

References

Aitkin, D. (1996). The astonishing rise of higher education. *Quadrant*, 40(1), pp.82–86.

Apple, M. (1996). *Cultural Politics of Education*. New York: Teachers College Press.

Apple, M. (1998). Under the new hegemonic alliance: Conservatism and educational policy in the United States. In K. Sullivan (Ed.). *Education and Change in the Pacific Rim: Meeting the Challenges*. Wallingford: Triangle Books.

Armitage, C. (1996, May 18–19). The threat to higher learning. *The Weekend Australian*.

Aronowitz, S. & Di Fazio, W. (1994). *The Jobless Future: Sci-Tech and the Dogma of Work*. Minneapolis, MN: University of Minnesota Press.

Ball, S. (1994). *Education Reform: A Critical and Post-structural Approach*. Buckingham/ Philadelphia, PA: Open University Press.

Bast, J. (2002, February). The year of school vouchers. *The Monthly Heartlander*. Retrieved from http://www.heartland.org/archives/heartlander/hlfeb02.htm.

Bayh-Dole Act (1980). Retrieved from http://www.cptech.org/ip/health/bd/

Belz, J, (1998, October 17). Death to schools. *World*. Retrieved from http://www.worldmag.com/ world/issue/10-17-98/.

Buchbindar, H. & Rajagopal, P. (1996). Canadian universities: The impact of free trade and glo-balisation. *Higher Education*, 31, 282–299.

Buchbindar, H. & Newson, J. (1990). Corporate-university linkages in Canada: Transforming a public institution. *Higher Education*, 20, 355–379.

Business-Higher Education Forum. (1983, April). *American Competitive Challenge: The Need for a National Response*. Washington, DC: The Business-Higher Education Forum.

Business-Higher Education Forum. (1986, January). *Export Controls: The Need to Balance National Objectives*. Washington, DC: Author.

Chubb, J. & Moe, T. (1990). *Politics, Markets, and America's Schools*. Washington, DC: Brookings Institution.

Dei, S. & Karumanchery, L. (2001). School reforms in Ontario: The 'marketization of education' and the resulting silence on equity. In J. Portelli & P. Solomon (Eds.). *The Erosion of Democracy in Education*. Detselig Enterprises Ltd.

Dewey, J. (1916/1985). *Democracy and Education*. New York: Macmillan.

Ebeling, R. (2000, February). *Its Time to Put Public Education Behind Us*. The Future of Freedom Foundation, commentaries. Retrieved from http://www.fff.org/comment/ed0200f.asp.

Freire, P. (1970). *Pedagogy of the Oppressed*. New York: Seabury Press.

Fulton, O. (1991). Slouching towards a mass system: Society, government, and institutions in the United Kingdom. *Higher education*, 21, 589–605.

Gamble, A. (1989). Privatization, Thatcherism, and the British state. *Journal of Law and Society*. 16(1).

Gluckman, A. (2002, January/February). Testing…testing…one, two, three: The commercial side of standardized-testing. *Dollars and Sense*, 239, 32–37.

Gouvernement du Quebec (1996). *The State of Education in Quebec, 1995–1996*. Quebec City: Author.

Government-University-Industry Research Roundtable (1992). *Fateful Choices: The Future of the U.S. Academic Research Enterprise*. Washington, DC: National Academy Press.

Great Britain White Paper (1993). *Realizing Our Potential: Strategy for Science, Engineering and Technology*. London: Her Majesty's Stationary Office.

Hatcher, R. (1998). Social justice and the politics of school effectiveness and improvement. *British Race, Ethnicity and Education*, 1(2), 267–289.

Hecht, J. (1994). Today's college teachers: cheap and temporary. *Labor Notes*, No. 188, November.

Jessop, B. (1993). Towards a Schumpeterian workfare state? Preliminary remarks on post-fordist political economy. *Studies in Political Economy*, 40, 7–39.

Johnes, G. (1992). Bidding for students in Britain – why the UFC auction "failed". *Higher Education*, 23, 173–182.

Lyotard, J. (1984). *The Post-Modern Condition: A Report on Knowledge*. Tr. G. Bennington & B. Massumi (Trans.). Minneapolis, MN: University of Minnesota Press.

McLaren, P. (2003). *Life in Schools: An Introduction to Critical Pedagogy in the Foundations of Education* (4th ed.). Boston, MA: Allen & Brown.

McPherson, M. & Schapiro, M. (1993). Changing patterns of college finance and enrollment. In D. Breneman, L. Leslie, & R. Anderson (Eds.). *ASHE Reader on Finance in Higher Education*. Needham Heights, MA: Ginn.

Mowery, D. (1994). *Science and Technology Policy in Interdependent Economies*. Dordrecht: Kluwer.

Osborne, K. (2001). Democracy, democratic citizenship, and education. In J. Portelli & R. Solomon (Eds.). *The Erosion of Democracy in Education*. Calgary: Detselig Enterprise Ltd.

Parker, W. (2003). *Teaching Democracy: Unity and Diversity in Public Life*. New York/London: Teacher's College Press.

Pratt, J. (1992). Unification of higher education in the United Kingdom. *European Journal of Education*, 27(1/2), 29–43.

Slaughter, S. (1998). National higher education policies in a global economy. In J. Currie & J. Newson (Eds.). *Universities and Globalisation: Critical Perspectives*. London/New Delhi: Sage.

Slaughter, S. & Leslie, L. (1997). *Academic Capitalism: Politics, Policies and the Entrepreneurial University*. Baltimore, MD: The Johns Hopkins University Press.

Shattock, M. (1994). *The UGC and the Management of British Universities*. London: The society for research into higher education/Open University press.

Stromquist, N. & Monkman, K. (Eds.). (2000). *Globalisation and Education: Integration and Contestation Across Cultures*. Towman & Littlefield.

Taylor, A. (2001). Education, business, and the 'knowledge economy'. In J. Portelli & R. Solomon (Eds.). *The Erosion of Democracy in Education*. Calgary: Detselig Enterprise Ltd.

World Bank (1994). *Higher Education: The Lessons of Experience*. Washington, DC: Author.

Zajda, J. (2005). Globalisation, Education and Policy: changing Paradigms. In J. Zajda (Ed.). *The International Handbook of Globalisation and Education Policy Research* pp. 1–22. Dordrecht: Springer.

Zajda, J. Majhanovich, S., & Rust, V. (2006). Education and social justice: Issues of liberty and equality in the global culture. In J. Zajda, S. Majhanovich, & V. Rust (Eds.). *Education and Social Justice* (pp. 1–12). Dordrecht: Springer.

Zajda, J., Davies, L., & Majhanovich, S. (2008a). (Eds.). *Comparative and Global Pedagogies: Equity, Access and Democracy in Education*. Dordrecht: Springer.

Zajda, J. Biraimah, B., & Gaudelli, W. (2008b). (Eds.). *Education and Social Inequality in the Global Culture*. Dordrecht: Springer.

Chapter 6
Globalisation of Education Policy: Its Effects on Developing Countries

Letitia Williams

6.1 Globalisation, Education and Development

Education has long been linked to national development and has been viewed as necessary not only for increased economic productivity, but also for promoting national unity and preparing young people for the rights and obligations of citizenship to their particular nation (Samoff, 1999; Zajda, 2005; Zajdaet al., 2008a; Morrow and Torres, 2000). To fulfill these roles in individual nation states, it is important that education policy formation remain, by and large, an indigenous process with the evolution of national educational systems reflecting the needs of particular societies. However, the increasing globalisation of education policy threatens the indigenous evolution of national education systems and implicitly suggests a global solution that ignores the fact that 'in practice education is interactive, replete with discontinuities and always locally contingent' (Samoff, 1996, p. 254). The globalisation of education policy reduces education's role in society by examining it in the context of the most globalised nations and their economies, and, in so doing, suggests that education's role is the same in all nations and the skills, values or type of citizen needed does not vary (Soudien, 2005). The assumption is that the 'the only suitable development strategy for the Third World is to imitate the industrialised countries at their present level of development' (Fagerlind & Saha, 1989, p. 44). With globalisation largely moving from industrialised nations and the international agencies located in them to developing nations, the objectives of Third World leaders and the needs of these nations may be ignored as education becomes a preparation for international rather than national development.

The education policy changes that result from the globalisation process can be viewed largely as the result of the neoliberal economic principles, informed by human capital theory, that characterise the global marketplace and are upheld by

L. Williams
University of Maryland, College Park, 3100 Hornbake Library, South Wing, College Park, MD 20742, USA

J. Zajda and V. Rust (eds.), *Globalisation, Policy and Comparative Research*,
DOI: 10.1007/978-1-4020-9547-4_6, © Springer Science + Bussiness Media B.V. 2009

the multinational corporations and international agencies that hold sway in the global economy (Zajda, 2005, 2007). The combination of human capital concepts that regard persons as human capital and education as an investment that raises chances of future income and can be measured in the same manner as investments in physical capital, and neoliberal economic principles that advocate reduced public spending, reliance on market forces and privatisation helps shape a global education reform agenda that has certain characteristics and potentially dire consequences for developing nations. These characteristics include most governments being put under pressure to reduce the growth of public spending on education and the resulting advocacy of decentralisation, privatisation and user fees, shifting emphasis from higher education to basic education, and the curriculum changes that reflect the focus of human capital theory with education being viewed as a tool for increasing economic productivity, while, for the most part, paying little attention to its other roles in society. While proponents of the neoliberal agenda, such as the World Bank, only highlight the benefits of the above-mentioned policies, the consequences may not be positive for developing nations and indeed may be in opposition to national goals and national needs. Each of these policies must be critically examined to see that they meet the needs of the local context instead of being swallowed wholesale as a bitter pill that will cure the aches of national educational systems around the globe and lead to development.

6.2   Globalisation Discourses

As Zajda, Biraimah and Gaudelli (2008b) remind us, 'Globalisation is not an easy term to define' (p. xvii). Some 3,000 definitions of globalisation were offered in 1998 alone (Zajda et al., 2008b, p. xvii). The definition of globalisation offered here is taken from *Global Transformations: Politics, Economics, Culture* (Held et al., 1999). The authors define globalisation as 'A process (or set of processes) which embodies a transformation in the spatial organisation of social relations and transactions – assessed in terms of their extensity, intensity, velocity and impact – generating transcontinental or interregional flows and networks of activity, interaction and the exercise of power' (Held et al., 1999, p. 16). This definition of globalisation can prove useful in that it recognises that the effects of globalisation are not uniform but rather may vary in extensity, intensity, velocity and impact. However, the reciprocal nature of the exchange suggested by use of the terms 'flows', 'networks' and 'interaction' is not accepted in this chapter. Instead, it is suggested that 'core-periphery relations remain highly relevant' (Klak, 1998, p. 6) for understanding the process of globalisation. It is argued here that globalisation largely moves from the center to the periphery, from more industrialised or developed nations to less industrialised or developing nations. Thus, while employing the above definition, my examination of the impact of globalisation on education focuses on developing countries because the 'flows' seem to move from developed to developing countries instead of being multidirectional and most developing countries are outside of the networks of activity, interaction and the exercise of power.

The term globalisation is a contested one and is not often precisely explained making any discussion of the topic difficult. In addition, there is a plurality of views with regard to the nature of the process ranging from homogenisation to hybridisation. Indeed, several authors caution against taking an overly simplistic view of globalisation because the process itself interacts with the histories and realities of different nations in different ways. Useful here is Leon Tikly's assessment of the different approaches to globalisation in the literature. Tikly (2001) suggests that there are three approaches commonly taken. First, the hyperglobalist approach that is premised on the idea that we are entering a truly global age 'involving the triumph of global capitalism and the advent of distinctively new forms of global culture, governance and of civil society. In this view we are witnessing the demise of the nation state' (Tikly, 2001, p. 153). In the hyperglobalist approach the demise of the nation state leads to the demise of the goals of national education and the creation of a national culture.

The second approach is what Tikly (2001) describes as the sceptical approach to globalisation. Advocates of this approach such as Andy Green (1997), argue that though there is a growing trend towards regionalisation in trade and politics this in no way signals the demise of the nation state. On the contrary, 'sceptics' contest the idea that in the globalised world the nation state is powerless and argue instead that the nation state is of even greater significance as it must manage the 'deepening crisis tendencies of capitalism' (Tikly, 2001, p. 153). With respect to education sceptics recognise that national education systems have been affected by globalisation but they resist the notion that globalisation means that national education systems are disappearing or that nation states have no control over them (Green, 1997). While aspects of the sceptical approach are useful for the purposes of this chapter in that it recognises that globalisation has not led to 'the erosion of North-South inequalities but, on the contrary, to growing economic marginalisation of many "Third World" states' (Held et al., 1999, p. 6), the usefulness of this approach is limited because many of the sceptics focus on Western industrialised countries with very little attention paid to less-developed nations. Therefore, while the arguments about the continued control and importance that the nation state still maintains in the global age may accurately depict governance in developed nations they may not be as valid when looking at the effects of globalisation on developing nations.

The third approach is the transformationalist approach. Like the hyperglobalists, transformationalists suggest that 'we are indeed experiencing unprecedented levels of global interconnectedness' (Tikly, 2001, p. 154), however, they question whether the global age we are entering is characterised by economic, political and cultural integration. Instead they see globalisation 'as an historically contingent process replete with contradictions' (Tikly, 2001, p. 154), and argue that globalisation's effects are not equal. Thus, while one can see greater integration in some areas, also evident is increased fragmentation and stratification in which 'some states, societies and communities are becoming increasingly enmeshed in the global order while others are becoming increasingly marginalized' (Held et al., 1999, p. 8). Transform-ationalists further make problematic the core-periphery relationship by arguing that though it is still valid, in contemporary globalisation it is no longer just about relationships between states but also involves 'new social relationships that cut across national boundaries' (Tikly, 2001, p. 154); core-periphery relations are evident between nation states and within nation states. Transformationalists argue that contemporary globalisation is 'reconstituting or 're-engineering' the power, functions and authority of national governments' (Held et al., 1999, p. 8). This is not to say that states have lost all control of their territories, however, the sovereignty of the state is juxtaposed, to varying degrees, with expanding jurisdiction of institutions of international governance, finance and law (Held et al., 1999). With respect to education transformationalists contend that globalisation works both on and through education policy. According to Leon Tikly (2001), 'not only is education affected by globalisation but it has also become a principle mechanism by which global forces affect the daily lives of national populations' (p. 155).

There are many advantages to employing the transformationalist approach when examining the impact of globalisation on developing countries. These revolve around the extent to which the approach recognises the complexity and lack of uniformity of the impact of globalisation both on and within different nations. Also useful is the role of the state as mediator of the influences of global forces articulated in this perspective. Tikly (2001) identifies the transformationalist approach as relevant for examining the globalisation of education policy as it allows one to look at the increased stratification between and within countries and how this is caused and exacerbated by the globalised education reform agenda. However, he argues, 'exponents of the transformationalist perspective fail to acknowledge the continuing impact and relevance of prior forms of globalisation, especially those associated with European colonization' (Tikly, 2001, p. 155). This is particularly important when examining the effects of globalisation on developing countries. In many ways I agree with Tikly's assessment of the usefulness of the transformationalist approach for understanding the impact of globalisation on education policy. Indeed, there are vast differences between nations in terms of how closely their national education policies mirror the globalised education policy agenda that is discussed in this chapter. In addition, this perspective recognises the complexity of globalisation and looks at what one can refer to as inter and intra core-periphery relations. As such, inherent in the focus of this chapter is the idea that globalisation has very different effects on Western industrialised core countries than it does in the countries on the periphery of the global economy which are becoming increasingly marginalised. Also in line with the transformationalists is the idea that, apart from globalisation having different effects between countries, persons within countries may also be affected differently. In looking at the globalised education policy agenda and its effects on developing countries, this chapter posits that, contrary to the neoliberal rhetoric that the policies promote equality, they in fact largely exacerbate inequalities in the society allowing a top tier of the society to benefit while more of the masses are left to join an educational and economic underclass (Hoogvelt, 2001). Also, in acknowledging Tikly's assessment this chapter attempts to supplement the transformationalist approach by looking at colonisation as a historical precursor to globalisation in developing countries.

However, there is also value in taking a hyperglobalist approach when examining the actual globalising process and the pervasiveness of the educational policies highlighted in this chapter. While this is not an attempt to argue that the impact on nations does not differ, or that we are witnessing the demise of the nation state with respect to its control over education policy formation, it seems clear that there is a move towards distinctively new forms of education policy formation; forms that rely on human capital concepts and neoliberal economic principles and reduce education's role in society to promoting a very narrowly construed form of national development that is for the most part economic. Thus, while the transformationalist approach provides a valid framework with which to assess the potential impact of the globalised policy agenda on different nations, the hyperglobalist approach can be used to examine aspects of the globalised policy itself, and the idea that because of the increasing interconnectedness between developed nations, developing nations and multilateral agencies one can question if we are entering some sort of global age with respect to education policy. The analysis presented here thus combines the transformationalist and hyperglobalist approaches drawing on the strengths of each while trying to address their weaknesses.

This chapter will focus on developing nations, looking in particular at the flows of educational policy reform and how they affect these countries. However, while much reference will be made to developing countries I am aware that these nations do not form a homogenous group; rather they differ economically, politically, historically and culturally. Also, the extent to which these nations are on the periphery and the extent to which they are dominated vary. For these reasons, at different points in this chapter reference may be made to specific regions or nations. With this being stated, I also believe it is possible to trace similarities in the way that globalisation is affecting the education policy agenda in many developing countries and to identify certain consequences of this process even amidst the varied nature of these nations.

It is essential to note that globalisation is more often discussed in the context of the economy, politics and culture than education. However, each relates to the globalisation of education policy in that education is invariably tied to the economy, politics and culture of any nation; the changes wrought by globalisation in these areas will affect education policy formation. Nicholas Burbules and Carlos Alberto Torres (2000) outline some of the ways globalisation manifests itself in these contexts. At an economic level these include changes in trade relations (the increasing internationalisation of trade), changes in factors of production, the presence of multinational corporations and international lending agencies, the mobility of companies and new patterns of consumption. These changes privilege neoliberal economic principles and increase the tendency to view education as primarily for promoting economic development thereby focusing the attention of policymakers on skill building, often to the detriment of values and national identity. At the political level the nation state while not powerless must now try to balance responses to global capital, responses to global political structures (e.g. the United Nations), responses to domestic pressures and responses to internal needs. Globalisation therefore, has complicated the role of the nation state as it attempts to balance these political imperatives. The globalisation of education policy reflects this difficulty in that governments in forming policy now have to consider the four political imperatives. Finally, in cultural terms, changes in global media and commercial culture mean that societies, while not completely absorbed into a global culture, must attempt to balance their own traditional values with the growing influence of an increasingly commercial culture (Burbules & Torres, 2000). In education, nations must now decide how much of the knowledge of their culture they are going to promote in the curriculum. While each of these contexts is important, this chapter will focus on the impact of the neoliberal principles that provide the rationale for economic globalisation on education policy formation.

6.3   Globalisation in Context

In many ways globalisation is an issue that transcends time. Though the term globalisation is a contemporary one and many writers address it as a modern phenomenon, others pinpoint the origins of globalisation in earlier centuries even while recognising the unprecedented speed of present-day changes. This chapter ascribes to the latter view. The tendency towards globalisation and its effects on education, particularly in developing nations, cannot be construed as a completely new phenomenon. In the book Globalisation and Neoliberalism The Caribbean Context Thomas Klak states, 'emerging global linkages come as no news to people of the Caribbean, which historically is perhaps the most globalized of world regions' (Klak, 1998, p. 6). Though referring specifically to the Caribbean it can be argued that the colonial experience of most developing countries meant that many aspects of their societies were 'exogenously constructed and transplanted' (Klak, 1998, p. 6). Indeed, a case can be made to support the idea that because of the wealth and progress that resulted from what Ankie Hoogvelt (2001) refers to as the 'hegemonic organization of international production relations' (p. 29) developed during colonialism, it was realised that despite the contradictions and pressures for change the 'continuity of global accumulation was to be safeguarded' (Hoogvelt, 2001, p. 29). Globalisation therefore can, in some ways, be viewed as an extension of the internationalisation process that had begun during the colonial period. Thus, while the issue of economic control and the need to develop global linkages, manifests itself differently in contemporary globalisation, the move towards internationalisation of the economy was certainly present before.

Similarly, the effects of globalisation on modern education in developing countries are also, in many respects, not a new phenomenon. Historically, modern education systems have developed as a result of national need. The needs may have ranged from skill building for economic development to the formation of citizens, but they were, by and large, indigenous. For example, Turner (1997), employing an institutional framework for the analysis of the development of education systems, argues that education, as an institution, has different forms and structures depending on the type or complexity of the societies in which it is found. Education systems develop based on the needs of local societies and while not necessarily equitably distributed, issues of the type of education, how it will be distributed and who would control it were largely determined locally. Globalisation represents a shift in this trend, because education policies, structures and curriculums are being increasingly determined or at least strongly influenced by the globalised neoliberal ideology in an attempt to prepare nations to fit into the new global economy, rather than to meet the needs of the nation state. However, education systems in developing countries were used in much the same way during colonisation; the organisation, control and distribution of education in developing countries was largely in the hands of the coloniser with the aim being that the educated would identify, not with the country of birth but with the colonising nation (Hoogvelt, 2001). One of the major differences in the contemporary globalisation of education policy as it affects developing countries is that instead of sovereignty of educational decision making passing into the hands of colonial masters it is now largely in the hands of multilateral agencies from which developing nations seek loans to finance educational developments (Miller, 1989). Later in the chapter, the consequences of the globalisation of education policy for developing countries will be examined; however, at this point it is important to note that the process is not unprecedented. In the book Education and the Colonial Experience Philip G. Altbach (1984) aptly surmises that though the present situation is more complicated than traditional colonialism because developing nations technically have the freedom to shape their own identities, it is clear that in many ways these nations are still under the influence of former colonial powers and other industrialised nations.

Whether one looks at the issue in its historical garb (colonialism) or its new attire (globalisation) it is clear that there are two fundamental issues involved. First there is the function of education. The question may be asked: 'what is the role of education in modern society?' The second issue is one of control – 'who determines the structure and organization of education systems, the content of these systems and how education is distributed?' The globalisation of education policy suggests that the purpose of education is primarily to fit the population of a nation with the skills they need to successfully allow the nation to operate in the global economic system. In the first place this newly constructed role for education places emphasis on teaching skills needed by the economy (global) so that production can be expanded and economic development promoted. Very little consideration is given to education's role of preparing citizens and promoting national culture and values. Martin Carnoy (1999) writes, 'education in general and higher education in particular are historically tied to inherently national objectives, such as promoting national culture' (p. 26), however, the changes in the world economy have provoked different responses in education systems. Secondly, globalised education policy increasingly removes the control of educational decision making out of the hands of the nation state making education a tool of the global economy.

6.4   Donor Agencies and Education Policy Formation in Developing Countries

The effect of globalisation on education policy in developing nation states cannot be fully understood without specific reference to multilateral lending agencies such as the World Bank. Reference will be made to the World Bank, though there are other lending agencies, because the World Bank is the largest single source of external financing for education in developing countries (Samoff, 1996), accounting for 'about a quarter of all aid to education' (World Bank, 1995, p. 14). The development of education is resource intensive and for many developing nations 'the external provision of assistance funds has become the center of gravity for education' (Samoff, 1999, p. 65). The influence of lending agencies on developing countries increased significantly in the 1980s1996 with the imposition of structural adjustment policies (SAPs). According to Joel Samoff (1996), 'effectively, structural adjustment offered access to capital in exchange for the adoption of externally specified national policies' (Samoff, 1996, p. 267). It is important to note that these policies reflected the neoliberal paradigm (Carnoy, 1999), thus it is not surprising that SAPs have often come with directives to reduce public spending on education. However, a rather less visible but more enduring effect of SAPs is the way they influence both the national education agenda and how it is set (Samoff, 1999). As reliance on foreign funds increases in developing countries so does the influence of external agencies. While there are differences among developing nations in their responses to the directives of funding agencies the trend seems to be that over time priorities are set less by government and party leaders and more by what aid organisations are willing to finance (Carnoy, 1999; Samoff, 1999). In this way policymaking acquires an increasingly external focus and educational planning becomes marketing. For example, in looking at the transformed role of the director for education planning in Tanzania Samoff (1999) writes, 'his task was less a process of exploring needs and developing strategies to address them than an effort to study the market of prospective funders. He then identified its priorities and value points, using that market knowledge to craft, advertise, and sell projects and programs' (p. 418). While this may be an extreme case it has implications for educational policy formation in all developing nations and in some ways provides an explanation for the emerging sameness of educational reform agendas in developing countries across the globe.

On reviewing World Bank financing Phillip W. Jones (1997) points out that by the end of the 1980s fewer and fewer bank education loans were free of obligations and these obligations rested heavily on the neoliberal economic agenda that viewed governments as inefficient and sought to promote the privatisation of education and the expansion of user charges. The sameness of the World Bank's strategies for development and for education policy has in no small way contributed to what this chapter refers to as the globalisation of education policy. In its most recent comprehensive policy document the World Bank has outlined six priorities and strategies for education: a higher priority for education, attention to outcomes, emphasis on basic education, attention to equity, household involvement and autonomous institutions (World Bank, 1995). While this chapter will not look at the Bank's 1995 education review in any detail it is enough to note that it paints a picture of what the Bank deems the preconditions for successful educational development. It is also interesting to note that this picture is 'in effect depicting its view of the ideal economy' (Jones, 1997, p. 127). The Bank argues for reduced public intervention in education, the setting of standards to help improve the quality of education (a movement very vibrant in developed countries), the setting of educational priorities based on economic analysis (not cultural, political or national needs), encouraging household involvement mainly by passing some of the costs of education to communities and parents, and decentralisation (Jones, 1997; World Bank, 1995). In his critique of Priorities and Strategies Joel Samoff (1996) asserts that the understanding of education presented in the chapter is narrow and limiting as it ignores the larger set of societal objectives for the education system reducing the functions of education to the preparation of workers and the promotion of economic growth. In addition, the chapter reflects a disjunction between the issues that the World Bank deems most important and the objectives articulated by many governments and educators in developing countries (Samoff, 1996). Despite this, the Bank presents its priorities and strategies as global solutions, implicitly suggesting that the same approaches and technologies can be used everywhere.

Trinidad and Tobago provides a clear example of the Bank's policy approach. In 1993 the Ministry of Education of Trinidad and Tobago produced its most recent comprehensive policy document, the Education Policy Paper 1993–2003, in which it outlined its vision for education in the country. The document explains the need for increases in government expenditure on education to improve school quality, teacher quality and increase access to schooling. The policy document articulates the need to provide instructional materials and facilities (such as textbooks, libraries and laboratories), provision of teacher training, increasing teacher salaries and reducing class size (Ministry of Education of Trinidad and Tobago, 1993). In a report by the World Bank entitled Trinidad and Tobago the Financing of Education, the Bank uses rate of return studies to show why the policy emphases in the White Paper are not sound. Instead of addressing the needs and conditions of Trinidad and Tobago specifically, the Bank report states that 'provision of laboratories, increasing teacher salaries, and reducing class size have been found to be effective in less that 40% of the cases' (World Bank, 1996, p. 45), and goes on to suggest the areas they feel are those in which the government can act effectively. While this was simply a report it gives a clear indication of what the Bank would be willing to fund and places pressure on the government to swerve from the aims and goals determined by the local stakeholders in education to embrace the concepts articulated by the finance brokers in the international arena. It also indicates the unbending nature of the Bank in endorsing its priorities and strategies rather than examining the local context. It is little wonder then that a globalised education policy seems to be emerging.

6.5   The Globalised Education Policy Agenda and Its Consequences for Developing Nations

In looking at the impact of globalisation on education in developing countries, special attention needs to be paid to the neoliberal economic principles, informed by human capital theory, that undergird globalisation and how these principles impact education policy in developing countries and with what consequences (see also Zajda, 2005; Zajda et al., 2008b). The concept of human capital refers to the fact that 'human beings invest in themselves, by means of education, training, or other activities which raises their future income by increasing their lifetime earnings' (Woodhall, 1987, p. 219). The concept has come to dominate the economics of education and when economists refer to expenditure on education as investment in human capital they are generally asserting 'that it is possible to measure profitability of investment in human capital using the same techniques of cost-benefit analysis and investment appraisal that have been traditionally applied to physical capital' (Woodhall, 1987, p. 220). This perspective of education impacts policy formation in a way that reduces the functions of education to economic development and largely ignores the other social functions that education plays in society. In explaining cost-benefit analysis Psacharopoulos and Woodhall (1985) state, 'Cost-benefit analysis is a technique by which factors can be compared systematically for the purpose of evaluating profitability of any proposed investment....The technique of cost-benefit analysis has been developed to make this evaluation as systematic, reliable, and comprehensive as possible' (Psacharopoulos & Woodhall, 1985, p. 29). However, cost-benefit analysis ignores the contested nature of education and it largely ignores the fact that nations may have other purposes for education to achieve apart from it contributing to economic development and therefore profitability. The World Bank uses cost-benefit analysis to determine its priorities (Psacharopoulos & Woodhall, 1985; World Bank, 1995) and in its most recent policy document the emphasis is clear, education for promoting economic development. The policies that are advocated are those with the highest rates of return, hence the Bank's constant emphasis on basic education while encouraging reduced public spending and increased reliance on private contributions and user fees for higher education (Psacharopoulos & Woodhall, 1985; World Bank, 1995).

While it is clear that many developing nations need to invest in basic education, higher education has been articulated as a focus of many developing governments that long to reduce their dependence on foreign experts (Ministry of Education of Trinidad and Tobago, 1993; Samoff, 1996). In addition, the changes in the global market place are demanding an increasingly skilled workforce. Thus, while many developing nations recognise the need to improve basic education they also see as imperative increasing the numbers of students gaining higher levels of education. Despite these factors the Bank placed attention to outcomes as one of its six priorities arguing that 'Educational priorities should be set with reference to outcomes, using economic analysis' (World Bank, 1995, p. 8). The Bank sets forth its priorities and strategies for education as scientific and based on sound economic analysis however, developing nations would do well to consider that in shaping public policy, societal values and goals must also be taken into account and these may not have the highest rates of return.

The neoliberal economic perspective is informed by human capital theory. Proponents of the neoliberal approach argue that governments have a poor track record in promoting development. Neoliberal economists suggest that the bureaucratic structure of governments inhibit change and that the political nature of governments limits their ability to promote either equity or efficiency since they are more concerned with staying in power (Zajda et al., 2008a). They argue that the market is much more efficient and therefore endorse cuts in government expenditure, user fees for public services, trade liberalisation, currency devaluation, reduction of price controls, export-oriented polices and increased privatisation. These are the main ingredients of SAPs which had been imposed on many developing nations by the World Bank and International Monetary Fund (IMF) since the 1980s. Referring specifically to Africa, Leon Tikly (2001) argues that SAPs relate to the new market principle advocated by neoliberal economists 'because they are intended to make countries more competitive through lowering production costs (through cuts in social welfare and reduced unit costs) and through making Africa more attractive to foreign investors (by means of trade liberalisation, reduced tax and other macro-economic reforms)' (Tikly, 2001, p. 160). Contrary to neoliberal arguments, many political economists suggest that these policies have very negative effects on developing countries.

Specifically with respect to education, neoliberals argue for the price system to allocate educational services with a much-reduced role for the state as provider and organiser of education (Colclough, 1997); policies ultimately aimed at reducing public spending. Three major tenets of the education reform agenda are decentralisation, privatisation and user fees. Decentralisation is framed as a reform that will increase productivity in education as it reduces the size of the educational bureaucracy and brings decision-making closer to parents and communities. However, often decentralisation, as advocated by neoliberals, is accompanied by a reduction in financial and technical assistance from central government. Thus, while it may achieve financial goals it tends to 'increase inequality in educational performance between the poorer states (municipalities) and the richer ones' (Carnoy, 1999, p. 55).

Privatisation is the second major tenet of the globalised reform agenda. Proponents suggest that the private provision of education at all levels of schooling should be encouraged, arguing that privatisation would improve management as well as ease the pressure on government to subsidise the system. Another reason used to justify this strategy is that private schooling has been found to be more cost-effective than public schooling. However, private provision means fees, which many of the poor will be unable to pay. In addition, while this measure is being advocated as something that would expand the education system in developing nations, most private schools tend to be established in urban areas, where the market is greatest, rather than in rural areas where the shortage of schools is most critical. It would mean the establishment of an even greater elitist element in the system (Colclough, 1996), increasing the divide between urban (core) and rural (periphery) areas, fostering uneven development and worsening already pervasive inequalities. In addition, the evidence supporting the claim that private schools are more cost-effective is controversial (Carnoy, 2000; Colclough, 1996). Often governments subsidise these schools, they are located in areas where it is cheaper to provide education and they offer a curriculum that requires cheaper resource inputs (Colclough, 1996). With privatisation, industry is likely to become more involved in the provision of education (as is increasingly the case in many developed countries), resulting in education becoming even more closely tied to preparation for work to the exclusion or significant reduction of the other purposes of education (Stromquist & Monkman, 2000). Referring specifically to higher education, it has been argued that privatisation will result in the depoliticisation of the university and the limiting of courses offered to those topics that donors deem of interest to economic development (Stromquist & Monkman, 2000). While skill building must be a necessary part of the focus of education in all countries, perhaps particularly developing nations, the tendency to limit the purposes of education to economic development may foster the continued dependence of developing nations, as they constantly must rely on an external knowledge base.

The third major tenet of the emerging global agenda for education is the charging of user fees primarily at the secondary and tertiary levels. It is argued that cost recovery at these levels is a practical solution for developing countries. Neoliberals argue that the majority of students at these levels tend to be from wealthier families that can afford to pay to send their children to school. In addition, the high private rate of return of these levels of education means that user fees could be introduced without much reduction in enrollment. These arguments often ignore the perceived development needs of nations. Once again Trinidad and Tobago will be used as an example. In its Education Policy Paper 1993–2003, the Ministry of Education of this country articulated, as part of its philosophy of education, the belief that 'a system of heavily subsidized and universal education is the greatest safeguard of the freedom of our people and the best guarantee of their social, political and economic well-being at this stage of our development' (Ministry of Education of Trinidad and Tobago, 1993, p. 17). However, in a report on financing education in Trinidad and Tobago made by the World Bank, it ignores the local philosophy in favour of neoliberal economic principles and suggests charging tuition fees at the upper secondary level (World Bank Report, 1996). It should be noted that the World Bank has gone so far as to endorse neoliberal economic principles in its most recent policy statement on education citing household involvement (user fees) as one of their six priorities. Political economists contest these arguments arguing that cost recovery schemes would reduce the number of poor persons gaining access to these levels of education and 'would affect enrollment rates in a highly inequitable fashion' (Carnoy, 1995, p. 408), further decreasing any chance of social mobility for the poor.

While the global education reform agenda is couched in the rhetoric of increasing quality, and efficiency and expanding access, the main aim is to reduce the government's involvement in and contribution to public education. Political economists argue that leaving the allocation of educational resources up to the market will exacerbate the inequalities in society. Indeed several economists point out that the capitalist economy is not perfect neither is it concerned with equity instead they suggest that by nature capitalism generates inequality (De Janvry, 1981; Thurow, 1996). Political economists argue that while the state is itself a tool in the capitalist structure, it also serves to mediate the contradictions in the system in the form of reformist policies. However, if the market were allowed free reign in the allocation of educational resources the poor would be further disenfranchised, while the rich, having money to purchase the good, would increase in power, privilege and prestige. The result would be greater social inequality and it is not clear that these reforms will foster development (Zajda et al., 2008b).

6.5.1   Are These Policies Globalised?

Many educational policy makers in developed countries may baulk at the education policies outlined above while others may argue that to suggest that these policies are globalised is erroneous because most of these policies are not found in all countries. To address this question both the hyperglobalist and transformationalist perspectives must be employed. In many nations the education policy agenda outlined in this chapter is what is set before them. In this sense, the hyperglobalist perspective is applicable in that the policies, and perhaps more so the concepts on which the policies are based, are becoming increasingly pervasive. Stromquist and Monkman (2000) provide an apt example of the applicability of the hyperglobalist lens when they suggest that the globalisation of education policy has also led to a shift in focus to what Stromquist and Monkman (2000) call 'economy-centered vocational training' (p. 12) with education being primarily viewed in terms of its contribution to national economic development; few nations continue to emphasise education for promoting shared culture and values. This transition may have a negative impact on developing countries since many of these nations are relatively newly formed and still need to focus on creating shared values and loyal citizens. In looking at Africa Joel Samoff states that after independence education 'was expected to be the principal vehicle for social change, both helping to define the new society and enabling citizens to function effectively within it....Education was to be the vehicle for redressing discrimination and inequality, both in daily practice and in popular understanding' (Samoff, 1999, pp. 395–396). After independence many leaders in developing countries viewed education as necessary for both accumulation and transformation, however, increasingly the narrow construction of the relevance of education has prevailed.

This chapter also ascribes to the transformationalists view of globalisation and suggests that as with the economic effects, the effects of globalisation on education policy are not uniform. As Leon Tikly argues, the 'particular form hegemonic projects will take within the state will depend on the outcome of political struggles at the national level and of the particular construction of national identity' (Tikly, 2001, p. 163). The ability to resist adverse effects of globalisation is mainly a privilege of developed nations. Developing countries are more dominated and more susceptible to global forces. Tikly's argument about the inability of African states to resist globalisation can be extended to developing countries in general, 'The fragility of the state and of the postcolonial status quo has ensured that most African states are much more susceptible to global forces than those of wealthier countries. This susceptibility provided the conditions for the imposition from the early 1980s of a new neoliberal orthodoxy in the economy and politics...as we have seen, this new orthodoxy has been severe in its implications for all areas of social welfare including education and has served to exacerbate social stratification' (Tikly, 2001, p. 165). Therefore, the extent to which the policies are implemented, or rather the impact of the policies on different nations must be viewed through the transformationalist lens (see also Zajda, 2005).

6.6 Conclusion

While education does function to develop skills and may prepare persons for the world of work, it must also play a transforming and liberating role in developing nations. In Joel Samoff's words, 'Education must enable people to understand their society in order to change it. Education must be as concerned with human relationships as with skills, and equally concerned with eliminating inequality and practicing democracy' (Samoff, 1999, p. 413). Postcolonial leadership in developing countries was committed to using education to foster social cohesion and to address inequality. The globalised education policy agenda therefore, in many ways, represents a shift in the direction that postcolonial leaders in developing countries may have desired and while the aim of these polices is to foster accumulation, implementation of these polices may threaten the ability of developing nation states to maintain their own legitimacy (Samoff, 1999; Zajda et al., 2008a).

References

Altbach, P. G. & Kelly, G. P. (1984). *Education and the Colonial Experience*. New Jersey: Transaction Books.
Burbules, N. C. & Torres, C. A. (2000). Globalisation and education: An introduction. In: N. C.Burbules, & C. A. Torres (Eds.), *Globalisation and Education: Critical Perspectives*. New York: Routledge.
Carnoy, M. (1995). *International Encyclopedia of Economics of Education*. New York: Elsevier.

Carnoy, M. (1999). *Globalisation and Educational Reform*. Paris: UNESCO International Institute for Educational Planning.

Carnoy, M. (2000). Globalisation and educational reform. In: K. Monkman & N. Stromquist (Eds.), *Globalisation and Education: Integration and Contestation Across Cultures*. New York: Rowman & Littlefield.

Colclough, C. (1996). Education and the market: Which parts of the neoliberal solutions are correct? *World Development*, 24, 589–610.

Colclough, C. (1997). Education, health, and the market: An introduction. In: C. Colclough (Ed), *Marketizing Education and Health in Developing Countries*. Oxford: Clarendon Press.

DeJanvry, A. (1981). *The Agrarian Question*. Baltimore, MD: The Johns Hopkins University Press.

Fagerlind, I. & Saha, L. (1989). *Education and National Development*. Oxford: Pergamon Press.

Green, A. (1997). *Education, Globalisation and the Nation State*. London: Macmillan Press.

Held, D., McGrew, A., Goldblatt, D. & Perraton, J. (1999). *Global Transformations: Politics, Economics and Culture*. Stanford: Stanford University Press.

Hoogvelt, A. (2001). *Globalisation and the Postcolonial World: The New Political Economy of Development*. Baltimore, MD: The Johns Hopkins University Press.

Jones, P. W. (1997). On World Bank education financing. *Comparative Education*, 33, 117–129.

Klak, T. (1998). Thirteen theses on globalisation and neoliberalism. In: T. Klak (Ed.), *Globalisation and Neoliberalism: The Caribbean Context*. Oxford: Rowman & Littlefield.

Miller, E. (1989). Contemporary issues in Jamaican education. In: C. Brock & D. Clarkson (Eds.), *Education in Central America and the Caribbean*. New York: Routledge.

Ministry of Education of Trinidad and Tobago (1993). *Education Policy Paper 1993–2003*. Trinidad & Tobago: Ministry of Education.

Morrow, R. A. & Torres, C. A. (2000). The state, globalisation, and educational policy. In: N. C. Burbules & C. A. Torres (Eds.). *Globalisation and Education: Critical Perspectives*. New York: Routledge.

Psacharopoulos, G. & Woodhall, M. (1985). *Education for Development: An Analysis of Investment Choices*. Washington, DC: World Bank.

Samoff, J. (1996). Which priorities and strategies for education? *International Journal of Educational Development*, 16, 249–271.

Samoff, J. (1999). No teacher, no textbooks, no chairs: Contending with crisis in African education. In: R. F. Arnove & C. A. Torres (Eds.), *Comparative Education: The Dialectic of the Global and the Local*. Oxford: Rowman & Littlefield.

Soudien, C. (2005). Inside but below: The puzzle of education in the global order. In J. Zajda (2005) (Ed.). *The International Handbook of Globalisation and Education Policy Research*. Dordrecht: Springer.

Stromquist, N. &Monkman, K. (2000). Defining globalisation and assessing its implications on knowledge and education. In: N. Stromquist & K. Monkman (Eds.), *Globalisation and Education: Integration and Contestation Across Cultures*. New York: Rowman & Littlefield.

Thurow, L. C. (1996). *The Future of Capitalism: How Today's Economic Forces Shape Tomorrow's World*. New York: Penguin Books.

Tikly, L. (2001). Globalisation and education in the postcolonial World: Towards a conceptual framework, *Comparative Education*, 37, 151–171.

Turner, J. (1997). Education. In: J. Turner (Ed.), *The Institutional Order: Economy, Kinship, Religion, Polity, Law, and Education in Evolutionary and Comparative Perspectives*. New York: Longman.

Woodhall, M. (1987). Human capital concepts. In A. H. Halsey, H. Lauder, P. Brown & A. S. Wells (Eds.), *Education Culture Economy Society*. Oxford: Oxford University Press.

World Bank (1995). *Priorities and Strategies for Education: A World Bank Review*. Washington, DC: World Bank.

World Bank (1996). *Trinidad and Tobago: The Financing of Education Report No. 16216- TR*. Washington, DC: World Bank.

Zajda, J. (Ed.). (2005). The *International Handbook of Globalisation and Education Policy Research*. Dordrecht: Springer.

Zajda, J. (2007). Credentialism in the 21st century: The importance of qualifications. *Educational Practice and Theory*, 29(2), 61–79.

Zajda, J., Davies, L. &Majhanovich, S. (Eds.). (2008a). *Comparative and Global Pedagogies: Equity, Access and Democracy in Education*. Dordrecht: Springer.

Zajda, J. Biraimah, B. & Gaudelli, W. (Eds.). (2008b). *Education and Social Inequality in the Global Culture*. Dordrecht: Springer.

Chapter 7
Globalization and the Challenges for Education in Greece

Petroula Siminou

7.1 Introduction

This chapter explores the impact of globalization on education in Greece and examines samples of challenges emerging from this process. More specifically, it examines and discusses the influence of globalization on educational changes in Greece with reference to recent associated phenomena such as international sports–cultural manifestations, unemployment and brain drain of scientists. The Europeanization of Greece is evident in the constant educational changes since its accession in the European Union (EU), especially after the 1997 educational reforms associated with the EU subsidies. Aspects of globalization are reflected in the increasing immigration of cheap labor and at the same time emigration of enterprises, unemployment of university graduates and further education restructuring attributed to the need for new skills in the "knowledge society" of a competitive European and world market (see Meselidis, 2008).

7.2 Public Education at a Crossroad

The process of globalization through global economy of the international elits, capital flow, scientization of the western world, the expansion of transnational companies, mass education and the new way of life as advertised and almost imposed my the mass media has reached almost every inhabited area on this planet. Calls in many countries for global education standards have generated a series of cross-national efforts to measure achievement in several subjects at different levels (Meselidis, 2007). Although they claim sensitivity to the unique characteristics of

P. Siminou
Institute of International Education, Stockholm University
e-mail: petra.siminou@interped.su.se

J. Zajda and V. Rust (eds.), *Globalisation, Policy and Comparative Research,*
DOI: 10.1007/978-1-4020-9547-4_7, © Springer Science + Bussiness Media B.V. 2009

specific national and local settings, by design those assessments seek to use and thereby institutionalize internationally particular assumptions about both content and the process of learning and teaching. Furthermore, the rapid change from the industrial society to the "digital society" (dominated by ICTs) has created the need for the upgrading of competencies and skills. Another upcoming tension in a system of mass education is the one between equality and quality. Equality of opportunity rapidly comes into conflict with quality (Meyer, 2000). According to Meyer (2000, p. 9), the new principles of "global education" emphasize the status, citizenship and human rights of all persons in the world, and the legitimate equality and empowerment of every national society. These forms are portrayed in education especially in the curricula which are generated by professionals and educational associations that construct changes in curricula potentially appropriate to an imagined "world society" (Anderson, 1991).

In the context of structural change and the evolution towards a knowledge-based "world society," education and training are considered the keys for reaching higher levels of employment and lower unemployment. Consequently, the need for a continuous updating of skills originated by the economic rationale for lifelong learning promotes a more active participation in the process of decision-making, for increased cultural diversity and social cohesion. Thus, education cannot escape being influenced by the process globalization (European Commission, 2000).

Human rights are now celebrated more than ever before (Zajda et al., 2008a). Access to education is a human right, but the challenges and the process of learning are now focused more on the "individuals" and less on the "system." In this respect, the "individuals" are the targets of economists, educators and political protagonists. The economists promote education vouchers and the freedom of choice of individuals on arguments of market efficiency. Educators believe that it is the learner who ultimately determines the construction of knowledge, on pedagogical grounds (Hallak, 1998, 1999).

The main utopian assumption of globalization is that there is a "world market" where "all individuals" can buy and sell, no matter where they live and how they live. Apart from "flexibility" imperatives in education include, for example, the cultural balance of the growing power of global mass media with confidence in the best of local culture, the design of small-scale enterprises that suit both local and global markets, the protection of human rights and protection of the environment. These goals are sought by collective networks of like-minded people operating globally and locally (Hickling-Hudson, 1999; Zajda, 2005).

However, if "a global free market is a utopia destined to fail" (Gray, 1998, p. 235) what we are seeing worldwide today looks like the end of it or what is mostly the globalization of poverty and problems associated with increasing poverty in most countries of the world (Vergopoulos, 2004). As Forrester points out:

> Businesses based in the North that set up in the so-called 'developing' countries, do not create jobs for the people of those countries, but generally make them work without any kind of social security protection and in medieval conditions. The reason is that the workforce- often underpaid women and children, as well as prisoners - costs less than automation would cost in the country of origin. This is colonization in another form. (Forrester, 1999)

7.3   Greece, Globalization and Education

According to the European Commission's 1996 annual economic report the EU is one of the strongest economic powers in the world and therefore it could play an important role in changing the world economy. The profits of European industrial enterprises, (especially the big ones) have clearly improved since 1994/1995. This was especially due to a decline in personnel costs because of a "wage-retention" scheme on the part of employees (Kreissl-Dorfer, 1996). Greece accessed to the European Community in 1981. Since then, the impact of the EU membership upon the economic role of the state fostered a reduction in its economic activities, as well as a gigantic size of bureaucracy in the state. It has also altered the regulatory pattern of the Greek economy, from one tightly controlled by the state into one conforming to the EU's regulatory regime (Ioakimidis, 2001, p. 80; see also Ioakimidis, 2002; Koliopoulos & Veremis, 2002).

Through accession to the European Monetary Union (EMU), Greece secured its institutional place within the evolving political system of the EU. It was also considered that accession to the Euro will make Greece a player in the international economic and financial system, as well as to strengthen its regional role (Ioakeimidis, 2002). Today, Greece is considered integrated into the EU, but, as the EU becomes more cohesive, the possibility of a small state like Greece to act independently decreases. Europeanization – more in the nominal-macroeconomic than in the structural sense – has been the most pronounced economic objective of Greek governments especially throughout the 1990s (Pagoulatos, 2001, p. 211).

As Greece is located in the southeast border of the EU a widespread immigration to Greece which began mostly in the 1990s is continuously taking place. Over one million people are seeking political asylum, and it is estimated that 9% of the population in Greece holds foreign passports; immigrants have come from 104 countries. About 1.5% of the population is considered to be "minority." To address indifference toward minority populations in primary and secondary schools, teachers can earn a 50% salary increase to teach in "minority" schools, but they must be bilingual and few teachers in Greece have developed language skills in the languages spoken by this population (Pitkänen et al., 2002).

Throughout the history of wars in the 1940s in Europe, and in Greece, many people were forced to emigrate in many countries of the world. Today there are Greeks living in 114 countries in all continents. They constitute an international network – the World Council of Greeks who live abroad (SAE) officially established in 1995 by a Presidential Decree of the Hellenic Republic. SAE is a global nongovernmental organization with its headquarters in Greece and serves as consultative body to Greece on matters of interest to the Greeks abroad and as their official body for the representation at the Greek state aiming to unite them assisting their cultural and educational activities (SAE, 2004). Yet, the Ministry of Education (MoE) supports education for the Greeks abroad in the following countries:

Units of Greek education abroad (MoE, 2004)

Europe	N. America	Australia	Africa
Berlin, Dusseldorf, Munich, Frankfurt, Stuttgart, Brussels, London, Paris, Kiev, Stockholm, Istanbul	New York, Chicago, San Francisco, Washington, Montreal, Toronto	Adelaide, Melbourne, Sydney	Cairo, Johannesburg

Unemployment is also one of the many reasons forcing people to emigrate abroad. In Greece unemployment and temporary work are the two words which accompany the graduates, especially women, with first those with a graduate degree in social sciences (30%). Graduates with a higher degree such as Master's or Ph.D. are not guaranteed any jobs, as the rate of unemployment at this level of education is 7.2%. Similarly 7% of graduates of technological higher institutions are also unemployed (Triantafyllou, 2004). Consequently, the phenomenon of "brain drain" is continuing in Greece showing that the majority of Greek scientists who complete their education in the USA and the EU never return, mainly due to the fact that in Greece they cannot practice their profession because of the high unemployment, meritocratic bureaucracy and the lack of equal opportunities. Some scientists who returned (mainly for family reasons) left the country again. There is small number of those who manage to survive having one-foot abroad and one in the country (Delithanasis, 2004). However, this is not only a Greek phenomenon. The "brain drain" of people born in the EU is increasing. About 75% of EU-born US doctorate recipients who graduated between 1991 and 2000 had no specific plans to return to the EU, and more and more are choosing to stay in the USA. The most important reasons keeping EU-born scientists and engineers abroad relate to the quality of work. Better prospects and projects, and easier access to leading technologies were most often cited as reasons behind plans to work abroad (European Commission, 2003, p. 2).

The attraction of scientists with high scientific qualifications (brain gain) constitutes a critical and decisive factor for development and wealth of a country. Unfortunately, the brain drain is not a simple academic problem. It restricts the possibilities of development in their country of origin and at the same time it reduces its productivity. There maybe many Greek "brains" ending up in Europe, but similarly many European "brains" end up in the USA. In Europe, at present, billions of euros and work positions are at risk due to the emigration of scientists, mainly to the USA. And as the relations between the industry and higher education are better in the USA, almost 50% of those receiving a doctoral degree from American Universities prefer to remain in the USA.

The EU is now trying to create a "common market" for research (the European research area) with the ambition to "repatriate" scientists who would also increase the standards of scientific research in Europe. Of course this does not mean that their repatriation is directed to their country of origin but to any member state.

Although states like Germany, France, the UK, Belgium, Sweden and Finland are leading in the creation of the a common European area, Greece remains last in investments in scientific research among 15 member states in the list of the 100 best academic institutions in Europe (ibid). Despite the progress achieved in setting up policy and improving legislation, raising the employment rate remains the main concern. The EU Commision Report (2003) suggests measures to reduce the non-wage labor cost, the offer of greater incentives to encourage part-time employment, and completing the reform of Public Employment Services appear necessary. It is also suggested that the economic relevance of education and vocational training could be improved by strengthening links to labor market needs. Further development and implementation of a lifelong education strategy, including promotion of active aging and implementation of the labor market reform seem necessary to ensure the modernisation of work and a balance between flexibility and security. There is a need to significantly improve female employment from both a quantitative and qualitative point of view in order to reduce the gender gap, especially in terms of both job segregation and pay gaps (Europa, 2002).

Hence new demands are being made on the presentation of any institution which tries to enter the "worldwide competition" especially in higher education. As electronic communication becomes easier, the idea of conquering the "world market" of educational products and services is attracting business-minded established institutions and profit-based new providers in a competitive race in which most traditional higher education institutions are "doomed" left far behind (Reichert & Wächter, 2000, pp. 9–10).

The recent educational reforms in Greece, since 1997, supported both by national budget and the European Social Fund, justified changes in education claiming that the reforms were necessary due to the need for new skills which demand flexibility that is required by the national and international labor market. These aspects of globalization were manifested in the education reforms actions and strategies such as the following:

- Increasing ICT and foreign languages in the curriculum
- Reforming the examination system in order to increase access to higher education
- Expanding of vocational training
- Introducing distance education and lifelong learning
- Establishing new departments in universities and upgrading the technological institutes to university level

Choice, decentralization and privatization in education are also attributed to the process of globalization and the increasing demand for local governance or a certain degree of autonomous decision making in order to reduce bureaucracy and costs. In Greece, there is still a slow process of decentralization in the level of administration. Although private education exists in a parallel way as cram schools, mainly in the secondary and upper-secondary level of education, the establishment of private higher institutions is not yet allowed.

Another aspect of globalization is that individuals can have more than one identity moving from national to international. This is apparent in the world of sports, which is commercialized, and without frontiers. The "wonder child" who could escape from poverty to pursue an international career in a famous sport is a dream for many of the youth also in Greece. This was manifested in the recent European football championship when the national team of Greece was nationally glorified for winning the cup although many of its players are at the same time professional players for teams of other countries.

Greece had the privilege of hosting the Olympic Games celebrating their "homecoming." On the occasion of the 2004 Athens Olympics, Greece has introduced a resolution on "Building a Peaceful and Better World through Sport and the Olympic Ideal" for adoption by the UN General Assembly. Since 1993, the UN assembly has adopted six such resolutions, calling for a truce during the Olympic Games (Papandreou, 2003). Unfortunately, there was no war or conflict which stopped due to the Olympics appeal for truce in 2004 and these games – as many other world sport events – revealed the international problem of doping addiction towards utopian competitions.

Hosting the Games in every country is generally seen as an opportunity for promoting national prestige, states of all political regimes have embraced the Olympics throughout their international history. Participation of as many states as possible is permitted without applying any standards. Nationalism, commercialism, competition, celebrity, technological intensification and government repression as well as sites of reduced civil liberties are obvious in all the modern Olympic Games (Martin, 1996).

Globalization led the return of the misconception: "economic growth at any price." Some political discourse in several EU countries became a little more "green," however concerning environmental consciousness or actions have not really increased across the world. Unemployment is endemic in many member-states of the EU, and millions of individuals are entitled, for an indefinite period to misery or the threat of it sooner or later, to the loss of a roof over their heads, to all loss of social respect (Forrester, 1999, p. 6).

Unemployment in Greece is 10.2% (ESYE, 2004), still a social problem, especially high for university graduates, while many of the unemployed accept temporary work irrelevant to their degree of studies (e.g., teachers or social scientists work as waiters in restaurants). Professional inflation in previously prestigious professions, such as for lawyers and medical doctors, forces them facing the dilemma to follow the difficult route of the "brain-drain" searching for further training and employment abroad.

7.4   Conclusion

Torres (1998) points out that the growing distrust in democracy poses problems for the process of educational reforms and its connections with citizenship. New educational models might emerge, such as new models of rural education for peripheral areas, (e.g., the education of the poor; immigrants, for street children and travelers, and so on. Different partnerships for education may emerge, (e.g., between state, NGO, third-sector, and in some instances religious or private organizations), new models for adult literacy and non-formal education; higher institutions and business relationships; and new ways of financing education (Burbules, 2000, p. 19). In the post-modern times the de-globalization of literacy, or the globalization of basic education, seems to be the challenge for all those involved in education planning including governmental, educational, or non-governmental organizations. Obviously, as far education is concerned, nothing less is at stake today than the role of public education for democracy (Burbules, 2000; Torres, 1998; Walters, 1997; Zajda et al., 2008a; Zajda et al. 2008b).

In Greece, educational changes are attributed to globalization coupled with the Europeanization process (Featherstone & Kazamias, 2001) and as borders are decreasing and both emigration and immigration are taking place, yet there is more attention for the education to Greeks abroad than to foreigners in the country. It is suggested that the educational system should turn from its "introverted" orientation to a more "extraverted" one. Creating a European citizen is called for, aiming at the maintenance of cultural and linguistic polymorphism through the projection of a "common cultural heritage" (Pitkänen et al., 2002).

References

Anderson, B. (1991). *Imagined Communities*. New York: Verso.

Burbules, N. (2000). Does the internet constitute a global educational community? In Burbules, N. & C.-A Torres (Eds.) (2000). *Globalisation and Education: Critical Perspectives* (pp. 323–355). New York: Routledge.

Delithanasis, M.(2004). *Greece Still Emigrating Scientists* (in Greek). Athens: Kathimerini, 19-09-04.

ESYE (2004). *Unemployment Figures: October–December 2004*. Athens: ESYE.

Europa (2002). Greece: New Commission analysis of labor market performance. *Press Release MEMO/02/240*. Brussels: Europa.

European Commission. (2000). *Commission Press Release IP/00/234*. Brussels: Author.

European Commission. (2003). Weakening growth in investment and increasing brain drain: two major threats to the European knowledge-based economy. *Commission Press Release IP/03/1594*. Brussels: European Commission.

Featherstone, K. & Kazamias, G. (Eds.) (2001). *Europeanization and the Southern Periphery*. London: Frank Cass.

Forrester, V. (1999). *The Economic Horror*. Oxford: Polity Press.

Gray, J. (1998). *False Dawn*. London: Granta.

Hallak, J. (1998). *Education and Globalisation*. Paris: UNESCO Institute for Education Planning.

Hallak, J. (1999). *Globalisation, Human Rights and Education*. Paris: UNESCO Institute for Education Planning.

Hickling-Hudson, A. (1999). Beyond schooling: Adult education in postcolonial societies. In Arnove, R. & C. A. Torres (Eds) (1999). *Comparative Education: The Dialectic of the Global and the Local*. Boston, MA: Rowman & Littlefield.

Ioakimidis, P. (2001). The Europeanization of Greece: An overall assessment. In Featherstone, K. & Kazamias, G. (Eds). (2001). *Europeanization and the Southern Periphery* (pp. 73–94). London: Frank Cass.

Ioakimidis, P. (2002). The political significance of the Euro in Greece. In Koliopoulos, J. & Th. Veremis (2002). *Greece: The Modern Sequel. From 1831 to the Present* (pp. 316–317). London: Hurst & Company.

Koliopoulos, J. & Veremis, Th. (2002). *Greece: The Modern Sequel. From 1831 to the Present.* London: Hurst & Company.

Kreissl-Dorfer, W. (1996). Giving globalisation shape: The role of Europe. International Communication Project. Bonn: Global Policy Forum Europe.

Martin, B. (1996). Ten reasons to oppose all Olympic Games. *Freedom*, 57 (15), 7–8.

Meselidis, S. (2007). Globalisation and National Identity in the Representations of Year 5 and Year 6 Core Greek Primary School Textbooks (1997–2005). Unpublished manuscript.

Meselidis, S. (2008). *History Wars: Year 6 School History Textbook.* Unpublished manuscript.

Meyer, J. (2000). Globalisation and the curriculum: Problems for theory in the sociology of education. In H. Fujita (Ed.), *Education, Knowledge, Power* (pp. 48–67). Tokyo: Shinyosha.

MoE (2004). *Ministry of National Education and Religious Affairs: Education Units abroad* (In Greek). Athens: MoE.

Pagoulatos, G. (2001). Economic adjustment and financial reform: Greece's Europeanization and the emergence of stabilization state. In Featherstone, K. & G. Kazamias (Eds.) (2001). *Europeanization and the Southern Periphery* (pp. 210–223). London: Frank Cass.

Papandreou, G. (2003). *Draft Statement by G. Papandreou Minister for Foreign Affairs of the Hellenic Republic.* New York: Permanent Mission of Greece to the UN. 26-9-03.

Pitkänen, P. Kalekin-Fishman D & Verma G. (Eds.) (2002). *Education and Immigration: Settlement Policies and Current Challenges.* London/New York: Routledge Falmer.

Reichert, S. & Wächter, B. (2000). The *Globalisation of Education and Training: Recommendations for a Coherent Response of the European Union.* Brussels: European Commission.

SAE (2004). *The World Council of the Hellenes* (In Greek). http://www.sae.gr. 25-11-04.

Torres, C.-A. (1998). *Democracy, Education, and Multiculturalism: Dilemmas of Citizenship in a Global World.* New York: Rowman & Littlefield.

Triantafyllou, E. (2004). *First in Europe in Secret Unemployment Because of the Exclusion of Women.* [In Greek]. Athens: Eleftherotypia-Economy, 19-9-04.

Vergopoulos, K. (2004). *The End of Globalisation.* [In Greek]. Athens: Investor's world, 19-12-04.

Walters S. (Ed.) (1997). *Globalisation, Adult Education and Training: Impacts and Issues.* London: Zed Books.

Zajda, J. (2005) (Ed.). The *International Handbook of Globalisation and Education Policy Research.* Dordrecht: Springer.

Zajda, J., Davies, L & Majhanovich, S. (2008a). (Eds.). *Comparative and Global Pedagogies: Equity, Access and Democracy in Education.* Dordrecht: Springer.

Zajda, J. Biraimah, B. & Gaudelli, W (2008b). (Eds.). *Education and Social Inequality in the Global Culture.* Dordrecht: Springer.

Chapter 8
Organizational Trends of Chinese Higher Education: The Influence of Strategy and Structure at Ten Case Study Universities

James Jacob

8.1 Chinese Higher Education: Introduction

Possessing the world's largest education system and potentially largest national higher education subsector, China merits the attention of global scholars, policy makers, educators, and investors. Chinese higher education institutions (HEIs) are surrounded by, and interact with, a local and global environment, which is virtually everything outside of the boundaries of the campus, its digital reach through distance education programs, and its network relationships established with university stakeholders, personnel, and students. Within this environmental rubric, the four key components that make up most organizations are represented in Chinese HEIs: organizational *strategy*; institutional *culture*; *technology*, including both hard technologies (all physical characteristics such as buildings, computers, and laboratories) and soft technologies (all human resources, institutional knowledge, senses, and everything that exists inside of the individuals that make up the HEI); and finally the *structure* of HEIs.

This study provides the reader with a summary of findings found at ten of China's leading universities stratified by geographic region.[1] Ultimately, this study aims to benefit students, educators, and policy makers about the status of higher education in China today and how effective and efficient universities are at adapting to the dynamic needs of an increasingly global market economy. All findings were supported by quantitative and qualitative data collected from a

J. Jacob
University of Pittsburgh's School of Education, 5905 Wesley W. Posvar Hall, Pittsburgh, PA 15260, USA

[1]The sample universities include East China Normal University, Fudan University, Huazhong University of Science and Technology, Jilin University, Peking University, Shenzhen University, Tsinghua University, Xiamen University, Xinjiang Normal University, and Zhongshan University. These universities represent many of the top-ranked HEIs in China stratified by geographic region.

J. Zajda and V. Rust (eds.), *Globalisation, Policy and Comparative Research,*   101
DOI: 10.1007/978-1-4020-9547-4_8, © Springer Science + Bussiness Media B.V. 2009

series of questionnaires and in-depth interviews using triangulation techniques. The questionnaires used in this study were based on UCLA's Higher Education Research Institute (HERI). This was the first time that these surveys had been administered to students ($N = 989$), faculty members ($N = 147$), and administrators ($N = 48$) at HEIs in China. Qualitative interview instruments were designed by the author in an attempt to strengthen quantitative findings from the HERI surveys. The set of questions in the interview instrument targeted social justice issues of educational equity and access (Jacob, 2006), socioeconomic status background, and various items relating to the organizational components aforementioned.

While much of my research has focused on these four internal organizational components, in this article I will address only two, namely organizational strategy and structure, as they relate to the Chinese higher education context. The key to a successful HEI's operation is if all of the components listed in Fig. 8.1 work together as a cohesive whole. This model can also be considered a framework for decision-making within HEIs. Although theoretically plausible, it is often difficult to realize synergy amongst all of the four key components in HEIs. The domestic and global environments further complicate this synergistic realization by changes and challenges that continuously bombard the higher education subsector. This article looks at the strategy and structure of HEIs in-depth and juxtaposes each in the Chinese higher education context. The final section of this article includes an analysis provided from the qualitative data collected from the ten case universities in this study.

From an international and comparative educational perspective, I have chosen an eclectic theoretical approach to examine these issues (Jacob and Cheng, 2005; Rust,

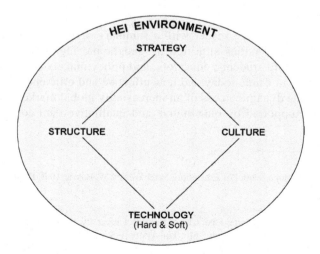

Fig. 8.1 Four essential components of HEIs

2004). There is also an underlying theme that addresses and critiques modernization, human capitalist, and dependency theories throughout the article. This thematic undercurrent highlights the impact market economics has on shaping higher education strategies and structures.

8.2 Guiding Strategies of Higher Education in China

Strategy is positioned at the top of the essential components framework because it is usually the guiding mechanism that formulates the other key components. The traditional organizational definition of strategy is the determination of the basic long-term goals and objectives of an organization, and the implementation of courses of action and the allocation of resources necessary for carrying out these objectives (Chandler, 1962; Beer, 1997). Strategies are often difficult to formulate in a higher education setting. Daniel Neyland and Claire Surridge (2003) have identified three ways in which HEIs often fail to produce a successful guiding strategy. The first strategic pitfall is due to a *distance of time* where the present is never sufficient to plan for the future of a university and the multitude of challenges and changes that will occur. Second is the *distance of space* between administrators and the departments and faculty members, who are either benefactors or instigators for implementing higher education strategies. This lack of ownership and security for a strategic plan that has been structured by a remote committee, administrative office, or government initiative often lacks the support it would otherwise receive if stakeholders were involved throughout the various stages of strategic planning, development, and implementation.[2] A final obstacle facing higher education strategists is a *distance of time* or a lack of a shared vision.[3] Having a shared vision is one of the most powerful ways to effect change in an organization.[4] Without involving key faculty members and stakeholders throughout each stage of the strategy formation process, it is often difficult to disseminate a shared vision of what is actually

---

[2]David K. Allen (2003, p. 71) considers the "'security'" or "'insecurity'" of HEI personnel as an essential element in determining the amount of ownership and motivation a faculty or staff member will put into supporting a strategic initiative or change. Allen later relates job security with the attribute of trust (see p. 84).

[3]The importance of *time* in organizational change is a well-documented, essential, and often neglected element in any sustainable and successful strategy or change effort (Beer, 1988; Fouraker and Stopford, 1968; Beer, 1988; Bateson, 1994).

[4]The term "'shared vision'" was made popular by Peter M. Senge (1990) in his book *The Fifth Discipline: The Art and Practice of the Learning Organization* (for additional reading please refer to Beckhard and Pritchard, 1992; Kanter, 1987; Kotter, 1996). Beckhard and Pritchard describe four key pieces of a vision-driven change: creating and setting the vision, communicating the vision, building commitment to the vision, and organizing people and what they do so they are aligned with the vision. They authors also provide a list of key activities for leaders to use in implementing vision-directed change in organizations, including developing a vision and commitment to it, ensuring the vision is communicated early, diagnosing the present condition

planned (Kotter & Schlesinger, 1979). Thus, actions may be interpreted in several, different ways, depending on the individual and the actual reading of the strategic documents to be implemented.

Although virtually impossible to propose a strategic planning model that can meet the needs of every HEI in China, there are a few points that can be implemented to cultivate a successful strategy-oriented institution. First, efforts can be made to identify and decrease the distances of strategy. This includes a greater emphasis on inclusion of key stakeholders in strategic planning and implementation, which will undoubtedly produce increased ownership for strategies that they would be included in the decision-making process. Second, rather than seen as an item to be discussed at a monthly university or department-level planning meeting, strategy could be an ongoing reflective process. This would help eliminate the eminent discord produced from all three pitfalls mentioned. It will also help presidents, administrators, and faculty members become more proactive in their efforts to think strategically by staying current in a dynamic higher education market and forming guiding strategies that are relevant to their respective contexts. A third point is to cultivate an atmosphere where strategies can be critically examined on a periodic and ongoing basis.

HEIs must beware of these challenges to effective guiding strategies and be open to ongoing changes and obstacles. An eclectic strategy is able to adapt to the dynamic forces of domestic needs, global competition, and technology shifts. Jay R. Galbraith (1974) has identified four strategies that HEIs can adopt in order to reach maximum results (Fig. 8.2).

First, the creation of slack resources where goals and objectives are adapted to better resemble institutional capacity, such as financial restrictions, enrollment abilities, faculty recruitment abilities, etc. Second, the strategy of self-containment shifts the locus of authority from one based on input, resources, skills, and department specializations to one based on output, geographic categories, social justice issues, and market needs. The third strategy is an investment in vertical information systems to create better communication and information mechanisms at all levels of the HEI. Prioritization of information flow will simultaneously become increasingly important, however, as an overload of information is sometimes as harmful as having no information at all. This is evident in the mass emails that circulate throughout HEIs today. This strategy is usually operational-

---

of the organization and identifying gaps, and managing the closing of the gaps. Kanter emphasizes that a shared vision is essential in any institutional change, along with other general principles such as coalition-building and effective communication. Kotter contends that organizations make eight key mistakes, and devotes a chapter to each step that should be taken for successful change: (1) establish a sense of urgency, (2) create a guiding coalition, (3) develop a vision and strategy, (4) communicate the change vision, (5) empower broad-based action, (6) generate short-term wins, (7) consolidate gains and produce more change, and (8) anchor new approaches in the corporate structure.

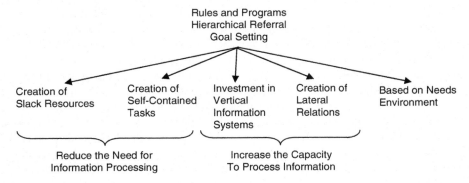

Fig. 8.2 HEI design strategies

ized by "creating redundant information channels which transmit data from the point of origination upward in the hierarchy where the point of decision rests" (Galbraith, 1974, p. 510). Finally, the creation of lateral relationships which cut across lines of authority. This strategy shifts the formal decision-making authority down the institutional hierarchy to where the information exists but does so without reorganizing around self-contained schools, departments, and other HEI centers. A fifth strategy might be to develop and implement strategies based on the needs put forth from the specific HEI environment as depicted in Fig. 8.1. Environmental needs will differ according to location, size, and the impact from both domestic and global forces on a given HEI.[5] Raymond E. Miles and Charles C. Snow (2001,[6] pp. 12–15) persuasively argue that there are only three approaches that organizations can adopt with respect to their environments – they can be "Prospectors," "Defenders," or "Analyzers." Prospecting HEIs are the creators of change in Chinese higher education. Defender HEIs are those that wait to change until the marketscape has stabilized and then attempt to build the products more efficiently by searching for economies of scale. The leading Chinese HEIs are analyzer institutions, which are somewhat of a hybrid of the

---

[5]Meeting the needs of a dynamic environment is a difficult task facing Chinese HEIs today. With an increasing shift from the traditional planned to a market economy equates to adapting the curriculum to help meet the needs of students who must find their own jobs through skills learned at the institution. For more information on how organizations adapt to environmental trends, see Raymond E. Miles et al. (1978), Miles and Charles C. Snow (1984), Richard Beckhard and Reuben T. Harris (1987), and Charles J. Fombrun (1992).

[6]Miles and Snow's definition of Prospector is highly associated with risk. If the strategy or change happens to be successful, then these organizations are generally the one's that will make it to the "'Hall of Fame'" or gain an extreme competitive advantage over its competitor institutions. Other authors are (Boxall, (1998),; Galbraith, (1995),; Scott, (2000),; and Wilkins, (1989).

two previous strategies. Analyzer HEIs are stable and well-planned before embarking on change. They are involved with innovations and changes, but are not generally the first to initiate a large institutional-wide change until it has proven effective in some degree or another. The challenge of the twenty-first century, or what Miles and Snow call "Future Fit," is to adopt organizational approaches to meet the environmental complexity introduced by the rapid evolution of new technology and the emergence of the global economy.

These strategies are necessary when dealing with large organizations, such as HEIs, that have several specialized schools, departments, and a large student body. Effective communication is a barrier in any large organization, and therefore requires integrating mechanisms that increase information-processing capabilities. The three ways Galbraith (1974, p. 506) recommends overcoming this increased communication uncertainty is through coordination by rules and programs, hierarchical referral, and goal setting.

Cynthia Hardy et al. (2003) argue that higher education strategy is determined based on the "realized" rather than on the "intended" strategies implemented by the HEI (see also Mintzberg, 1978; Mintzberg & Waters, 1983). For instance, an HEI that places a strong emphasis on scientific research on all of its activities could be described as pursuing a scientific research strategy. Another university may focus its resources and initiatives into teaching programs, thereby pursuing a strategy favoring teaching. Thus, according to Hardy et al.'s definition, an HEI can have a "realized strategy without having an intended one" (p. 170). This leads to the existence of two major types of strategies in higher education – *emergent* and *deliberate* (see Fig. 8.3).

Emergent strategies are those that form arbitrarily rather than by preplanned initiatives. They are similar to Galbraith's (1974) first strategy of creating slack resources that match actualities in an institution. Deliberate strategies have predisposed intentions or plans that result in realized actions. Both can fit within the definition of higher education strategy, yet they may have entirely different beginnings.

Instigators of higher education strategies are not always easy to identify (Hardy et al., 2003). In some instances strategies can be linked to the HEIs administration, a college or school within the university, a specific department, or even a single professor. In other instances, students can have a significant impact in realized higher education strategies.

Where Hardy et al. argue that HEIs are at odds with the traditional model of organizational strategy, I would say that the case is traditionally different in China.

Fig. 8.3 Various types of higher education strategies

Because of its centralized background since the formation of the People's Republic, higher education has experienced a great deal of centralized planning, or strategic planning if you will.

Ultimately, strategies are determined by those who possess decision-making power within HEIs. Hardy et al. (2003) identify three primary levels of decision-making power in HEIs – *administrative fiat*, *collective choice*, and *professional judgment*. I adapt these strategic decision-making processes to the Chinese HEI context, as portrayed in Fig. 8.4. The first level of higher education decision-making can be termed administrative fiat, where higher education board of regents, presidents, chancellors, or the equivalent to these individuals and their close associates, provide institutional goals and strategies from a top-down decision-making approach. The Chinese government plays a substantial role in the prerogatives of HEI leaders.

As an organizational environment, HEIs cultivate the second level of strategic decision-making – professional judgment. This academic cultivation stems from the specialization of countless fields of thought and industry; HEIs offer faculty members and researchers the opportunity to delve into new areas of research and teaching. In the Chinese higher education context, faculty members have an increasing level of

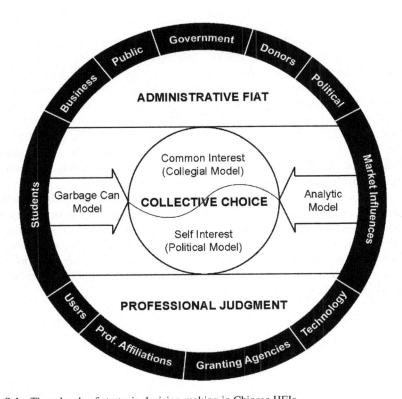

Fig. 8.4   Three levels of strategic decision-making in Chinese HEIs

autonomy. For the most part, gone are the days of government-curtailed research that prevailed during the Hundred Flowers Movement, Great Leap Forward, and Cultural Revolution. Yet faculty restrictions still exist in explicit government critique, as evidenced by the recent reform efforts to pass a law in Hong Kong prohibiting faculty members from publishing negative criticism of the Chinese government (McMurtrie, 2001). But, faculty autonomy exists to some degree in Chinese higher education, so long as it conforms to government initiatives and existing policies.

The third level of decision-making, collective choice, is subdivided into four existing models in Chinese higher education – common interest (or the collegial model), self interest (or the political model), garbage can processes, and analytic processes. Decisions are made by a collective group of higher educational administrators, Party officials, and faculty members who in the collegial model, by a group of individuals share a common vision and goals for the HEI (Taylor, 1983). This represents a decentralized strategy that gives autonomy to faculty and departments in the decision-making process. Although theoretically appealing, the collegial model has received a great deal of criticism as being far too altruistic. An opposing model also exists in China whereby differences of HEI groups and individuals are based on political and increasingly economic agendas. While the current status of Chinese higher education decision-making resides primarily in the political model, a combination approach also exists that draws from both the common and self-interests of all higher educational parties.

The third model is what James G. March and Johan P. Olsen (1979) call a decision-making strategy which acts like "garbage cans" providing a place for all to vent their feelings and provide suggestions and constructive criticisms on just about any subject.[7] If the subject of discussion is of importance to the primary strategy and decision-making players within a Chinese HEI, then the subject cannot fit into this model and would most likely shift to the collegial or political model as a topic of significance. Thus, the garbage can metaphor displays the frustrations that exist in higher education strategy formation where individuals voice their opinions ultimately to no avail – similar to throwing an idea that immediately or eventually winds up in the trash.

The final model of this third strategic decision-making paradigm resides in analytic research processes. This model can be adapted and used by the political, collegial, and garbage can models, as just about every decision made in HEIs require some sort of analytical backing. Although Hardy et al. focus primarily on quantitative data, I argue that both qualitative and quantitative analyses offer sound support for strategic higher education decision-making. The analysis model acts more as a supportive rather than a purely decision-making model.

---

[7] For more information regarding the garbage can process model, see M. D. Cohen, James G. March, and Johan P. Olsen (1972) and Cohen and March (1974).

8.3 Organizational Structure of Universities in China

Many scholars view organizational structure as the primary means for organizing work divided in a variety of ways; how that organization is realized – by whom and with what – determines what the institutional structure will resemble (Mintzberg, 1981). Alfred D. Chandler (1962) states that structure follows institutional strategy, as portrayed in the HEI framework in Fig. 8.1. Chandler defines structure as the design of an organization through which the institution is administered. This design can be disaggregated into two parts. First, the lines of authority and communication between the different administrative offices and officers. Second, the information and data that flow through these lines of communication and authority (see p. 25).[8] The link between structure and strategy is an intuitive one according to Charles Perrow (1967). He also insists that the only way to measure institutional technology is by identifying its organizational structure. Thus, in higher education, individuals at all levels must interact with one another. The form in which this interaction takes place can be termed as the structure of the HEI. It involves the arrangements or the relationships that permit the coordination and control of work (p. 196). Unless structure follows strategy, inefficiency results according to Chandler (1962). Yet structure often fails to follow strategy, a common dilemma among HEIs, government bureaus, and organizations.

Providing a framework on the origins of formal organizational structures (see Fig. 8.5), John W. Meyer and Brian Rowan (1977, p. 345) note that the "growth of rationalized institutional structures in society makes formal organizations more common and more elaborate."

Meyer and Rowan also described the loose coupling between formal organizational structures and their respective activity structures. Structural boundaries begin

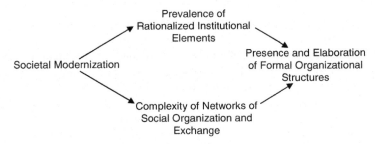

Fig. 8.5 Origins and elaboration of formal organizational structures

---

[8] Alfred D. Chandler (1962) targeted effective strategy and structure development among U S based organizations. A follow-up study by Lawrence E. Fouraker and John M. Stopford (1968) tested whether Chandler's foundational organizational structure thesis would hold up in international contexts. Their findings concurred with Chandler, supporting his thesis that diversification of organizations leads to the need to develop a strong organizational structure. It also supported the hypothesis that strategy is an essential precursor to establishing successful organizational structures.

to expand from large organizations, such as HEIs, into the local and global environments in which they interact. According to Meyer and Rowan, "organizations structurally reflect socially constructed reality" (p. 346).[9] Organizations are bound to social contexts through material resources and legitimacy. This conformity is reflected in the formal structure of an organization. Acting as a buffer from external pressures, the formal structure is only loosely coupled to the activity structure of an organization.[10] HEIs that establish formal structures that adhere to the institutional environment are better able to function within a volatile environment than those with no formal structure established (Meyer and Rowan, 1975). Yet, as HEIs get larger, their institutional structures and technologies become increasingly complex (Woodward, 1965).

Henry Mintzberg (1981) gives nine elements of organizational structure, which I adapt to HEIs:

- Specialization of tasks
- Formalization of procedures (job descriptions, rules, departmental policies, and so forth)
- Formal training, cultural adaptation, and socialization process required of students, faculty, administrators, and support staff
- Grouping of units (i.e., departments, schools, administrative bodies, and study groups) within the HEI, notably by function performed or market served
- Size of each of the units (i.e., the span of control of the top-level administrators)
- Action planning and performance control systems
- Liaison devices, such as task forces, ad hoc committees, integrating administrators, and matrix structure
- Vertical decentralization of power (from the top-level administrators of the HEIs to the lowest level in the administrative structure) and
- Horizontal decentralization of power (delegation of power out from that chain of authority (i.e., schools, departments, divisions, etc.) to nonadministrators (p. 95)

Mintzberg also identifies five basic organizational structure configurations based on when the institutions were established, the size of the organization, and the situations in which they were founded: (1) simple structure, (2) machine bureaucracy, (3) professional bureaucracy, (4) divisionalized form, and (5) adhocracy.[11] There are five component parts that make up all organizations (Fig. 8.6).

---

[9] This view is supported by Talcott Parsons (1956a, 1956b), Stanley H. Udy, Jr. (1970), and Goerg Krücken (2003).

[10] Fred L. Emery and Eric L. Trist (1965) see strong organizational structures as a means for controlling volatile environments and buffer organizations from failure.

[11] Mitzberg argues that these five basic organizational structures "'serve as an effective tool in diagnosing the problems of organizational design, especially those of the *fit* among component parts'" (p. 105). Yet he also cautions that sometimes the right structure may not work in every context. This is particularly important in this study where we are looking at the need to see if the appropriate HEI structure among elite universities in urban centers like Beijing, Shanghai, and Guangzhou would be appropriate for predominantly rural provinces like Xinjiang, Xizang, and in some regards Jilin. Thus, Mintzberg concludes that achieving consistency, coherence, and fit – what he terms as organizational "'harmony'" – are critical factors in organizational structural design.

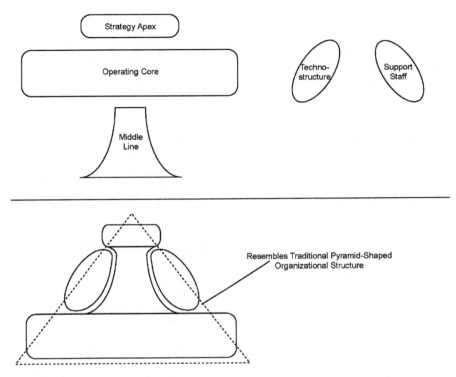

Fig. 8.6 Five basic components of an organization's structure

These parts include the *administration*, which is made up of either a person or group of persons; *operating core*, made of people who actually do the work of the organization; *middle line* or intermediary administrators, such as department heads; *technostructure*, made up of systems design analysts who oversee the formal planning and control of the work, such as software designers and R&D researchers; and finally the *support staff*, who help all areas of the institution. The traditional organizational structure closely resembles a pyramid-shape. Traditional HEIs resemble and fall within Minzberg's divisionalized organization configuration as portrayed in Fig. 8.7.

The divisionalized organization is a combination of rather independent entities loosely coupled together. Middle line administrators in a divisionalized structure are called divisions, departments, or even entire schools that make up an HEI. Mitzberg sees divisionalization as a "structure of semiautonomous market-based units" (p. 101). Mark Granovetter (1985) warns, however, that too much structural emphasis on a market-based environment often leads to a reduction in moral values, a position often taken by Chinese scholars about shifting toward a purely market economy. Tom Burns and G. M. Stalker (1961) feel that the type of structure an organization should adopt hinges on whether or not the organization is in a stable

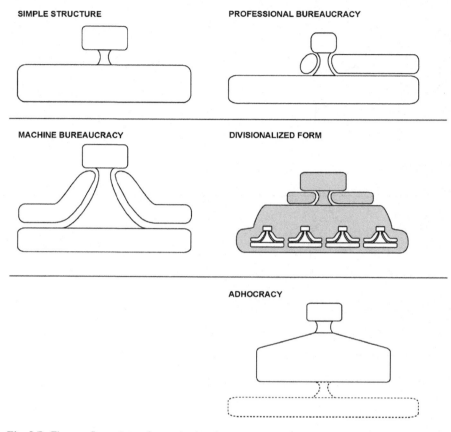

Fig. 8.7 Five configurations of organizational structures

or dynamic local and global environment. Mechanistic management systems are best for stable environments they contend, while an organic form, like the loosely coupled system, is most appropriate in changing environments.[12] Note how all of the organizational structures take on a pyramid-like shape, from the top-level administrators down through divisions and departments, until they finally reach the normal employee. The very shape suggests a stable environment.

Raymond E. Miles and Charles C. Snow (2001) include two additional organizational structures known as the traditional matrix structure and currently evolving and increasingly popular network structure. The matrix form is a hybrid of other

---

[12] Other scholars (Fombrun, 1992; Krücken, 2003; Mohrman & Cummings, 1989; Kotter, 1996) contend that organizational strategy, culture, technology, and structure should be continually revisited and adapted to the changing needs of increasing pressures from the market and the external environment.

organizational structure types, with multiple operating divisions, departments, or schools (Fig. 8.8).

Resembling Mintzberg's divisionalized organization structure portrayed in Fig. 8.7, the matrix form has multiple organizational substructures simultaneously within one mega-framework.[13] This enables organizations to maintain several emphases and specializations within different departments and divisions. For more information on the matrix organizational structure, see Paul R. Lawrence and Jay W. Lorsch (1967), Jay R. Galbraith (1974, 1995), and Mariann Jelinek et al. (1986). Many HEIs are adopting facets of a new organizational form, which includes a new way of packaging

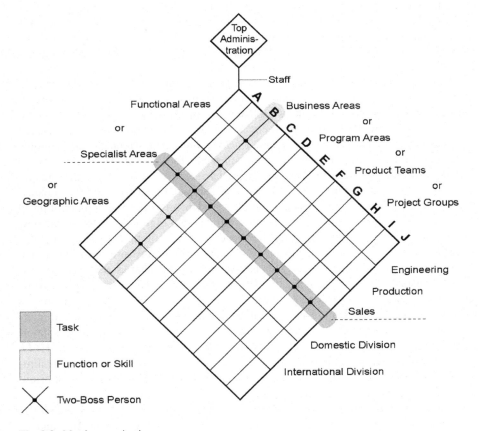

Fig. 8.8 Matrix organization

---

[13] Matrix organizational structures are particularly robust in terms of encouraging innovation, flexibility, and adaptive behavior. Drawbacks include functional teams retaining most of the organizational power, which in many cases leads to the establishment of teams within an overly bureaucratic framework that is not easily broken. Such hindrances actually stifle innovation rather than promote it. For more on matrix organizations, see Warren G. Bennis (1993), Harvey F. Kolodny (1981), and Gareth Morgan (1997).

strategy, structure, culture, and technology. Miles and Snow (2001) use the following images to portray this new network organizational structure (see Fig. 8.9).[14]

Under this newest form, key components for HEIs include strategic alliances, distance learning, outsourcing, location based on core competencies, and where possible the substitution of market forces for hierarchical controls. While Chinese HEIs have not entirely evolved into network organizations, many elements of this newest form are becoming increasingly evident. For instance, Miles and Snow (2001) view network organizations as examples of "substituting internal market mechanisms for centrally planned administrative mechanisms" (p. 57). Russell L. Ackoff (1993) has called this process of substituting internal market mechanisms with centrally planned administrative mechanisms "corporate perestroika." This is particularly relevant to China as it currently maintains a balance between market and planned economic forces in higher educational structures. A more realistic organizational framework for Chinese HEIs is portrayed in Fig. 8.10, which combines several features of the divisional and networks forms.

In many ways it is difficult for Chinese HEI structures to adopt network organizational structure attributes because of their relatively recent entry into a global-based economy. Yet the constant change of market and technological forces requires Chinese HEIs to adapt their curricula, teaching methods, and research agendas to keep pace or be left behind. Local and international businesses continue to look to the Chinese higher education subsector for basic skills development in the workforce. Meeting the needs of these businesses is essential as students are forced to compete for jobs within the country and on an international level. Finally, as China continues its preeminent economic growth, an increasing number of international HEI partnerships and exchanges will emerge. Figure 8.10 also shows how incoming students are essential for the success of an institution. After all, the ultimate product of HEIs is their students. Local communities often have links that support and contribute to HEIs. This is essential for financial as well as other reasons. Distinct core competencies of HEIs often revolve around their ability to draw from a strong cohort of faculty, administrators, and staff. These soft technologies are essential for reaching research goals and attracting the top domestic and international graduate students. These push and pull factors will continue to support more flexible organizational structure frameworks among Chinese HEIs. Recognizing that both opposing factors are essential for the lifeline of the institution, administrators will most likely choose to maintain a structural equilibrium along the higher educational value chain.

The key to organizational structure success according to Miles and Snow (2001) centers on discovering and maintaining fit – strategic fit between the HEI and its environment, and internal fit among strategy, structure, and management processes.

---

[14] Adhocracy organizational structures were coined by Warren Bennis to label organizational structures that are temporary by design. This structure is most appropriate in a highly volatile environment. Sometimes this kind of organization is called a 'virtual' or 'network' organization. Miles and Snow (2001) expand on this definition and focus on the unique aspects of a network organization in our contemporary global society.

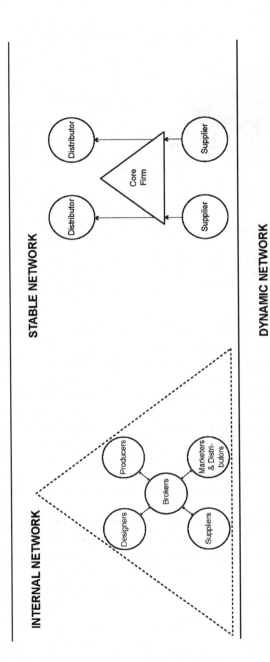
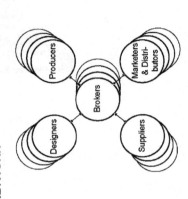

Fig. 8.9 Common network structures

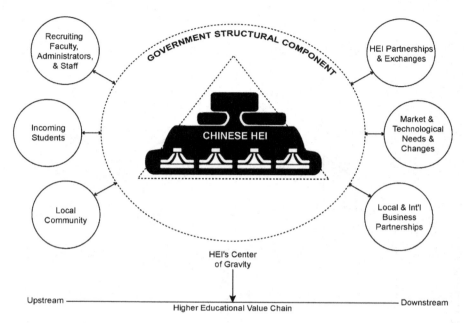

Fig. 8.10 Organizational structure of Chinese HEIs

Thus, for each strategy, there is an appropriate structure. There are four categories of organizational fit according to Miles and Snow – misfit, minimal fit, tight fit, and early tight fit. A limited fit with the market economy, between an organization's strategy and structure, is considered *minimal fit*. Minimal fit structures never reach their highest potential as they seem caught in a vicious cycle of struggle, mediocrity, and minimal survival. HEIs that obtain excellence achieve a *tight fit* with the market economy, and between their organizational strategy and structure. They are successful in virtually everything they do, and achieve a high level of human resource satisfaction and market value in their respective environments. Occasionally HEIs reach an *early tight fit* that ultimately can lead to what Miles and Snow coined as the "hall of fame." Early entry into a specific marketplace gives an HEI a distinct competitive advantage. Through the principle of continual improvement and innovation, these institutions tend to maintain their lead. An even larger advantage is enjoyed "by those firms that first put together the new strategy-structure-process package demanded by major changes in markets and technology" (Miles & Snow, (2001, p. 23). *Misfit* occurs when HEIs fail at what they were organized to do. They never seem to adapt to their environment and are simply out-strategized and out-structured by their competitors.[15]

---

[15] For additional information on the dynamics of organization structural fit, see Raymond E. Miles, Charles C. Snow, Alan D. Meyer, and Henry J. Coleman, Jr. (1978); Robert H. Miles (1980, 1997); Raymond E. Miles and Charles C. Snow, (1984); and Benjamin Schneider, Arthur P. Brief, and Richard A. Guzzo (1996).

In a study of ten universities in Germany, Goerg Krücken (2003) concluded that German universities remained highly decoupled from local reality. The rate of external change far exceeds the rate at which many large universities are able to adapt to the changes. Thus, universities generally deal with this dynamically changing environment by adapting and not changing their organizational structures to meet the necessities brought on by the external pressures.

Environmental forces have become so relevant that the basic shift in the structure of education has changed (Gumport & Sporn, 1999). Kathryn Mohrman (2003) sees many Chinese universities shifting from an organizational system in which all departments reported to an academic vice president, to one in which schools and colleges have been instituted to put decision-making closer to the individuals involved. Chief academic officers on those campuses would welcome fewer required reports, although the additional structural layer increases the bureaucracy at a time when institutions are seeking greater efficiency.

In an attempt to maintain a loosely coupled organization, HEIs can decouple elements of the formal structure and structural activities (Meyer & Rowan, 1977). Decoupling processes help avoid overly excessive departmental evaluations, loss of legitimacy, and loss of autonomy. Currently, Chinese HEIs are in a transitional stage between tight to loosely coupled organizational structures, whereby greater autonomy is slowly penetrating the subsector. This is manifested in the rapid rise of *minban* HEIs in recent years. Minban HEIs help fill the demand for students who want to enroll in higher education but are not able to get into the prestigious government-supported schools.[16]

Adjusting the traditional higher education accreditation structure to the global credit system has been tedious for many administrators. The credit system has not penetrated all universities in China thus far. Students who have completed the required credit hours cannot necessarily graduate earlier than other students within their cohort who have not completed an equivalent amount of hours. And, students who are unable to complete the required credit points within a specified time frame cannot defer to graduate. If students cannot complete the credit points necessary for graduation, or they do not have enough money to pay the required tuition fees, they must first work for a while and then return when they have saved enough money to put up their fees. Thus, graduation can take a long time. It can take upwards of 5–8 years for a normal 4-year degree, simply because of the student's inability to pay for tuition fees upfront.

---

[16] For the purposes of this study, the term *minban* refers to all nongovernment supported HEIs in China. Minban schools receive no direct government support. This is to say that there is no subsidy of costs associated with infrastructure or with instruction. The government continues to bear the cost of the general and professional education of all teachers, even those hired ultimately by minban schools. The term *government* or *public* refers to a government-aided HEI; I use the terms public and government interchangeably in this study (see also Rust, 2000; Holsinger et al., 2004).

8.4 Qualitative Relations to Chinese HEI Strategy and Structure

In this final section of the article, I provide several qualitative findings that relate to the organizational strategy and structure of HEIs in China. When asked about the efficiency of their respective organizational strategy, many interviewees responded that their university had as its primary goal to become a world-renowned university within a few years. Several faculty and administrators considered higher education as the "final castle" to be erected at the conclusion of the Chinese reform effort toward establishing a market economy. Similarly, nine of the ten universities felt that the overall university strategy was good but could be better. A total of eight interviewees from half of the institutions expressed concerns about the lack of a shared vision toward university goals and objectives. One faculty member commented: "Every administrative level within the university has established its own and often contradictory strategies. This creates a plethora of challenges to achieving the over-arching goals of the university." Another faculty member elaborated on this point by adding: "I miss the unified strategy we enjoyed prior to the merger; now it is difficult to identify the goals of each division within the new and sometimes conflicting structure of the university." Several interviewees expressed that they were not aware of any clear university-wide strategies. Somewhat venting when a faculty interviewee commented on the current strategy of the university, she said: "Our university is not as clear as it was in the past where successors of the proletariat were cultivated; now it is not as clear where the students will end up and to what means we will help them achieve their unforeseen end." Understanding the need to align their university strategies to better meet the needs of the market economy and the environmental forces that are facing HEIs today, several interviewees felt that their universities were lacking in this area. One graduate student commented about this need by saying:

> We need to continue to emphasize university education goals to reach world-wide excellence as an institution. Such goals include teaching English as a second language to the student body, which will help us be more prepared when entering the workforce upon graduation. So far our institution has only expressed this and other university goals in theory, but we need to see these goals put into action.

This pragmatic perspective, linking theory and action, was supported by one faculty member who cited John Dewey's impact on Chinese education during the early decades of the twentieth century. In this regard, Dewey taught that education should provide meaning and equip students with a practical means for relating and surviving in the economic context of the world economy (Dewey, 1899, 1916). Only three interviewees expressed widespread participation of all stakeholders in establishing university goals at their universities. This amplifies the need to increase stakeholders – students, faculty, administrators, and support staff – at all levels of the university, thereby increasing ownership and support to see strategies realized by putting them into practice.

Recognizing the ideal notion that organizational structure should be aligned with, and follow, strategy (see Chandler, 1962), one administrator said: "The organizational structure is in many ways prohibiting us from realizing our primary university goal—to become a world-renowned university." Adapting the structure to meet the goals of the university is essential to strategy and goal realization.

In some instances, the existing university structure was able to adapt to the dynamic environmental needs. An undergraduate student related how his university dealt with the SARS epidemic. "[My] university had already had a solid preparation," he said. "And the strategy to prevent SARS at the time was implemented well throughout the organization. Students were trained on hygiene and feedback mechanisms were installed to relay information from the bottom levels of the university to the top administrators." Other interviewees felt that the organizational structure should be directly aligned with the market's rapid development. Yet, they also recognized that changing the university structure requires a significant amount of time and effort.

Yet most interview participants agreed that Chinese HEIs are too bureaucratic. For instance, one faculty member commented that in order to attract elite faculty members to teach at a specific university, often the recruiting university will have to provide a place not only for the new faculty member but also for his or her spouse. Thus, administrative positions are given to these spouses, whether or not the spouse is qualified for the position. Another faculty member said: "Although most school and department administrative positions can be handled by 5 or so administrators, the average number of administrators at the school level at our university is 20. This is what John Dewey called the phenomenon of educational waste." Students feel the same about this excessive bureaucratic structure:

> Administrators are too many on campus. Some management staff are entirely unnecessary. Take for example the case of student dormitory management staff. One of their duties is to give services to students, but they do not always do this well. A very simple example is portrayed while students are looking for employment. Students are always looking for obtaining a job. In their continual pursuit of employment, students leave their dormitory postal address as a primary means of contact with companies when they are granted job interviews. When companies reply to the students, often the administrative staff will fail to deliver the mail to the students. The dormitory staff members feel that mail delivery is the responsibility of the campus postal service staff. Thus, students are being withheld job opportunities because they cannot maintain reliable correspondence with potential employers.

The bureaucratic nature of large organizations is represented in the immense organizational charts of most universities. Yet, excessive and unnecessary bureaucracy was the single most reported issue from the majority of those interviewed.

Other interviewees felt that their university structure was outdated. One administrator noticed the conflict that arose between his university structure – which was based upon the Russian model of the 1950s – and the market-oriented model prevalent in Western nations and much of the rest of the world. Contrasting this viewpoint, a faculty member said: "Our university still has shades of the traditional planned economy, which in many cases provides rules, a necessary division of labor, and leads to organizational effectiveness."

Rapid structural changes can lead to discord in the higher education settings. One university in our sample had in recent years merged with several other HEIs. This created mixed feelings reflected by the interviewees. All argued that the merger reform, though helpful in some ways, has also hindered the development of the university. One administrator said: "The merger created an aircraft carrier among HEIs in China. Yet, it has also led to increased inefficiency. The organizational structure is superfluous and has too many administrative staff." Another faculty member at the same institution said: "Comparatively speaking, the previous organizational structure before the merger was better. Current structural barriers, such as distance between the merged institutions, restrict our administrative staff from being as effective as before." Students have struggled with the restructuring process as well. One student expressed frustration of having to commute between several campuses for required services. She felt that "It is unnecessarily time-consuming; it was not this way before the merger. Without fundamental services set up at each campus location, students must spend a lot of precious time going back and forth between campuses." Regarding too many administrative staff, one faculty member pointed out:

> There are only 2,100 teachers at this institution, while we have an abundant 4,000 plus administrators on board. The proportion of administrators to teachers is not beneficial to a university setting. For example, there are twenty teachers in our school and twelve administrators. The proportion is not the worst in our university by any means. There are two accountants, though we only need the services of one. We even have too many gate entrance guards, who receive higher bonuses than many teachers. And while many administrative support staff receive full benefits, our young faculty members have to buy their apartments.

This overstaffed scenario was a common expression of several interviewees. Excessive personnel leads to inefficiencies and in many cases causes an unproductive mentality among support staff members at the universities. Almost half of the respondents felt that although their universities had come a long way, they needed additional structural reforms to lead to a desired level of organizational efficiency. Currently, issues such as too many administrative staff and the dissonance between the structure and strategy are difficult issues that these HEIs must deal with.

8.5   Conclusion

This chapter provides an overview of how Chinese higher education institutions are adapting to dynamic local and global forces. All higher educational institutions have the four essential components of organizations – strategy, culture, technology, and structure. While the models relating to these elements in this article have been for the most part created from a contemporary Western background, others like the systems models, *Tai-Ji*, and Janusian paradigms, are derived from Eastern and ancient Roman perspectives. Clearly Chinese higher education is evolving. Trends indicate that these changes are becoming more aligned with the market economy. Yet several features still remain unchanged. Where many societies have already made a complete market-economic transition, Chinese higher education has taken a more gradual route. This has left in place strong governmental regulation within each of the four organizational components. And while HEIs consist primarily of loosely coupled systems, those that have guiding strategies, targeting internal and external issues, will most readily be able to cope with the dynamic needs of the future. While in a transitional state, Chinese HEIs have established a unique organizational structural trend that combines the traditional divisional form with the more fluid network framework. If all four of these essential elements are operating in an efficient and coordinated manner, Chinese HEIs have the potential to keep the economic power of the future rejuvenated. True efficiency, however, cannot sacrifice global needs at the expense of local political and social contexts. The balance between the local and the global is an organizational dialectic that will need to be continually addressed among Chinese HEIs.

References

Ackoff, R. L. (1993). Corporate Perestroika: the internal market economy. In W. E. Halal (Ed.), *Internal Markets: Bringing the Power of Free Enterprise Inside Your Organization* (pp. 15–26). New York: Wiley.

Allen, D. K. (2003). Organisational climate and strategic change in higher education: organisational insecurity. *Higher Education*, 46(1), 61–92.

Bateson, M. C. (1994). *Peripheral Visions: Learning Along the Way*. New York: HaperCollins.

Beckhard, R. & Harris, R. T. (1987). Organizational Transitions: Managing Complex Change. Reading, MA: Addison-Wesley.

Beckhard, R. & Pritchard, W. (1992). Leading a vision-driven change effort: a commitment to the future. In Changing the Essence: The Art of Creating and Leading Fundamental Change in Organizations. (pp. 25–35). San Francisco, CA: Jossey-Bass.

Beer, M. (1988). Leading Change. Cambridge, MA: Harvard Business School.

Beer, M. (1997). The transformation of the human resource function: resolving the tension between a traditional administrative and a new strategic role. *Human Resource Management*, 36(1), 49–56.

Bennis, W. G. (1993). Beyond Bureaucracy: Essays on the Development and Evolution of Human Organization. New York: McGraw-Hill.

Boxall, P. (1998). Achieving competitive advantage through human resource strategy: towards a theory of industry dynamics. *Human Resource Management Review*, 8(3), 265–288.

Burns, T. & Stalker, G. M. (1961). The Management of Innovation. London: Tavistock.

Chandler, A. D. (1962). Strategy and Structure: Chapters in the History of the Industrial Enterprise. Cambridge, MA: MIT Press.

Cohen, M. D. & March, J. G. (1974). Leadership and Ambiguity: The American College President. New York: McGraw-Hill.

Cohen, M. D., March, J. G., & Olsen, J. P. (1972). A garbage can model of organizational choice. *Administrative Science Quarterly*, 17(10), 1–25.

Dewey, J. (1899). The School and Society. Chicago, IL: The University of Chicago Press.

Dewey, J. (1916). Democracy and Education: An Introduction to the Philosophy of Education. New York: Free Press.

Emery, F. L. & Trist, E. L. (1965). The causal texture of organizational environments. *Human Relations*, 18(1), 21–32.

Fombrun, C. J. (1992). Turning Points: Creating Strategic Change in Corporations. New York: McGraw-Hill.

Fouraker, L. E. & Stopford, J. M. (1968). Organizational structure and the multinational strategy. *Administrative Science Quarterly*, 13(1), 47–64.

Galbraith, J. R. (1974). Organization design: an information processing view. *Interfaces*, 4(3), 28–36.

Galbraith, J. R. (1995). Designing Organizations: An Executive Briefing on Strategy, Structure, and Process. San Francisco, CA: Jossey-Bass.

Granovetter, M. (1985). Economic action and social structure: the problem of embeddftness. *American Journal of Sociology*, 91(3), 481–510.

Gumport, P. J. & Sporn, B. (1999). Institutional adaptation: demands for management reform and university administration. In J. C. Smart & W. G. Tierney (Eds.), Higher Education: Handbook of Theory and Research (vol. 14) (pp. 103–145). New York: Agathon Press.

Hardy, C., Langley, A., Mintzberg, H., & Rose, J. (2003). Strategy formation in the university setting. In J. L. Bess (Ed.), College and University Organization: Insights from the Behavioral Sciences (2nd ed.) (pp. 169–210). Amherst, MA: I&I Occasional Press. Original edition, 1984.

Holsinger, D. B., Jacob, W. J., & Mugimu, C. B. (2004). Private Secondary Education in Uganda. Paris: International Institute for Education Policy.

Jacob, W. J. (2006). Social justice in Chinese higher education: issues of equity and access. *International Review of Education*, 52(1), 149–169.

Jacob, W. J. & Cheng, S. Y. (2005). Mapping paradigms and theories in comparative, international, and development education (CIDE) research. In D. P. Baker & A. W. Wiseman (Eds.), International Perspectives on Education and Society (pp. 231–268). New York: Elsevier.

Jelinek, M., Litterer, J. A., & Miles, R. E. (Eds.) (1986). Organizations by Design: Theory and Practice. Plano, TX: Business Publications.

Kanter, R. M. (1987). Moving Ideas into Action: Mastering the Art of Change. Cambridge, MA: Harvard Business School Press.

Kolodny, H. F. (1981). Managing in a Matrix. *Business Horizons*, 24(2), 12–24.

Kotter, J. P. (1996). Leading Change. Cambridge, MA: Harvard Business School Press.

Kotter, J. P. & Schlesinger, L. A. (1979). Choosing Strategies for Change. *Harvard Business Review*, 57(2), 106–114.

Krücken, G. (2003). Learning the 'New, New Thing': on the role of path dependency in university structures. *Higher Education*, 46(3), 315–339.

Lawrence, P. R. & Lorsch, J. W. (1967). Organization and Environment: Managing Differentiation and Integration. Boston, MA: Harvard Business School.

March, J. G. & Olsen, J. P. (1979). Ambiguity and Choice in Organizations (2nd ed.). Bergen: Universitetsforlaget.

McMurtrie, B. (2001). In the new Hong Kong, scholars fear a loss of academic freedom. *Chronicle of Higher Education, March* 30, A52.

Meyer, J. W. & Rowan, B. (1975). Notes on the structure of educational organizations. Paper read at Annual Meeting of the American Sociological Association, at San Francisco.

Meyer, J. W. & Rowan, B. (1977). Institutionalized organizations: formal structure as myth and ceremony. *American Journal of Sociology*, 83(2), 340–363.

Miles, R. E. & Snow, C. C. (1984). Fit, failure, and the hall of fame. *California Management Review*, 26(3), 99–115.

Miles, R. E. & Snow, C. C. (2001). Fit, Failure, and the Hall of Fame: How Companies Succeed or Fail. New York: Free Press.

Miles, R. E., Snow, C. C., Meyer, A. D., & Coleman, H. J. (1978). Organizational strategy, structure, and process. *Academy of Management Review*, 3(3), 546–562.

Miles, R. H. (1980). Organization boundary roles and units. In The Dynamics of Organizational Theory. Glenview, IL: Scott, Foresman & Company.

Miles, R. H. (1997). Leading Corporate Transformation: A Blueprint for Business Renewal. San Francisco, CA: Jossey-Bass.

Mintzberg, H. (1978). Patterns in strategy formation. *Management Science,* 24(9), 934–948.

Mintzberg, H. (1981). Organization design: fashion or fit. *Harvard Business Review*, 59(1), May–June, 93–109.

Mintzberg, H. & Waters, J. A. (1983). Of Strategies, Deliberate and Emergent. Working Paper. Montreal: McGill University.

Mohrman, K. (2003). Center and periphery: changes in the relationship between Chinese universities and the central government. *International Higher Education*, 33(1), Fall, 24–25.

Mohrman, S. A. & Cummings, T. G. (1989). Self Designing Organizations: Learning How to Create High Performance. Reading, MA: Addison-Wesley.

Morgan, G. (1997). Images of Organization (2nd ed.). Thousand Oaks, CA: Sage.

Neyland, D. & Surridge, C. (2003). Information strategy stories: ideas for evolving a dynamic strategic process. *Perspectives*, 7(1), 9–13.

Parsons, T. (1956a). Suggestions for a sociological approach to the theory of organizations-I. *Administrative Science Quarterly*, 1(1), 63–85.

Parsons, T. (1956b). Suggestions for a sociological approach to the theory of organizations-II. *Administrative Science Quarterly*, 1(2), 225–250.

Perrow, C. (1967). A framework for the comparative analysis of organizations. *American Sociological Review*, 32(2), 194–208.

Rust, V. D. (2000). Educational reform: who are the radicals. In N. P. Stromquist & K. Monkman (Eds.), Globalisation and Education: Integration and Contestation Across Cultures (pp. 63–76). New York: Rowman & Littlefield.

Rust, V. D. (2004). Postmodernism and globalisation: the state of the debate. Paper presented at annual meeting of the Comparative and International Education Society, March 2004, Salt Lake City, Utah.

Schneider, B., Brief, A. P., & Guzzo, R. A. (1996). Creating a climate and culture for sustainable organizational change. *Organizational Dynamics*, 24(4), 7–19.

Scott, P. (2000). Higher Education Reformed. London/New York: Falmer Press.

Senge, P. M. (1990). The Fifth Discipline: The Art and Practice of the Learning Organization. New York: Currency Doubleday.

Taylor, W.T.(1983). The nature of policy making in universities. *Canadian Journal of Higher Education,* 13(1), 17–32.

Udy, S. H., Jr. (1970). Work in Traditional and Modern Society. Englewood Cliffs, NJ: Prentice-Hall.

Wilkins, A. L. (1989). Developing Corporate Character: How to Successfully Change an Organization Without Destroying It. San Francisco, CA: Jossey-Bass.

Woodward, J. (1965). Industrial Organization: Theory and Practice. London: Oxford University Press.

Chapter 9
Intellectual Property and the Cultural Aspects of Collaboration in the Global Culture: Comparisons Between Mexico and the United State

Armando Alcantara and Margaret M. Clements

9.1 Intellectual Property and the Cultural Aspects of Collaboration: Introduction

Institutions of higher education, particularly in the developing world, increasingly look to other countries to develop, through research collaboration, new technologies that contribute to knowledge and institutional development as well as increase revenues. Furthermore, the pressures and benefits of a global economy have motivated the expansion of international research alliances. However, these alliances are frequently constructed between unequal partners in terms of both intellectual and material resources. This disequilibrium ultimately reinforces the social construction of marginality as dependency on scientific and technological resources is cultivated. This chapter explores the international and institutional aspects of university collaboration on research and technology transfer between Mexico and the USA. To do so, we first examine international issues concerning intellectual property policy for universities in the developing world. Second, we explore challenges and dilemmas that universities in the USA currently face in their academic culture regarding intellectual property management and commercialization. Issues such as academic freedom, scientific communication, community service, financial reform, freedom of inquiry, and policy are all implicated in this rapidly changing academic culture. Third, we describe a series of regulatory changes implemented at Mexico's UNAM to protect intellectual property rights (industrial property and copyright). Finally, we broadly describe programs for technology transfer between Mexico and US institutions of higher education. Some of the implications of the collaborative initiatives are discussed as well.

A. Alcantara
National Autonomous University of Mexico
M.M. Clements
Indiana University

J. Zajda and V. Rust (eds.), *Globalisation, Policy and Comparative Research,*
DOI: 10.1007/978-1-4020-9547-4_9, © Springer Science + Bussiness Media B.V. 2009

9.2   Global Issues of Intellectual Property Policy in the Developing World

The notion of intellectual property as private property varies around the globe. In the nineteenth century, very heated debates ensued in Europe over the patent system developed in Italy and in England between the fifteenth and seventeenth centuries (Machlup & Penrose, 1950). Despite efforts to unite procedures involving international patent protection through international organizations such as the North American Free Trade Association (NAFTA) and the European Union (EU), in practice individual countries remain divided over policies involving the protection of intellectual property. Furthermore, especially for historically communist, socialist, and developing nations, intellectual property has a strong element of community investment in which the society perceives a right to share in the resulting profits (Isla, 2000; Noetinger & Veirano, 2000; Masuda, 2000; Poltorak, 2000; Von, 2000; Villarreal, 2008). Since the fall of the former Soviet Union, however, most countries have been aligning their intellectual property laws and policies with those espoused by a market economy and the industrialized world (Altbach, 1996; Sell, 1995; Olivas 1992). Specifically, the USA has applied significant pressure on other countries to strengthen and protect intellectual property rights through multinational corporations and international forums such as the United Nations Conference on Trade and Development, the World Trade Organization (WTO), the Trade and Tariff Acts of 1984 and 1988, and the NAFTA (Gereffi, 1978; Sell, 1995). While political pressure has helped curb pirating and intellectual property theft and infringement, the research literature suggests that through actual involvement and profit from research activities, other countries are beginning to perceive and enforce the spirit of the laws protecting intellectual property (Altbach, 1996; Anton, 1996; Haas, 1996; Sell, 1995; The Task Force on Higher Education and Society, 2000). As an historically vulnerable trading partner, Mexico has been especially susceptible to pressures to realign intellectual property laws more closely to those of the USA (Gereffi, 1978; Sell, 1995)

Recently, a team sponsored by the World Bank and UNESCO argued for reforms in intellectual property rights protection for higher education. The special team contends that in an increasingly global world it is important to protect investments made in the production of knowledge. However, most patents protect a variety of advances and inventions made in industrial nations – not developing nations. Furthermore, licensing fees for product development are quite expensive. Table 9.1, below, shows the difference between Canada and Mexico in both receipts and payments of royalties and license fees to the USA generated from industrial processes in millions of US dollars.

This table illustrates that while US receipts from Canada have actually declined over the last 10 years, Mexican dependency on technology has evidently grown. By contrast, US payments to Canada have increased while payments to Mexico are either negligible (*) or undisclosable due to corporate privacy (D) rights. Universities and research institutions throughout the developing world likewise face significant

Table 9.1 US receipts and payments of royalties and license fees generated from the exchange and use of industrial processes (National Science Board, 2000)

Year	Canada	Mexico	Canada	Mexico
	US Receipts		US Payments	
1987	87	14	9	3
1988	60	13	11	
1989	62	18	8	
1990	79	23	16	
1991	62	31	11	
1992	47	29	10	1
1993	41	28	8	
1994	54	33	11	1
1995	55	24	13	D
1996	81	26	57	
1997	82	25	76	D

and similar financial hurdles to research as those experienced by Mexico. It is foreseeable, given this example, that entire regions may find themselves excluded from participation in the global system of innovation (The Task Force on Higher Education and Society, 2000).

The Task Force warns that although this problem is not yet serious, there is growing recognition that such barriers to participation in innovation will be aggravated as the commercialization of university-based international intellectual property becomes more formalized. The Task Force suggests, among other measures, that a wider use of a sliding scale for licensing agreements that takes into account a country's level of development would be helpful. Another possibility should be to promote North–South joint ventures in which industrial and developing country participants earn and share intellectual property rights. A few years ago, the UK's National Endowment for Science, Technology, and the Arts (NESTA) explicitly committed itself to exploring creative partnerships with innovators in developing nations. Basically, in exchange for bearing some of the risk and providing financial support, NESTA would receive a percentage of the intellectual property rights derived from those creative partnerships. In this manner, profits are fed back into the funding loop. The Task Force recommends that where models do not exist, developing nations should be prepared to innovate. There is a belief that, as the knowledge economy demands new and quite different institutions, emergent economies may be better poised to respond to those demands than mature economies (The Task Force on Higher Education and Society, 2000).

The OECD underscores the fact that access to the protection mechanisms of intellectual property, for the "country of origin" as well as the country to which technology is transferred, constitutes a fundamental prerequisite to stimulate cooperative activities. These activities ultimately lead to specific agreements on technology transfer and foreign investment in countries that are technology importers. Strict laws for intellectual property protection and enforcement, are critical elements in this direction (OECD, 1997). However, these very laws are frequently in conflict with strong cultural traditions of communal ownership as well as an academic ethos of "the intellectual commons."

9.3   Intellectual Property and the University

9.3.1   Implications for Academic Culture

As institutions and nations confront the challenges of higher education financial stringency, decentralization, and reform, they likewise wrestle with the challenges of financing higher education. Thus, issues involving property rights have become progressively more pertinent for research and industrial outcomes of the education venture. Higher education institutions as well as individual countries struggle with the notion of private gain for publicly funded research. However, as the costs of operating the university become decentralized, universities must look to their outputs in order to raise revenue. In 1999, US universities filed for 7,612 US patents, were granted 3,079 patents, executed 3,295 licenses or options with commercial companies, and collected more than $641,000,000 in royalties on inventions (AUTM, 2000). Obviously, confidentiality is paramount to the production and protection of proprietary interests. But because university collaboration aspires to the ideal of a free and open exchange of scholarly ideas, this recent change to proprietary rights has a resounding impact across the university, and indeed, around the globe. Different opinions exist, however, regarding the risks and advantages of intellectual property commercialization for higher education.

Advocates for the commercialization of university-developed intellectual property argue that the knowledge production process (social or individual) is not harmed by providing legal protection to the property rights of intellectual products – particularly to those subject to patents. Furthermore, the knowledge production process is ultimately strengthened due to the reduction of conflicts caused by unfair competition. Property rights aim at granting to intellectual producers a privilege – regulated and within specific limits – over the knowledge they create. This line of argumentation also stresses that most of the typical academic "products" such as scientific and technological research, teaching, and the diffusion of knowledge through all sorts of publications – are not usually candidates for commercialization. Advocates also argue that legal protection for intellectual property is an indispensable aspect of stimulating and promoting scientific and technological activities. Thus, national and international patenting patterns are a valuable indicator in assessing science and technology system's productivity (PECYT, 2001).

Critics of intellectual property commercialization point out that proprietary rights accrue more quickly for the already advantaged. In the USA, university commercialization has resulted in the construction of marginality for universities that don't emphasize research over teaching. Likewise, the gap between developing countries and industrialized countries continues to widen as a result of more strict protection programs (Aboites, 1993). For example, between 1990 and the year 2000, more than 700,000 patents were granted to persons, institutions, firms, or residents in the USA. Mexico was only granted 522, while Brazil obtained 711, Spain 1,937, and Korea 17,570. In the same time period, more than 50,000 patents were granted in Mexico, of which only 3,200 were granted to Mexicans (less than 6% of the total) (PECYT, 2001). Tables 9.2 and 9.3 illustrate the enormous disparities in patent production between the three NAFTA economies (Canada, Mexico, and the USA).

Aboites argues that one implication for the least developed of the three NAFTA partners is that protection of intellectual property may lead the Mexican economy to warrant that knowledge that has been accumulated for multinational corporations would be protected by the Mexican government. Another implication is that, as most research and development (R&D) in Mexico is conducted at public universities and research institutes, their agendas and research priorities would be set up in accordance to commercial rather than academic interests (Aboites, 1993).

9.3.2   Commercialization and Community Service

Given the potential of intellectual property commercialization to imperil the liberal university's future, Claire Polster (2000) points out the importance of exploring how it works and how it may be resisted. She argues that dynamics set into motion by the commercialization of intellectual property are eroding the university's ability to draw on and to replenish the intellectual commons – a fundamental precondition to the survival of the university. Because commercialization of intellectual property changes the reward structure for faculty within the university, these ventures also prevent academics from fulfilling their public service mission. As the academy decreases its service to the public, the very popular support that is essential to its survival will be challenged. In her view, these two mutually reinforcing develop-

Table 9.2 US patents by inventor residence (National Science Board, 2000)

	1985	1990	1995	1998
US origin	39,556	47,390	55,739	80,294
Canadian origin	1,342	1,859	2,104	2,974
Mexican origin	32	32	40	57
Other foreign origin	30,731	41,083	43,536	64,195
Total	71,661	90,364	101,419	147,520

Table 9.3 Patents granted in other countries of US origin (National Science Board, 2000)

	1985	1990		1994		1996	
	Patents to non-residents as percentage of total	Patents to USA as percentage of total	Patents to non-residents as percentage of total	Patents to USA as percentage of total	Patents to non-residents as percentage of total	Patents to non-residents as percentage of total	Patents to USA as percentage of total
Canada	92.8	54.8	92.2	52.2	92.7	51.3	90.1	52.2
Mexico	93.4	56.3	92.0	63.4	93.4	58.0	96.4	67.9

ments are making it increasingly difficult for the liberal university to continue on as it has. Intellectual property management ultimately produces a qualitative transformation of the institution that is economically and socially costly to society. Polster argues that although current developments pose very serious threats to the liberal university's future, there is still time to intervene in order to preempt or to alter them. She advocates for a strategy of pursuing broad IP exemptions for universities.

9.3.3 Academic Freedom

In a similar vein, M. M. Scott (1998) compares the potential harm of intellectual property rights in academia to a ticking time bomb. Scott points out that for a long period of time, ideas have been owned by the person who produced them. Recently, however, universities have begun to act like corporations, attempting to claim ownership of professors' ideas in order to market them. This change may have two devastating consequences for academics. In the short run, the new market-based strategies abridge academic freedom; in the long run, they have the potential to diminish the human knowledge base. Scott argues that not only scientists and those who deal with patents have to concern themselves with intellectual property rights. She has observed that many administrators and trustees are already examining the arts and humanities for ideas and products they can sell. Scott underscores, however, that it may be possible to defuse the bomb. She brought to the discussion the experiences of the Indiana University's Intellectual Task Force as an example of one way the academic community has responded to the problem. Scott describes the debates ensued about intellectual property, the policies governing it, and their implications for the long-term health of the university. The IU Task Force developed a set of four principles governing intellectual property:

1. The university is first and foremost an academic institution whose fundamental missions are research, teaching, and service in furtherance of its principal aim of the advancement of knowledge and toward the ultimate aim of the greater public good.
2. Academic freedom is one of the most basic principles governing academic institutions and in maintaining their role in society as an independent critic.
3. The free and open exchange of ideas and information is fundamental to the very reason for being a university.
4. There shall be no requirement that any intellectual property be exploited commercially; the university cannot transfer intellectual property to a third party without the permission of the creator/faculty member.

In accordance with these principles, Scott concludes that it is important for universities to recognize their mandate to conduct free and open research and maintain an environment of unrestricted exchange of ideas for the greater common good (Scott, 1998).

Unfortunately, the ability for any university to foster an unrestricted exchange of ideas for the greater common good is increasingly tied to university commercialization efforts. For example, of the 3,600 institutions of higher education in the USA, 200 universities account for 95% of all research and development expenditures. Furthermore, the top 10 institutions received 17% of all academic research and development funds; the top 20 institutions spent 30% of all research and development funds; and the top 50 institutions spent 56% of all R&D funds (National Science Board, 2000). This concentration of funds in top-tier universities tends to reinforce the structure of marginalization between university types. While some institutions like Indiana University at least pay lip service to the importance of academic freedom, other more competitive universities are establishing structures such as business incubators and spin-off companies to improve the status of their institution. It should be noted that Indiana University has subsequently strengthened its technology transfer initiatives and is taking more aggressive measures toward commercializing intellectual property.

9.4   Policy Implications

Several aspects of the implications of intellectual property for universities have been documented through empirical research. Slaughter and Rhoads (1993) observed the way the state has helped shape the climate for the commercialization of science in a public university, and how this – in turn – has shaped the terms of professional labor for faculty. They examined patent policies of a public research university and of its Board of Regents, and the relevant state statutes from 1969 to 1989. Slaughter and Rhoads stressed that policies and statutes moved from an ideology that defined the public interest as best served by shielding public entities from involvement in the market, to one that saw the public interest best served by public organizations' involvement in commercial activities. In their view, claims to the ownership and rewards of intellectual property shifted dramatically in that time, from faculty owning their products and time to complete ownership by the institution. The contract between the university and faculty became increasingly formalized and specified. Slaughter and Rhoades also believed that such development augured significant changes in professional labor and in the relationship between the state and higher education (Slaughter & Rhoades, 1993).

In their 1999 study Daza Campbell and Slaughter (1999) explored areas of possible tension between faculty and administrators engaged in university–industry activity by investigating the key sources from which tensions are more likely to emerge: issues related to conflicts of interest (conflict over financial issues, e.g., revenue-generating opportunities through patents and licensing); conflict of commitment (conflict over competing faculty responsibilities, e.g., whether faculty allocate more time to their traditional academic duties or to their industrial sponsor); and conflict over internal equity (conflict over the university's internal distribution of rewards and workload).

Their study compared two groups of academics and administrators (those involved in university–industry collaborative activity and those who were not). A fundamental premise of their research was that a significant number of American universities are seeking resources from industry, and at the same time firms are seeking knowledge, know-how, and people from universities. Analysis of the several groups' responses to the survey pointed to two sets of tensions that stem from increased university–industry activity primarily centering on autonomy, resources, and flexibility to capture financial gain. The first was between involved faculty and involved administrators, the second between involved faculty and noninvolved faculty. The authors conclude that the manner in which these tensions are resolved will have important implications for the organization of faculty work, students' experience with the educational system, and administrators' efforts to respond to pressures from federal and state regulators. Furthermore, the numerous ambiguities suggest that these issues are unresolved and perhaps volatile (Dazaet al., 1999).

Although this section of the paper examined a number of implications of establishing organized intellectual property management in several US universities, we believe that higher education institutions in the developing world will also face, sooner or later, some of the challenges and dilemmas reviewed here. Especially, as private and technological institutes continue to increase throughout Mexico and as Mexico's UNAM continues to produce a significantly higher number of graduates in science and engineering programs.

9.5 Intellectual Property at Mexico's National University

A number of legal regulations concerning IP have been established since the 1990s at Mexico's National University (UNAM). Issues such as editorial works, discoveries, inventions, and artistic works expressed in a variety of forms constitute a great deal of UNAM's most valuable assets. Due to its huge size and long tradition in several fields of scientific and social research as well as strong programs in the arts and humanities, issues of intellectual property have become increasingly important. Although several governmental offices and departments in charge of dealing with the legal aspects of copyright and industrial property already exist in Mexico, UNAM has just opened a University Registration Office for Intellectual Property. This office has been attached to UNAM's Attorney General Office. The new office's purpose is to coordinate all the guidelines and regulations concerning intellectual property at UNAM and to serve as a liason with other government offices and departments dealing with IP issues. (UNAM, 1994, Gaceta UNAM, 2002).

Not surprisingly, Sylvan Learning Systems is purchasing controlling interests in Mexican private universities and hotel management schools. This "deal" combined with the current emphasis and prioritization of distance learning initiatives in Mexico are indications that the commercialization of the university in Mexico has already begun. Furthermore, a study by Rogers, Yin, and Hoffman (2000) indicates that there is a correlation between the maturity of such offices and the increased awareness of the problems and possibilities of commercialization for the university. Age of such programs in the USA varies from 77 years (University of Wisconsin) to 1 year. Most US technology transfer offices, however, sprung up within the last 5–20 years. Comparatively, then, UNAM's technology transfer office is just now beginning this process of commercialization and capitalization.

9.6 Technology Transfer Collaboration Between Mexico and the USA

A comprehensive inventory of technology transfer agreements, patent production activity and licensing agreements between US universities and institutions in Mexico is not available – most likely because very few exist. We contacted 10% of the 139 respondents to the Association of University Technology Manager's annual survey to ascertain the landscape of such joint commercial ventures. The technology managers acknowledged that tracking such information would be very difficult to do because the purpose of the Bayh-Dole Act was to increase university partnerships with US industry. For instance, if a US university participates in research with industry, it is quite possible that the industry could license that patent in another country without the knowledge of the university. Instead, the technology managers indicated that co-authorship on journal articles might be the best indicator of cooperative research efforts that could result in intellectual property.

In order to glean some insight into the nature and extent of collaborative efforts between universities and higher education institutions – in addition to the implications that IP has for academic life – it is worth looking at collaborative efforts between US and Mexican universities and higher education institutions. Likewise, collaborative efforts between higher education institutions and government agencies in both countries help to illustrate the current cooperative posture[1]. What follows is only a sample of those mutual efforts.

An agreement between Universidad Autonoma de Nuevo Leon (UANL) and the University of Arizona concerning technology transfer, is currently in progress. At a more governmental level, the Association Liaison Office for University Cooperation in Development (ALO), established in 1992, coordinates the efforts of the country's six major higher education associations[2] to build their partnership with the USAID, and to help their member institutions plan and implement devel-

---

[1] We are grateful to Francisco Marmolejo, executive director of the Consortium for North American Higher Education (CONAHEC) for providing us with very useful advice about this topic.

[2] The American Association of Community Colleges (AACC), the American Association of State Colleges and Universities (AASCU), the American Council of Education (ACE), the Association of American Universities (AAU), the National Association of Independent Colleges and Universities (NAICU), and the National Association of State Universities, and Land Grant Colleges (NASULGC).

opment programs with colleges and universities abroad. It is within this framework that six US institutions entered in partnership with the same number of Mexican institutions. The aim is to develop collaborative programs seeking cooperation with business and industries through teaching, research, and service activities.

Recently, the US Government announced the launching of the US–Mexico Training Internships, Education and Scholarship (TIES) partnership. The goals of this program are to facilitate pursuit of the common agenda for development that is emerging in the US–Mexico bilateral relationship. TIES will be focused principally on education and human capital development, natural resources management and environmental science, information technology for development, health, agriculture, humanitarian assistance, transparency and decentralization, micro and small business development, international finance, public policy, and administration. The program is a 6-year, $50 million public–private alliance designed to stimulate social and economic growth in Mexico by supporting institutional strengthening in higher education through education programs, scholarships, and university linkages. TIES will provide about 750 scholarships for Mexicans to study in the USA. Most of the scholarships will be awarded to master's degrees or special graduate programs in American colleges and universities; other scholarships will fund enrollment of Mexicans in undergraduate courses. A number of master's degree candidates will participate in internships in governmental agencies, NGOs, or the private sector as an integral component of their academic study program (US–Mexico TIES Partnership, 2001).

Border PACT is another initiative whose motto is: "Border higher education institutions fostering change in the U. S. – Mexico borderlands." The conveners in this collaborative effort are CONAHEC, American Council of Education (ACE), and Mexico's ANUIES (National Association of Universities and Institutions of Higher Education). Border PACT members underscore that despite the important structural differences between the Mexican and US higher education systems there are many similarities in the challenges and areas of opportunity that each country faces. There are four principal issues that constitute the agenda of borderlands higher education institutions:

- Expanding access to higher education and serving "new" clients
- Maintaining and improving quality
- Increasing higher education institutions' involvement in their host communities and elevating their role in economic development, and
- Improving accountability and effectiveness

Although some of these challenges are much more critical in Mexico, they continue to be of significance for higher education policy in the US (Border PACT Network home page, 2001). The US–Mexico Foundation for Science has as its mission "to promote and support bilateral collaboration in science and technology using contacts and strategic alliances within the scientific, political, and academic communities to strengthen bilateral collaboration." The Foundation's goal is to address "the problems in areas such as health, poverty, agriculture, education and the environment" (FUMEC web page). In December, 1999, a $13.9 million endowment was established, allowing the foundation the establishment of bilateral programs that respond to issues of mutual concern to the USA and Mexico. The US–Mexico Foundation for Science has established as its main priority issues related to sustainable development. Some of these issues are part of the environmental degradation that are so prevalent in large cities and fast growing regions like the US–Mexico borderlands (The US– Mexico Foundation for Science web page, 2001). The following problems are included in the Foundation's agenda:

- Water (water and health along the US– Mexico border; technological innovation support for water utilities; and clean water in small communities).
- Sustainable Industrial Development (science, technology, and industrial sustainable development along the US–Mexico border).
- Sustainable Urban and Rural Development (Sustainable urban development along the US–Mexico border; air quality in large cities [the Foundation supports the study of atmospheric pollution in Mexico City by a bilateral group, led in the USA by the MIT and in Mexico by a consortium of eight research groups]; and exploratory activities in agriculture and rural sustainable development).
- Enhancement of Human Resources in Science and Technology (Visiting senior scientist program; summer fellowship program for young scientists; training of specialists in science and technology policy and strategy; and workshops on advanced research techniques).
- Bilateral Research Projects (each project strengthens bilateral collaboration by fostering productive relationships between US and Mexican researchers).

Finally, during the last decade Mexico's National Council for Science and Technology (CONACYT, its Spanish acronym) and the National Science Foundation (NSF) signed a memorandum of understanding in order to facilitate the exchange of experience in different areas of science and technology. The development of a joint financial program was also included. However, no further information on these issues is available thus far[3].

The experiences of university collaboration between American and Mexican institutions of higher education that were widely reviewed in this chapter show an increasing significance in the bilateral agenda. This is so because they represent, up until now, the beginning of valuable efforts aimed at tackling issues of mutual concern, particularly those related to issues of sustainable development such as water; urban, rural, and industrial sustainable development; and so on. In addition to knowing the results and assessment of the specific projects, what is to be seen is whether the academic approaches to the issues under inquiry – expressed in policy recommendations – would not conflict with the interests of corporations. Some of these contradictions would appear on issues such as disposal of water residual and other forms of industrial pollution along the US–Mexico borderland.

---

[3] This information was provided by Francisco Marmolejo in personal communication with the authors of this paper.

9.7   Conclusion

This chapter has reviewed some of the complex issues surrounding university involvement in the production of intellectual property in the global culture. Recent changes that foster and encourage commercialization in the university have significant implications for university academic life and centrally held values such as academic freedom, scientific communication, community service, and freedom of inquiry. While these dilemmas are experienced most strongly at the leading research universities in the developed countries, they create implications for universities and other higher education institutions in the developing world. While joint research collaborations between US universities and institutions in Mexico provide social promise, adequate protections in strictly commercial ventures must be established to prevent economic exploitation and cultural domination. Currently, there are a number of genuine efforts between US universities and Mexican institutions of higher education to study and resolve common problems. These programs provide promise for tackling critical issues for both countries through mutual efforts. However, the overarching needs of each country and the spirit of authentic reciprocity in the development of common projects should extend to the commercial sphere as well.

References

Aboites, H. (1993). El derecho al conocimiento y la propiedad intelectual. Constitución y Tratado de Libre Comercio. *Umbral XXI*. No. 13, Otoño 1993, 27–34.

Altbach, P.G. (Ed.). (1996). The *International Academic Profession: Portraits of Fourteen Countries*. Princeton, NJ: The Carnegie Foundation for the Advancement of Teaching.

Anton, M.G. (1996). The Mexican academic profession. In P.G. Altbach (Ed.), *The International Academic Profession*: Portraits of Fourteen Countries (pp. 307–342). Princeton, NJ: The Carnegie Foundation for the Advancement of Teaching.

Association of University Technology Managers (AUTM) Licensing Survey: FY 1999 (2000) November 24). *Licensing Revenues and Patent Activity at 139 Universities, Fiscal 1999*.

Border PACT Network home page (http//borderpact.org).

Campbell, D., Isabelle, T. & Slaughter, S. (1999). Faculty and administrators' attitudes toward potential conflicts of interest, commitment, and equity in university–industry relationships. *The Journal of Higher Education*, 70(3), 309–352.

Castro, C.M. & Levy, D.C. (1997, December). Higher Education in Latin America and the Caribbean: A Strategy Paper (Report No. EDU-101). Washington, DC: Inter-American Development Bank.

Consejo Nacional de Ciencia y Tecnología (2001). *Programa Especial de Ciencia y Tecnología (PECYT) 2001–2006*. México: CONACYT, 2001.

Fundación México-Estados Unidos para la Ciencia/The U. S. – Mexico Foundation for Science (http://www.fumec.org.mx/).

Gaceta UNAM, No. 3, 519, 7 de febrero de 2002.

Gareffi, G. (1978). Drug firms and dependency in Mexico: The case of the steroid hormone industry. *International Organization*, 32(1), 237–286.

Haas, J.E. (1996). The American academic profession. In P. G. Altbach, (Ed.), *The International Academic Profession* (pp. 343–390). Princeton, NJ: The Carnegie Foundation for the Advancement of Teaching.

Isla, G. (2000). Technology transfers into Mexico. Paper presented at the Conference on Technology Transfers, June 21–23, 2000, New York.

Masuda, J. (2000). Technology transfers into Japan. Paper presented at the Conference on Technology Transfers, June 21–23, 2000, New York.

National Science Board (2000). *Science and Engineering Indicators.* Arlington, VA: National Science Foundation, 2000 (NSB-00-1).

Noetinger, F. and Veirano, R. (2000). Technology transfers into Argentina and Brazil. Paper presented at the Conference on Technology Transfers, June 21–23, 2000, New York.

Olivas, M.A. (1992). The political economy of immigration, intellectual property, and racial harassment: Case studies of the implementation of legal change on campus. *Journal of Higher Education*,63(5), 570–598.

Organización para la Cooperación y Desarrollo Económicos/Organization for Economic Co-operation and Development (OECD) (1997). *Propiedad Intelectual, Transferencia de Tecnología y Recursos Genéticos. Un Estudio de la OCDE sobre Prácticas y Políticas Actuales. Serie Perspectivas OCDE.* París: OCDE.

Polster, C. (2000). The future of the liberal university in the era of global knowledge grab. *Higher Education*, 39(1), 19–41.

Poltorak, A. (2000). Licensing and Acquiring Technology in Russia and Israel. Paper presented at the Conference on Technology Transfers, June 21–23, 2000, New York.

Rogers, E.M., Jing Yin & Hoffman, J. (2000). Assessing the effectiveness of technology transfer offices at U.S. research universities. *Journal of the Association of University Technology Managers*, 12, 47–80.

Scott, M.M. (1998). Intellectual property rights: a ticking time bomb in academia. *Academe.* May–June, 84(3), 22–26.

Sell, S.K. (1995). Intellectual property protection and antitrust in the developing world: Crisis, coercion, and choice. *International Organization*, 49(2), 315–349.

Shugurenski, D. (1999). Higher education restructuring in the era of globalization. In R. Arnove & C.A. Torres (Eds.), *Comparative Education: The Dialectic of the Global and the Local* (pp. 283–304). Lanham, MD: Rowman & Littlefield.

Slaughter, S. & Rhoades, G. (1993). Changes in intellectual property statutes and policies at a public university: Revising the terms of professional labor. *Higher Education*, 26(3), 287–312.

The Task Force on Higher Education and Society (2000). *Higher Education in Developing Countries: Peril and Promise.* Washington, DC: The International Bank for Reconstruction and Development/The World Bank.

Universidad Nacional Autónoma de México (UNAM) (1994). *Propiedad Industrial y Derechos de Autor en la UNAM.* Mexico City: UNAM (Oficina del Abogado General).

US–Mexico TIES Partnership (2001) (http://usembassy-mexico.gov/eTIESdescrip.html).

Villarreal, R. (2008). La propiedad intelectual, el conocimiento y las actividades de docencia e investigación.

Von, B.S. (2000). Technology transfers into Asia. Paper presented at the Conference on Technology Transfers, June 21–23, 2000, New York.

Chapter 10
Globalisation and Mathematics Teaching: The Global Importance of Local Language Contexts

Philip C. Clarkson

10.1 Notions of Globalisation and Implications for Mathematics Education

Globalisation is impacting on education, even in the very localised site of the classroom. One aspect of this process is what and the way language is used in the teaching of mathematics. This chapter draws attention to mathematics teaching, which inevitably relies on deep communication, in various multilingual contexts. Examples are given of the variety of possible contexts that do exist. Little research on teaching has been completed that takes these possible different language contexts into account. The question is raised as to whether research results such as, the use of informal or exploratory talk in the students' first language is vital before moving to formal mathematical language, and that exploratory talk may be a situation of broken communication which may not be recognised by participants, are applicable across all contexts.

When dealing with notions such as globalisation, there are difficulties of definition (Zajda, 2005; Zajda et al., 2008b). In a review of an edited comparative education book, the framework used centred on '[t]he problem of how the global affects the local ... one of the most important areas of research interest within global studies'. Yet the editor commented that 'nowhere in the book is there an accepted definition of globalisation or any common analysis of its relationship to education' (Woock, 2000, pp. 163–164). Waters (1995) defined the term globalisation as 'a social process in which the constraints of geography on social and cultural arrangements recede and in which people become increasingly aware that they are receding' (Waters, 1995, p. 3). He noted that globalisation is often associated with 'forces [that] are impersonal and beyond the control and intentions of any individual or groups of individuals' (Waters, 1995, p. 2). McGinn (1995) also

P.C. Clarkson
Australian Catholic University (Melbourne Campus) School of Education, 115 Victoria Parade, Fitzroy Vic 3065, Australia.

J. Zajda and V. Rust (eds.), *Globalisation, Policy and Comparative Research*, DOI: 10.1007/978-1-4020-9547-4_10, © Springer Science + Bussiness Media B.V. 2009

makes the point 'that the processes of globalisation are compelling rather than invitational, and therefore require careful scrutiny' (McGinn, 1995, p. 78; see also Zajda, 2005; Zajda et al., 2008a).

There has been little research on the issue of globalisation in relation to mathematics education. Although there are some references in the literature, more often than not illusions are made to the process without explicitly using this term. The term 'globalisation of mathematics education' is taken to refer to the phenomenon of knowledge, values, principles and curricula, developed in a local context gaining a global adherence in such a way as to be perceived as being an inevitable outcome. Briefly noted here are just three issues, among a number of others, in which globalisation is having an impact. They are the mathematics school curriculum, mathematics education research and the reaction of mathematics educators in universities.

Robitaille and Travers (1992) have discussed the relative similarity of content of school mathematics curricula around the world, and the near universal importance in which it is held. What has given rise to this has been debated at length. Clarkson (1992) has noted how curriculum decisions can change depending on which cultural group is dominant within a country, and the political decisions of the ruling group. The colonisation of education systems in developing countries has been noted by Begg (1995) and Clements (1995), and stands in contrast to calls for increased collaboration from developing countries (Sawiran, 1995). Further to this, Nebres (1995) has argued that developing countries often modelled their curricula on that of developed countries that colonised them, often of course because they had no choice in the matter. In a response to such global imperatives, he has argued for what he calls 'an axiom of collaboration. ... The more global and multicultural we seek to become, the deeper must be our local cultural roots' (p. 39). Bishop (1992) has argued how the 'growing mutual international influences of ideas, methods, practices, and expectations' (p. 710) has lead to the difficulties in identifying national perspectives of mathematics education in the different countries. Usiskin (1992) also noted 'the extent to which countries have become close in how they think about their problems and, as a consequence, what they are doing in mathematics education' (p. 19). Yet, he goes on to hope that there is no development of 'a common world-wide curriculum; our differences provide the best situation for curriculum development and implementation' (p. 20). Rogers (1992) shared this concern about uncritical globalisation of school mathematical curriculum issues. He opined that 'the assumptions that mathematics is a universal language, and is therefore universally the same in all cultures cannot be justified. Likewise, the assumptions that our solutions to local problems ... will have universal applications is even further from the truth' (p. 23). It appears that although globalising forces have given many countries with diverse cultures and languages similar mathematical curricula based on Western Mathematics, there is ongoing debate as to whether this is justifiable from an educational point of view.

Turning to research in mathematics education, international research conferences have been criticised in that they are dominated by American and European researchers and their views (Bishop, 1992). Further, these forums often consist of brief reports of research projects that do not allow the discussion of the complexity of issues affecting mathematics education (Silver & Kilpatrick, 1994). One example of this was when the author experienced two South African researchers at an annual conference of the International Group for the Psychology of Mathematics Education starting to discuss the crucial methodological differences that come into play when conducting research in South Africa, which at times are quite at variance with notions of good research in western countries (Valero & Vithal, 1998). However, the time devoted to such an important issue was swamped by the needs of the conference timetable. There has also been criticism of the other major way that research ideas are disseminated. It was noted sometime ago that most articles in the *Journal for Research in Mathematics Education* were authored, or at least co-authored, by educators affiliated with universities in North America or Europe (Silver & Kilpatrick, 1994). This situation does not seem to have changed, and it is probably true for the other major research journals in our field (e.g. *Educational Studies in Mathematics, For the Learning of Mathematics* and *Mathematics Education Research Journal*). Again, it appears that the forces of globalisation are making an impact on how we disseminate our research. It should not be assumed that globalisation is short hand for Americanisation, or more generously westernisation. However, in the cases outlined above this is clearly the case.

More recently, in a project focused on higher education, Clarkson and Atweh (2002) set out to research the impact of globalisation in mathematics education. In analysing focus group data gathered from colleagues in Mexico, Brazil, Columbia, New Zealand and Australia, there have been a number of consistent topics that participants have discussed. These include issues that have their origins in the economic/political debates on globalisation, but which have been reflected on in terms of mathematics education practice in higher education. An example that has emerged consistently as an issue is the impact of technology, and in particular e-mail contact with peers in other countries. A political issue has been the influence of aid or research projects funded by such bodies as UNESCO or the World Bank. It has been noted that such projects often assume that western theories of education and western forms of curriculum, including assessment practices and their results, must be useful, important or indicate appropriate change in all countries. Another issue to emerge, more aligned to education, has been the nature of mathematics and whether it is a type of universal language, or whether Western Mathematics is a cultural tool being used, albeit unwittingly but often, as a hegemonic, globalisation form of disempowering local mathematics and/or mathematical practice. As a counter to this, one group spoke of the rise of ethnomathematics, which in some way arose as a local disruptive force to the all-embracing push of Western Mathematics.

In turn ethnomathematics itself has spread beyond its original local environs (see Atweh & Clarkson, 2002a, b,c). Clarkson and Atweh (2003) used a survey to follow up some of these issues with colleagues in Australia and New Zealand. They found that participants thought it was to be expected in mainly English-speaking Anglo-western cultures, such as those found in Australia or New Zealand, that most resources they used, and indeed the research they carried out, would be from within this cultural basis. However, some suggested it was a different thing if we uncritically viewed, for whatever reason, that what we practice and believe is, or indeed must be, universal or perhaps the best possible option, no matter what the cultural context. The results suggested that there was quite a divergence of views that respondents held on this issue. There did seem to be a trend for colleagues who had experienced at some depth non-western cultures to appreciate more deeply some issues thrown into relief by the notions of globalisation, such as this one. There also seemed to be a wish for global collaboration (see also Atweh & Clarkson, 2001; Atweh et al., 2003). Hence, there is disquiet with what appears to be the impact of the global, and that this will leave no room for the local. The talk of collaboration may be an answer, or it may simply pave the way for the triumph of the global.

10.2   Language as a Global Issue for Mathematics Education

The role of language is clearly another issue involved in the globalisation debate. When the United Nations (UN) came into being in 1945, there were a number of languages that would be deemed to be the languages of common use within the UN. For practical purposes of communication, some designation had to be made. This is not unusual and happens in many places throughout the world. However, with such decisions comes the danger of dominance of the cultural milieu within which that language exists. It is not surprising then that a language debate in the context of the broader globalisation controversy should be a matter for mathematics education as well. Little has been written directly on this issue. However, there are two issues that can be examined. The first is the dominant use of English in research conferences and in research journals. Here I will concentrate on the other, language use in the mathematics classroom.

It may be useful to start by sketching in one view of the mathematics teacher in a classroom. In a recent forum that the author attended, deliberation was given to what might be some characteristics of an effective mathematics teacher. Some of these were that the teacher:

- Understands mathematical reasoning, connections and proof
- Understands how these manifest in learners and how to scaffold such learning
- Encourages student inquiry and thinking for themselves
- Allows students to negotiate their own learning
- Recognises and enhances students' mental strategies and
- Understands the sequencing of mathematical development

One of the interesting characteristics in this list is the way they depend on effective communication between teacher and student(s). It is one thing for the teacher to understand this or that about mathematics, but the skills to recognise a particular ability in this learner, or provide scaffolding for that learner, in part depends on adequate communication. How do you encourage a student to negotiate their own learning, and recognise and help a student hone their preferred mental strategies and then explore others, if you cannot effectively communicate with them? These characteristics assume that there is meaningful and deep communication between the teacher and students. Such communication moves beyond the surface conversation of greetings, and perhaps chatting about the weekend sport that might be of interest to the student, or even of commenting on the current news in newspapers or on the Internet, although being able to do this is also important for teaching. But the type of communication embedded in the above list of characteristics deal with cognitive functioning at a much deeper level when nuances of academic ideas not only elaborate the students' thinking, but also become the heart of the mathematical concept that gives it its power.

In one sense, one might argue that these characteristics are universal in the teaching of mathematics. But what if the culture we are considering does not condone children asking questions of adults? What if the culture prefers memorisation to scaffolding? Will these characteristics still apply? In my view it may well be that this is quite open to question. However, it also seems to me that some type of clear communication between teacher and student is crucial to effective teaching no matter what the culture, and hence this notion of communication can be recognised as a universal aspect. How to communicate may be an issue more for the local than the global to dictate.

10.3 New Classrooms as a Global Issue

Before delving into the issue of why it is useful to look at the impact of globalisation on the language of the classroom, and in particular the teacher in this context, it is useful to review recent changes in classrooms, or at least the recognition of these changes. For present purposes these revolve around cultural, linguistic and social issues in learning, issues that until recently have been often seen as distant to, and having little impact on, the teaching and learning of mathematics.

Culture can be understood as knowledge, beliefs and conceptions about particular situations. However, they can also be understood as a pattern of meanings, historically constructed and socially transmitted, that are embodied in symbols and language, through which human beings communicate, perpetuate and develop their knowledge and their understanding of life. The social transmission of such is clearly, what happens in a classroom. However, in many classrooms this is not as straightforward as it might often be supposed. For many teachers and schools, as well as much educational research, the common understanding of the 'normal' learning context for students is it will be a classroom that is 'monolingual', students will belong to the dominant culture, and they will have the social habitus of the middle class. If students are different in any of these three factors, then they, that is the student, will need to change. It is simply assumed that students know the 'norms' of the school, and the norms are often built around what middle class members of the dominant culture expect of children. As well, it is taken for granted that students have already a mastery of the language of the instruction and its subtleties, and this is somehow automatically linked by the students to the discourses of different subject taught in the school. Interesting in such classrooms and schools, the assumption is often held that mathematics is free of culture, beliefs and values, and hence it is a small step to make the subsequent assumption that mathematics can be taught in the absence of a common language because it is 'universal'.

But this scenario is simply not the case for most classrooms throughout the world. In most places, students who are monolingual are not the total population of a classroom. Although there will be classrooms that have most children from a dominant culture, most classrooms will have students from a mix of cultures. And clearly again most classrooms will have a mix of socio-economic classes in them, although there will be many exceptions to this. Hence, most classrooms will be places where different cultures are present that is multiculturalism in a microcosm.

This clearly brings challenges for pedagogical traditions of teaching, including mathematics teaching. It is no longer acceptable to assume that the answer is simple; that is, the students will have to change. Multiculturalism also has interesting ramifications for the broader school contexts within which individual classrooms sit, such as the forms of socialisation that the organisation and management of such schools promote, that in their turn clearly flow into the classroom, although we do not have room to pursue this notion here. Why this simplistic notion of the classroom has grown up and become the dominant view in the research literature, against which other situations are judged and either similar or vastly different, is an interesting question. It may be with the domination of research by American and European academics, they are reflecting what they take to be the common view for them, and this becomes the norm for the rest of the world. This is an example of the globalisation of an idea. The rest of this discussion examines this notion more fully and shows that this is clearly not the case for many, if not most, classrooms. Hence, there is a need for change to what our research attends.

There are a number of processes that may bring about a mix of cultures, and for this discussion, languages, in a classroom. The phenomenon of migration is one of these. Migration can no longer be considered only as an 'emergency situation' for refugees, although there is a global increase in the number of refugees. However, whether migrants are refugees or not, the result is we do have many adults and children living in places where the language and the culture are different from that of their origin. Clearly, this has implications for classrooms. Another mixed culture/language classroom situation arises when the teacher may be from one culture, probably the dominant culture, but the students come from a non-dominant culture. There was a short documentary shown on Australian television recently that showed three Vietnamese women from an urban area, travelling to a remote mountain district of Vietnam to start three primary schools in adjacent rural villages. Each of them had to cope first with learning some of the local vernacular of 'their' village, and then begin teaching the children Vietnamese, and through Vietnamese some other areas of the curriculum including mathematics. Clearly, there was an interesting mix of cultures operating. Other situations will be noted below. However, these two examples, particularly that of migration, show how a global force impacts at a very local level, and the result is never a simple mix of cultures, but indeed the process of hybridity is set into motion. It remains in the rest of this discussion to explore more of the details of the local context, the classroom in this instance, and the teacher's role in particular.

10.4   The Variability of Mathematics Multilingual Classroom Contexts

What then of the mathematics classroom, set within a multilingual scenario? It is clear now that mathematics teaching and learning is a process where cognitive, affective, emotional, social, cultural and linguistic factors are deeply intertwined (Bishop, 1988; Ellerton & Clarkson, 1996; Lave, 1988). Further, the multiple links among these factors makes the teaching of mathematics a complex task, which becomes even more complex in multilingual or multicultural situations. In a classroom, neither the teacher nor the researcher may now assume that they are part of a homogenous group. Indeed, there should be recognition by the teacher and the researcher that there is a great heterogeneity amongst the several multilingual or multicultural situations that can, and probably do exist in any one classroom. As an aside, this complexity of the research context requires the use of a multi-layered theoretical perspective, and a great sensitivity towards the different cultures that may be present. But more centrally, the critical question becomes, what does this heterogeneity do to the free flow of ideas in a mathematics classroom, difficult at the best of times given the abstract nature of the mathematical domain, and normally dependent on language?

The notion of the multilingual context of many classrooms is itself misleading. In fact, there is not such 'a' context, but this term should be used as a general term covering many different contexts, something that has not been noticed in the research literature. Some of these contexts are:

- Monolingual teachers teaching a stable mixture of monolingual and multilingual migrant students, with the multilingual students speaking a number of different languages (e.g. urban schools in Australia)
- Monolingual teachers teaching classes of multilingual students all speaking the same language (e.g. Caucasian teachers and Hispanic students in parts of USA)
- Predominantly monolingual teachers faced with an influx of new migrant students with different languages (e.g. various urban areas of Italy, Spain and Portugal) and

- Multilingual teachers teaching multilingual students in a specified teaching language being neither the first language of either teacher or students (e.g. Papua New Guinea, West Timor)

These examples are real life situations. To extend this notion a little, it is useful to start trying to generate theoretical teaching contexts by considering some of the possible interacting sources of language in a mathematics classroom. Clearly one of these is the students' language or languages, then there is the teacher's language or languages, as well as the official teaching language, and less often languages, that will be deemed to be so by the government. There is also the common language that will be used in normal conversation, which may be quite different to the official teaching language, or may be just a variant of it. For convenience, this will be termed the lingua franca. Then there is the language used to teach mathematics, which varies in a distinctive manner to both the official teaching language and the lingua franca, although it will probably overlap both. A first attempt to show these components of the teaching situation is found in Table 10.1.

Table 10.1 has been devised to try and show the potential language complexity of a classroom. However, a particular classroom may well be a context where some of the columns included to the right may in fact overlay the first three. Take the situation in Australia where we have a student who is a monolingual speaker of Australia's version of English. The teacher is also such a monolingual speaker. The official teaching language is also English. Now even in this situation most teachers will argue, I think quite correctly, that the language used between students out of the classroom, and probably between the teacher and students out of the classroom, will be a variant of the official teaching language. Hence, I will still use the term lingua franca in this context, although the term is used loosely at this point. We also know that the language actually used to teach mathematics is not identical to either of the official teaching language, nor the lingua franca. Sometimes the differences are subtle when a common English word takes on a particular fixed meaning in a mathematical context (e.g. set, circular, half). There will also be more use, for instance, of logical connectives (e.g. but, if, and) because of the mathematics (see Clarkson, 2003). Within this context, it is common teaching advice to move from the lingua franca, perhaps through the official teaching language, and onto the particular teaching language for mathematics. This strategy seems to be a good one for these students. If Table 10.1 was used to chart what languages the student and/ or teacher was experiencing, then only the first three columns would be needed.

Table 10.1 Languages used in the teaching contexts for mathematics

Languages	Official teaching language	Lingua franca	Language of teaching for mathematics	Student's first language	Student's second language	Teacher's first language	Teacher's second language
Student							
Teacher							

We would have a very simple chart indeed. One in fact that resembles the traditional view of a classroom described above.

But this simple picture is not all there is to say. Again, take my own situation in Melbourne in Australia. In many primary classrooms, the teacher will be a monolingual English speaker, the official teaching language, who is also well versed in the English lingua franca, and may have a reasonable grasp of the mathematical language that is needed. However, one of her students is from a recent migrant family from Vietnam. The first language this female student learnt at home was Vietnamese, and this is the language normally used in the home. She actually never really started to learn English until she went to school. Now in grade 2 she is able to have conversations with other students in the English lingua franca of the playground. However, she uses her first language with her Vietnamese classmates both in and outside of the classroom, and of course in Saturday school that they attend at the Vietnamese community hall. With the language she has learnt and still uses at home, Vietnamese, she has also learnt many norms of behaviour that may be quite different to others in the classroom. On the next table in this classroom, a boy sits who has a similar story. But his family came from Greece 20 years ago, and although he was born in Australia, Greek is still spoken in the home and most family friends and activities are within a strongly knit Greek community. And so on around the room where we may well find something like ten or more languages represented. Table 10.1 cannot hope to capture all of this variation. However, if a chart like Table 10.1 was drawn up for each student, then within the pile of charts we may start to see the complexity with which each student has to deal, and the teacher likewise.

Many have seen this complexity as a difficulty. And if the teacher makes the traditional assumptions of teaching in a homogeneous context already briefly outlined above in an earlier section, there is no doubt a very great difficulty. But trying to map the complexity is one way of being able to deal with it, and perhaps see that there can be advantages within the complex nature of this classroom context. In the first approximation attempted here, there are aspects of the context that have not been addressed. For example, there has been some hint in the description of the classroom that the competencies with the different languages may be variable for students and teacher, but this is not shown on any student chart based on Table 10.1. There are also other sources of language in a classroom. Clearly written language is one, be it board work, books, either texts or more general, and computer screens to list three possibilities. But these may be considered as derivative sources since each is at least in part dependent on the official teaching language and perhaps the language of the teacher. Hence, although charting the context in the above manner may be useful, it is still too simple and should not be taken as the reality. However, for the purpose of this discussion the above process does start to detail the nature of the language complexities in many classrooms in which mathematics is taught most days of the year.

10.5   The Role of Mathematics Teachers
in Multilingual Classrooms

It seems useful to start the consideration of the role of the teacher in this often complex, linguistic situation by looking at available research. To this end, volumes from 2000 to 2003 of four international research journals (*Journal for Research in Mathematics Education, Educational Studies in Mathematics, For the Learning of Mathematics* and *Mathematics Education Research Journal*) where scanned. In looking through the English written contributions (about 300 articles) there are a reasonable number, and perhaps understandably so, which have students as the central foci. However, there are very few articles that focused on the teacher's role. That in itself is worth noting, with the clear implication that more research is needed to clarify the roles that teachers may play in multilingual classrooms. Secondly, there seemed to be little if any importance attached to the specific language context that the teacher was in, and the impression is given, may be inadvertently, that all such contexts can be treated as the same. It is this issue that forms the crux of this discussion. It has been shown above that there are many different contexts that have been clustered together under such headings as, 'Teaching mathematics in a multilingual situation' as occurred at a recent research conference. This issue will be pursued by noting a number of different contexts that are portrayed in the literature, even though the authors of the contributions did not see the specific context as an important notion in itself on which to comment.

10.5.1   *Multilingual Teachers, Multilingual Students Who Share a Language*

South Africa, where students' normal out-of-class talk (their lingua franca) is in a non-English language but where the official teaching language is English, was the setting for research undertaken by Setati and Adler (2000). They discussed the language practices of teachers in some primary schools, and in particular their code-switching behaviour. Although they suggest that it makes a lot of sense for teachers to encourage students to code-switch, and to actually use this as a teaching strategy, they also note that there are challenges in this practice that can not be overlooked. At times it seemed to the authors that teacher talk is down played in some curriculum reforms, that incidentally have their origin in non-multilingual situations, and yet it is teacher talk they suggest that often illuminate ideas for students. Hence such an emphasis in official documents may well be counterproductive. The authors note that it is important to understand the role of different types of discourses. For example, starting with informal talk in the students' first language, leading through to more formal mathematical talk finally in English, is a critical path to use in such complex lingual communicative situations (but see also Adler, 1998, 1999; Setati, 1998).

10.5.2   Multilingual Teachers, Multilingual Students, Teacher/Students May Share a Language

In Papua New Guinea, typically students in a classroom will share a lingua franca, although this may not be their first language and indeed they may well speak a number of other languages too. The teacher may speak the common student language if he/she comes from the same region, but will also be multilingual. Up to year 3, schools can choose which teaching language, but from year 3 the official teaching language is English, although teachers are encouraged to use a mixture of languages if possible through years 3, 4 and even 5 (Clarkson et al., 2001). Of interest to this discussion, there is a suggestion based on classroom observations that although there is a judicious use of languages in social studies, religion and so on, teachers seem to prefer English only when it comes to teaching mathematics. It seems that it is often difficult dealing with mathematical concepts in a vernacular or Melanesian Pidgin. This raises another interesting question. Teachers are encouraged to use indigenous mathematics in the school curriculum. However, what has not been answered satisfactorily as yet is whether crucial nuances will be lost in the very act of translation into English of say a measurement practice, and hence embedded cultural meanings may well be marginalised. Should then the Ministry's rule of using English be sidestepped so that the cultural meanings can be explored, if the teacher has command of the appropriate first language?

10.5.3   Bilingual Teachers and Students with Languages Common to Both

Moving to the USA, Khisty and Chval (2002) contrast the teaching styles of two bilingual teachers who were teaching groups of Latino students. The two classes were of different levels in English proficiency, and hence there was more frequent use of English in one classroom than in the other. However, that is not the critical thrust of their paper. The authors write that the main issue was the way one teacher in contrast to the other used precise and extended mathematical language in her verbal discourse with her class, and promoted an expectation that the students would also use such language. The results of the investigation suggested that students did in the end use the formal mathematical language promoted by this teacher. The underlying emphasis is that bilingual students will not learn this type of English, which they need, unless they are witnesses to quite deliberately displayed examples of such discourse.

10.5.4   Multi or Monolingual Teachers, Multilingual Students Speaking the Same Language

In some areas of the Northern Territory in Australia through the 1980s and early 1990s, there was political support for the use of the people's first language to be used as the teaching language, at least in the early years of schooling, with a gradual move to English in later primary years. Further, there was insightful curriculum work carried out to devise mathematical curricula that commenced in the early years of schooling with Aboriginal ideas. Hence in one area in the desert, indigenous spatial ideas became the basis of the early years curriculum (Harris, 1991), where as on the north coast the notions of relationships were used as the key framework concept (Watson, 1988). In these instances not only were the teaching languages changed to that of the students and community, but the mathematics curriculum too was totally transformed. What then of the teacher? If the teacher was also of the local indigenous people then clearly there is the situation that they share the same first language, and switches into English could be negotiated within a particular classroom situation. However, where the teacher was not of the same language group, and then more often than not, a monolingual English speaker, such negotiation was not an option. Thus there are sometimes similar aspects to these situations to that of classrooms in Papua New Guinea, and yet as well, distinct differences.

10.5.5 Monolingual Teachers, New Migrant Students with a Mixture of Different Languages

Gorgorio and Planas (2001) were working in classrooms, where the teaching language was Catalan. The students were a mixture of Catalan, and immigrant students who spoke a variety of languages at home. The authors suggest it was very hard to separate the social, cultural and linguistics aspects of mathematics teaching and learning, something already noted from Papua New Guinea and Australia. Indeed they took the view that it was better to think of broader communication within the classroom than a narrow linguistic one, although language aspects could not be ignored. In particular they suggested that in such situations as these the informal or exploratory talk could often be broken communication, particularly for the teacher, since this inevitably occurs in the students' first languages. Therefore helping students to move to the more formal mathematical talking and writing, which often involves a switch to the language of the classroom, can be fraught with unknown linguistic set backs for both teacher and students. Others who have also commented on this situation are Alro, Skovsmose, and Valero (2003), Favilli, Oliveras, and Cesar (2003), and Moreira (2003).

10.5.6 Monolingual Teachers, Stable Mixture of Monolingual/ Multilingual Migrant Students

In Australian urban schools, many monolingual teachers teach a mix of multilingual students. It would seem however that few teachers realise the role that a first language plays for these students. This is summed up by the total surprise of a primary school teacher, who had recently completed graduate studies in Teaching English as a Second Language, when she discovered how often her year 4 Vietnamese students were switching languages when doing mathematics in her class. Although there has been advice on the difficulties non-English speaking migrants can face in mathematics classes, little has been done to study the teaching of them in any comprehensive manner (Clarkson, 2002).

10.5.7   Advice for a New Context?

In Malaysia at the beginning of the 1970s in Malay schools, the teaching language was changed from English to Bahasa Malay. This was done mainly for political purposes. However, from 2003, due again to a political decision, although the main teaching language in classrooms remained Bahasa Malay, the teaching of mathematics and science reverted to English. This has clear ramifications for teachers of mathematics. It is an interesting exercise to wonder what advice, if one was asked, could be given to the teachers. The context is that the teacher are at least bilingual, although their command of mathematical English varies in quality (Clarkson & Idris, 2008). The teachers share a non-English language with their students. The students are also multilingual, but their command of mathematical English is not great. So this situation is probably akin to the context of bilingual teachers, teaching multilingual students who share a language. On this analysis the Malaysian situation is perhaps closer to that of Papua New Guinea than the USA, but given the different use of teaching languages for different subjects, it really is yet again a new category.

10.5.8   A Note of Caution

In Pakistan, Halai (2004) has been working with students who share Urdu as their first language, as does the teacher. The official teaching language in these schools however is English. The teacher has been taking the notion of understanding the language of the problem seriously and hence encouraging the students to code swap and to use informal English before moving into formal mathematical application. This approach is described as 'classrooms where the teachers were using reform-oriented teaching approaches', clearly influenced by US teaching reforms. However, she comments:

> My observation … showed that the teacher's use of everyday words for mathematical concepts led to difficulties for the students. … [U]sing discursive strategies to teach mathematics where students are expected to build on their knowledge of the everyday context and language takes on an added complexity in a multilingual context. This complexity arises because of possibly unquestioned assumptions regarding students' familiarity and understanding of the language of the language of instruction. (p. 3)

Again the apparently good notions for teaching taken from one context and applied to another may not be such a direct translation process as is so often implied in the literature by omission of the detailed language context.

10.6 Problematising the Issue

In a first attempt at problemitising and thus addressing this issue, it is instructive to consider the commonly used model to describe the progression through forms of language that teachers are encourage to use (see Fig. 10.1). In the original form of this model there was depicted a simple downward flow from informal language use (students are encouraged to discuss the mathematics problem in their own way and

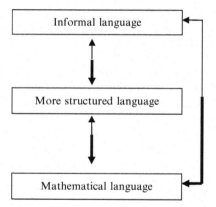

Fig. 10.1 A modification to the language use in mathematics learning model

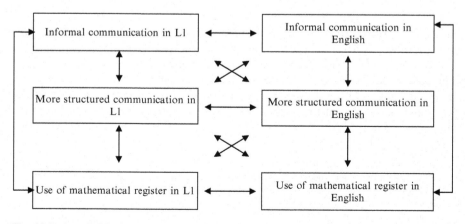

Fig .10.2 A model for language use in mathematics learning for bilingual students

own language) through to the use of the more mathematical language with embedded use of correct mathematical terms (e.g. Clements & Del Campo, 1987). However, a more realistic model, as shown with double-headed arrows, acknowledges the common switches between the language forms, although the overall flow is still down the model shown by the more intense downward pointing arrows.

Further modification is needed once the bilingual contexts of classrooms are recognised as important (see Fig.10.2).

In this model (Fig. 10.2) the double-headed arrows indicate most interactions between the language modes that teachers could encourage students to use. Some potential interactions are not displayed. There is no linkage between the top left and bottom right cells, a linkage that is probably not very useful. Some interactions shown may be better indicated with broken lines, or indeed not at all. For example, it may be that the bottom left-hand cell for some languages is essentially empty for some students if they are not conversant with the mathematical register in their first language. In this case the arrow would be deleted. However, Clarkson (2002) has shown that some ELL students in Melbourne have a fragmentary knowledge of the mathematical register in their first language. In this context a dotted line may be better. Although the model in Fig. 10.2 may be judged better than that in Fig. 10.1 since it tried to incorporate the bilingualism of some students, it no way does justice to the complexities outlined in the subsections above of the potential multiple languages used in some classrooms. As with the use of Table 10.1, the teacher may well be in a position where a number of Fig. 10.2 models may be needed in their particular classroom. However, this model does show that in classrooms the local complexity must be addressed, a complexity sometimes imposed by global processes.

10.7 Evaluation

These brief descriptions emphasise that the issues of teaching in multilingual contexts is not straightforward. The teachers need to cope in situations where they will not have full control of the discourse, unless they too are proficient in the students' language(s), the lingua franca, as well as the teaching language. However, the flow from informal verbalizing of ideas through to their formalising in the rich mathematical language, both verbal and written, seems to be a given across the contexts. How to manage the flow across differing languages is the issue that needs further insightful research. In particular, what implications the particular differing contexts will have on this needs exploration.

A further issue that becomes self evident in looking through the literature is the use made of English in so many contexts. The same criticisms that have been made of research conferences and journals in mathematics education may well apply to the policies invoked in many countries. A number of supportive arguments can be made for the deeming of English as the official teaching language for mathematics. However, there are negative arguments as well, which do not always seem to be considered to any extent. One of them clearly demonstrated here is the complexity this adds to the language environments of many classrooms. Another negative argument, only touched on in this discussion, is the added difficulty of cogently teaching the mathematics that is embedded in the students' culture(s) when a foreign teaching language is used. A further issue is the ease with which curriculum developed in an English speaking environment can flow that much more easily to multilingual contexts (and rarely in the reverse direction). This may well be intended of course. But the potential danger is that in this process the values, which may be unarticulated and deeply embedded in that curriculum, will also, flow although and not be explicitly recognised and examined by the recipient group. Hence the recipients may be accepting values for which they are not prepared.

This chapter began by using some notions that are important in the ongoing debate concerning globalisation. It was shown that the ways languages are used both in disseminating research on mathematics education and indeed what happens in the classroom are influenced by differing degrees by this process. Many classrooms in which mathematics is taught are indeed micro sites of multiculturalism. With the recognition that mathematics itself, and more clearly what and how mathematics is taught, is influence by culture, language and the social milieu of the classroom, school and the wider society, deeper and complex issues for research immediately become the foreground.

10.8   Conclusion

In this chapter, the global importance of local language contexts in mathematics teaching was discussed. The different contexts and situations that arise with language in the global culture have been briefly explored. There was no attempt here at deeply analysing the implications of such complexity, suffice to say the differing types of contexts that give rise to multilingual situations should become an important variable considered in future research. This recognition should also give pause to policy makers and curriculum developers before wholesale implementation of good practice in one setting is transferred to a new context. The often unspoken assumptions of globalisation imply that all contexts are the same. But the local, particularly that of language, is just as important, if children are to learn something of mathematics that will be of use to them and their society.

References

Adler, J. (1998). A language of teaching dilemmas: Unlocking the complex multilingual secondary mathematics classroom. *For the Learning of Mathematics, 18*(1), 24–33.

Adler, J. (1999). The dilemma of transparency: Seeing and seeing through talk in the mathematics classroom. *Journal of Research in Mathematics Education, 30*(1), 447–64.

Alro, H., Skovsmose, O., & Valero, P. (2003). *Communication, Conflict and Mathematics Education in the Muticultural Classroom*. Paper presented at Third Conference of the European Society for Research in Mathematics Education, Bellaria, Italy. [available from website http://dlibrary.acu.edu.au/maths_educ/cerme3.htm].

Atweh, B., & Clarkson, P. (2001). Internationalisation and globalisation of mathematics education: Towards an agenda for research/action. In B. Atweh, H. Forgasz, & B. Nebres (Eds.).

Sociocultural Research on Mathematics Education: An International Perspective (pp. 167–184). New York: Erlbaum.

Atweh, B., & Clarkson, P. (2002a). Some problematics in international collaboration in mathematics education. In B. Barton, K. Irwin, M. Pfannkuch & M. Thomas (Eds.), *Mathematics Education in the South Pacific* (pp. 100–107). Auckland: Mathematics Education Research Group of Australasia.

Atweh, B., & Clarkson, P. (2002b, November). *Globalisation and Mathematics Education: From Above and Below*. Paper presented at annual conference of the Australian Association of Research in Education, Brisbane.

Atweh, B., & Clarkson, P. (2002c). Mathematics educators' views about globalization and internationalization of their discipline: Preliminary findings. In P. Valero & O. Skovsmose (Eds.), *Proceedings of the Third International Mathematics Education and Society Conference* (pp. 166–174). Copenhagen: Centre for Research in Learning Mathematics, University of Copenhagen.

Atweh, B., Clarkson, P., & Nebres, B. (2003). Mathematics education in international and global contexts. In A. Bishop, C. Keital, J. Kilpatrick & K. Clements (Eds.), *Second International Handbook of Mathematics Education*. Dordrecht: Kluwer.

Begg, A. (1995). Collaboration: Cooperation or colonization. In R. Hunting, G. FitzSimons, P. Clarkson & A. Bishop (Eds.), *Regional Collaboration in Mathematics Education* (pp. 97–106). Melbourne: Monash University.

Bishop, A.J. (1988). *Mathematical Enculturation*. Dordrecht: Kluwer.

Bishop, A.J. (1992). International perspectives on research in mathematics education. In D. Grouws (Ed.), *Handbook of Research on Mathematics Teaching and Learning* (pp. 710–723). New York: Macmillan.

Clarkson, P. (1992). Language and mathematics: A comparison of bi and monolingual students of mathematics. *Educational Studies in Mathematics, 22*, 417–429.

Clarkson, P.C. (2002). Bilingual students learning mathematics in Australia: A review. In H. Dhindsa, I. Cheong, C. Tendencia, & M. Clements (Eds.), *Realities in Science, Mathematics and Technical Education* (pp. 266–275). Brunei Darussalam: Universiti Brunei Darussalam.

Clarkson, P.C. (2003). Language, logical thinking and communication in school mathematics: Whose responsibility? In H.S. Dhindsa, L.S. Bee, P. Achleitner, & M.A. Clements (Eds.), *Studies in Science, Mathematics and Technical Education* (pp. 99–116). Brunei Darussalam: Universiti Brunei Darussalam.

Clarkson, P.C., & Atweh, B. (2002). Examining internationalisation and globalisation in the context of mathematics education in higher education. In D. Edge & Y. Ban Har (Eds.), *Mathematics Education for a Knowledge-Based Era* (pp. 217–223). Singapore: Association of Mathematics Educators.

Clarkson, P.C., & Atweh, B. (2003). More perspectives on the impact of globalisation on mathematics education in higher education in Australasia. In L. Bragg, C. Campbell, G. Herbert, & J. Mousley (Eds.), *Mathematics Education Research: Innovation, Networking Opportunity* (pp. 238–245). Geelong: Mathematics Education Research Group of Australasia.

Clarkson, P.C., & Idris, N. (2008). *Reverting to English to Teach Mathematics: How are Malaysian Teachers and Students Changing in Response to a New Language Context for Learning?* (submitted)

Clarkson, P.C., Owens, K., Toomey, R., Kaleva, W., & Hamadi, T. (2001). *The Development of a Process for the Evaluation of Teacher Education*. Paper presented at the annual conference of the Australian Association of Research for Education. <http://www.aare.edu.au/index.htm >

Clements, K. (1995). Restructuring mathematics teacher education: Overcoming the barriers of élitism and separation. In R. Hunting, G. FitzSimons, P. Clarkson, & A. Bishop (Eds.), *Regional Collaboration in Mathematics Education* (pp. 1–10). Melbourne: Monash University.

Clements, K., & Del Campo, G. (1987). *Beginning Mathematics*. Melbourne: Catholic Education Office.

Ellerton, N., & Clarkson, P.C. (1996). Language factors in mathematics. In A. Bishop, K. Clements, C. Keitel, J. Kilpatrick, & C. Laborde (Eds.), *International Handbook of Mathematics Education* (pp. 991–1038). Dordrecht: Kluwer.

Favilli, F., Oliveras, M., & Cesar, M. (2003). *Maths Teachers in Multicultural Classes: Findings from a Southern European Project.* Paper presented at Third Conference of the European Society for Research in Mathematics Education, Bellaria, Italy. [http://dlibrary.acu.edu.au/maths_educ/cerme3.htm].

Gorgorio, N., & Planas, N. (2001). Teaching mathematics in multilingual classrooms. *Educational Studies in Mathematics, 47,* 7–33.

Halai, A. (2004). Action research to study impact: is it possible? *International Journal Educational Action Research* 12(6), 515–534.

Harris, P. (1991). *Mathematics in a Cultural Context.* Geelong: Deakin University.

Khisty, L., & Chval, K. (2002). Pedagogic discourse and equity in mathematics: When teachers' talk matters. *Mathematics Education Research Journal, 14*(3), 154–168.

Lave, J. (1988). *Cognition in Practice: Mind, Mathematics & Culture in Everyday Life.* New York: Cambridge University Press.

McGinn, N. (1995). The implication of globalisation for higher education. In L. Buchert & K. King (Eds.), *Learning from Experience: Policy and Practice in Aid to Higher Education* (pp. 77–92). The Hague: CSEDC.

Moreira, D. (2003). *Portuguese Immigrant Children and Mathematics Education.* Paper presented at Third Conference of the European Society for Research in Mathematics Education, Bellaria, Italy. [http://dlibrary.acu.edu.au/maths_educ/cerme3.htm].

Nebres, S.J. (1995). Mathematics education in an era of globalisation: Linking education, society an culture in our region. In R. Hunting, G. FitzSimons, P. Clarkson, & A. Bishop (Eds.), *Regional Collaboration in Mathematics Education* (pp. 31–41). Melbourne: Monash University.

Robitaille, D.F., & Travers, K.J. (1992). International studies of achievement in mathematics. In D. Grouws (Ed.), *Handbook of Research on Mathematics Education* (pp. 687–709). New York: Macmillan.

Rogers, L. (1992). Then and now. *For the Learning of Mathematics, 12*(3), 22–23.

Sawiran, M.S. (1995). Collaborative efforts in enhancing globalisation in mathematics education. In R. Hunting, G. FitzSimons, P. Clarkson, & A. Bishop (Eds.), *Regional Collaboration in Mathematics Education* (pp. 603–608). Melbourne: Monash University.

Setati, M. (1998). Code-switching in a senior primary class of second-language mathematics learners. *For the Learning of Mathematics, 18*(1), 34–40.

Setati, M., & Adler, J. (2000). Between languages and discourses: Language practices in primary multilingual mathematics classrooms in South Africa. *Educational Studies in Mathematics, 43,* 243–269.

Silver, E., & Kilpatrick (1994). Challenges of diversity in the future of mathematics education research. *Journal for Research in Mathematics Education, 25,* 734–754.

Usiskin, Z. (1992). From 'Mathematics for Some' to 'Mathematics for All'. 17–23 August, ICME-7, Québec City.

Valero, P., & Vithal, R. (1998). Research methods from the "north" revisited from the "south". In A. Oliver & K. Newstead (Eds.), *Proceedings of the 22nd conference of the International Study Group for the Pyschology of Mathematics Education* (Vol. 4, pp. 153–160). Stellenbosch, South Africa: International Study Group for the Psychology of Mathematics Education.

Waters, M. (1995). *Globalisation.* London: Routledge.

Watson, H. (1988). Ganma Project: Research in mathematics education by Yolgnu Community in the schools of Laynhapuy, North East Arnhamland. In R. Hunting & G. Davis (Eds.), *Language Issues in Learning and Teaching Mathematics* (pp. 33–50). Melbourne: La Trobe University.

Woock, R. (2000). Review of Torres, C. (Ed.), Comparative education: The dialectic of the global and the local. (Lanham, MD: Rowman & Littlefield, 1999). *Melbourne Studies in Education, 41*(1), 163–164.

Zajda, J. (2005). Globalisation, Education and Policy Research. In J. Zajda (Ed.), The *International Handbook of Globalisation and Education Policy Research.* Dordrecht: Springer.

Zajda, J., Davies, L., & Majhanovich, S. (2008a). (Eds.). *Comparative and Global Pedagogies: Equity, Access and Democracy in Education.* Dordrecht: Springer.

Zajda, J. Biraimah, B., & Gaudelli, W. (2008b). (Eds.). *Education and Social Inequality in the Global Culture.* Dordrecht: Springer.

Chapter 11
States, Markets and Higher Education Reform: The Netherlands and England

Rosamunde F.J. Becker

11.1 Globalisation and Higher Education

In many countries pressures of globalisation have led to major changes in relationships between the State, the market and higher education. These changes have consequences for the roles and organisation of higher education, and of universities in particular (Butera, 2000; Cowen, 2000; Fulton, 2002, 2003; Zajda, 2005, 2006; Henry et al., 2001; Schugurensky, 1999). This chapter explores aspects of higher education reform in the Netherlands and England, with a particular focus on market regulation. It is clear to everyone that in several OECD countries there has been a shift to market-framing of higher education (Clark, 1998; Jongbloed, 2003). Various governments have taken the view that institutional autonomy should be increased and that higher education institutions would become more effective and efficient, more responsive to economic imperatives, more productive and better managed if institutions are urged to compete more directly within a market (Goedegebuure & Westerheijden, 1991; Williams, 1992; Dill, 1997; Weiler, 2000; King, 2004; Kogan & Hanney, 2000; McNay, 1999; Slaughter & Rhoades, 2004). Market-framing is also expected to lead to particular kinds of innovation and adaptation to 'customers', such as students and companies.

However, market-framing not only refers to linking higher education closer to business and industry, but also to organising higher education institutions *themselves* as a business (Cowen, 1991). It involves large changes in the funding and management of higher education. Government initiatives to frame higher education institutions within markets have included deregulation of financial autonomy, the introduction of performance-based models of resource allocation, an urge for institutions to attract external funding and encouragement of competition between (and within) institutions. In a number of countries higher education institutions now operate in several markets: there are markets for students, teaching and research staff, research council

R.F.J. Becker
Institute of Education University of London

J. Zajda and V. Rust (eds.), *Globalisation, Policy and Comparative Research,*
DOI: 10.1007/978-1-4020-9547-4_11, © Springer Science + Bussiness Media B.V. 2009

grants, funding and company training. Higher education institutions have to compete for external funding, which leads to more market-related activities. Institutions also increasingly have to compete for state funding. The formulae for state funding send a powerful message about what is (and what is not) considered to be important in the higher education system. The markets in which higher education has been framed are not free markets because the Government intervenes in several ways by setting the rules and boundaries of the market (see also Williams, 1997).

In a market-framed higher education system, new forms of management are necessary (Cowen, 1991; Gordon & Whitty, 1997; Henkel & Little, 1999). As actors in markets, higher education institutions need to be able to develop strategies and 'products', and they need to adapt to changing environments and to be able to perceive and to grasp new market opportunities. Therefore, 'efficient' and entrepreneurial management structures are introduced so that institutions can adapt themselves more rapidly. This trend to introduce managerialist structures in higher education can be seen in several countries (Deem, 2001). It is important to note that there is considerable resistance to the widespread use of market models for higher education (King, 2004). This resistance is based on the belief that higher education should not be provided on the basis of an individual exchange agreement between a 'producer' and a 'consumer'.

The broad shift to market-framing of higher education has been accompanied by the development of new modes of state regulation. In several countries higher education has received increased institutional autonomy in financial aspects, while there also has been widespread introduction of national systems and procedures to evaluate the 'quality' and performance of higher education institutions and to find ways of 'improving' it (Vught van, 1993, 1997). Usually, this has involved the creation of a national agency to manage the assessment processes. The development by the State of centralised and regular cycles of quality assessment has been referred to as the 'rise of the evaluative State' (Neave, 1998).

However, if we look carefully at a couple of cases, the general proposition of a shift towards market-framing is more or less true, but it is the ways in which higher education institutions are reformed (and shaped around and within markets) that are different. This can be illustrated by taking a closer look at recent higher education reforms in the Netherlands and England. While both countries have been among the first in Europe to emphasise 'quality' and responsiveness to markets, they have done so in very different ways.

11.2   Market-Framing of Higher Education in the Netherlands

Since the mid-1980s the Dutch Government has introduced market mechanisms in higher education and developed new forms of government regulation. This section analyses shifting relationships between the State, the market and higher education in the Netherlands, with particular attention to market-framing of higher education institutions. These changes will be examined by looking at (i) barriers to the development of new institutions and programmes, (ii) institutional and financial autonomy,

(iii) government funding of higher education, (iv) tuition fee arrangements, and (v) changing relations between higher education institutions and the State.

Dutch higher education institutions have considerable freedom to specify the aims and contents of curriculum programmes (Maassen et al., 1993). However, the Government imposed two restrictions on the establishment of new higher education institutions and degree programmes. Firstly, the Government set minimum standards that (public and private) higher education institutions and programmes have to meet in order to be established. Secondly, there is a test of 'macro-efficiency', which means that new programmes should not duplicate already existing ones. To receive government funding for a new programme, institutions must first demonstrate a demand for such a programme (taking into account similar programmes offered elsewhere). This can make it difficult to get new programmes approved.

Recently, a number of government representatives started to argue for abolition of the 'macro-efficiency' test and for leaving decisions to start new programmes to the higher education sector itself. However, the issue is still undecided because of resistance of several academics and higher education interest groups to leaving the offer of higher education programmes to the 'demands' of the market. Advocates of deregulation point to the possibility of inefficient central planning and funding of higher education programmes. Opponents argue that the Government should protect students by keeping some regulation of the range of programmes on offer, for instance to protect a programme that does not attract many students but that is the last of its kind in the country (such as a specialist programme in Asian languages or archaeology).

In other respects, the Dutch Government has given higher education institutions considerable autonomy, for instance in their financial decision-making. Since the early 1980s Dutch higher education institutions receive block grant funding from the government, while they are encouraged to generate external income by operating in external markets. Institutions may take up private loans or seek out donations, and they are free to develop and maintain business start-ups, engage in contract teaching (i.e. short professional development courses for companies and other external organisations), build research partnerships with industry, and do private consulting. In the past years institutional contract-based income has increased enormously. Between 1997 and 2001 university income from external sources increased by 312% from €8.1 million to €33.5 million. In the same period, revenues from contract teaching went from €40.8 million to €95 million (132%) while income from industry-sponsored research grew from €71.1 million to €125.1 million (76%) (Salerno, 2004).

Institutional autonomy was increased in other ways too. At the end of the 1990s the Dutch Government has decentralised decision-making on terms of employment of staff to the higher education sector (see also Weert de, 2001b). The institutions themselves now negotiate with their staff on pay rises and other terms of employment. Employment relationships thus have shifted from public to private contractual ones.

In general, institutions do not have the autonomy to select their students. The Dutch higher education system is characterised by open entry: all qualified students are free to enrol on programmes in the institution of their choice. The only instances where institutions can refuse entry can be found in the case of *numerus fixus* programmes in medicine and dentistry, areas that have a limited capacity of student places based on labour market conditions. In recent years, the Government allowed institutions to experiment with a system of decentralised admission in these programmes (Vossensteyn, 2002). This experiment was allowed after intense public debates and strong opposition against the existing lottery system in *numerus fixus* programmes from prospective students with brilliant secondary school grades, who had failed to get a place on one of these programmes. In consequence, institutions can now select a percentage of students who will be granted access to *numerus fixus* programmes, although this experiment is restricted to a maximum of 30% of the available places for first-year enrolments (70% of the places will continue to be allocated by lottery) (Jongbloed, 2003).

Policies of market-framing did not only encourage institutions to attract increasing amounts of external funding, but they have also included changes in the ways in which higher education is funded by the Government. Among OECD countries the Netherlands has been a pioneer in the introduction of formula funding (Weiler, 2000). The introduction of market elements was intended to increase competition for funding between institutions on the basis of performance criteria. In the last decade institutional competition for government funding of specific research programmes has increased. However, from a comparative point of view, the funding approach of the Dutch Government is not strongly market-oriented. This has three main reasons. Firstly, Dutch university research is still relatively dependent on government funding (although this has been declining in the past decade). In 2000, university research income consisted of 72% government funding, 8% research council funding (government funding distributed on a competitive basis) and 20% external funding (de Weert, 2001a). Secondly, quality assessment outcomes have no strong influence on the basic government funding of higher education institutions. Government funding for teaching is for 50% dependent on the number of degrees awarded, 37% consists of a stable funding allowance for teaching and 13% is allocated on the basis of the number of registered first-year students. Government funding for research includes a stable amount of funding for each university (15%), and is further dependent on degrees awarded (12%), the number of research schools (13%) in a university and 'strategic considerations' (60%) (Ministerie van OCW, 1999). Initially, the allocation for 'strategic considerations' was intended to be given to the universities on the basis of the 'relevance' of their research to society, but it was never linked to research assessments, and now it is a stable amount of funding per institution. Thus, the proportion of total public research income that Dutch universities receive on the basis of competition and quality assessment outcomes is relatively low.

The nature of market-framing of Dutch higher education can also be seen in tuition fee arrangements. Dutch higher education institutions are not allowed to determine their own tuition fee rates. The Government sets the rate of tuition fees, which is uniform across all levels and programmes. Differential tuition fees are strongly resisted because a long history of liberal politics in the Netherlands has fostered a belief that higher education is a public good, which therefore should be heavily subsidised by the Government. Although fees have been raised slowly but gradually (following the Government's arguments pointing at the private benefits of higher education), efforts to make substantial changes have met with stiff public resistance (Salerno, 2004). This was clearly demonstrated by revolts in the mid-1990s. In 1995 the Government proposed raising the tuition fees by 1,000 guilders (approximately €450). In protest, thousands of students went to the city of Utrecht's central train station, one of the largest and busiest stations – and the most central – in the country, and sat on the train tracks, which effectively halted train services across most of the country. Faced with this resistance, the Dutch Government reconsidered and decided to raise tuition fees only by 500 guilders and to spread the increase over 3 years.

The tuition fee arrangements are combined with a system of student grants. Since 1996 student grants have been allocated as initial loans. These loans are converted into grants if students meet study progress requirements. Although the Government has imposed stricter performance requirements on students' financial aid, these requirements are not very demanding; students have to pass at least 50% of their first-year exams, or complete their course within 2 years after its official duration.

At the moment, the Dutch Government still considers fixed tuition fees in combination with open admission to higher education and financial aid policies as the best way to promote equal access to higher education. However, recently a debate has started about whether institutions should be allowed to set their own fees. While several university rectors are in favour of this, there are widespread concerns about the financial barriers that it may impose on students from disadvantaged backgrounds. In addition, higher education institutions fear that price flexibility may be used by the Government as an excuse to reduce its institutional funding.

Uniform fees do not act as signals of price/quality differentials across programmes. However, the Netherlands does not have a tradition of quality differentials between universities and between institutions for higher professional education. Open admission policies and fixed tuition rates have historically hindered the rise of an institutional hierarchy. There have never been any elite universities in the Netherlands, and overall levels of quality are still considered to be roughly similar between institutions, although the focus of their programmes can differ. In consequence, from an international comparative viewpoint, the publication of national rankings of 'institutional performance' has had little influence on the choices of Dutch students and staff for particular institutions.

However, there is some evidence that several Dutch institutions are now trying to attract 'high-performing' students. An example of this is the recent establishment of a 'university college' located at the University of Utrecht. Its curriculum relies heavily on small-class teaching. In contrast to normal Dutch practice in higher education, admission to the college is selective, based on interviews and letters of recommendation. While the university can only charge the government-set tuition rate, all students have to pay boarding expenses. Nevertheless, such new institutional opportunities to set up such colleges for 'excellent' students demonstrates the willingness of the Dutch Government to allow gradually more institutional freedom to select parts of their student intake (Jongbloed, 2003; Salerno, 2004; Huisman et al., 2004; Maassen, 2002).

Finally, government attempts to frame higher education within a market have coincided with other important changes in the relationships between higher education and the State. By the mid-1980s the Government argued that in return for increased institutional autonomy a quality assessment system should be developed to guarantee minimum standards and to ensure institutional accountability for public funds. Originally, the Government had intended the Higher Education Inspectorate to perform the quality assessments. However, this was strongly opposed by the universities, and in subsequent discussions their umbrella organisation, the Association of Co-operating Dutch Universities (VSNU), succeeded in taking up that responsibility. After initial struggles, the Government and the universities agreed that the universities themselves would develop a quality assessment system that would include periodic internal and external evaluations of teaching, research and (in some cases) public services, and that would meet a number of procedural requirements set by the Government. Through that compromise the Inspectorate was bypassed and largely left with the task of 'meta-evaluation': supervision of the evaluation procedures and of the actions taken by the universities in response to the assessment outcomes and recommendations. The Government has created a legal possibility of direct quality assessment in case it would doubt the evaluations, but in practice, this has not happened.

The Dutch universities understood that the development of a quality assessment system was a condition for increased institutional autonomy (see also Boer & Huisman, 1999). The Government in turn allowed the universities to be responsible for the quality assessment system because that was in line with the more distant form of government regulation, without the Government losing its possibilities to intervene if it considered it 'necessary' to do so. Thus, while the Government insisted on the development of a formal system of quality assessment, the higher education institutions themselves managed to take the responsibility for the development of the system, subject only to broad procedural requirements set by the Government.

The development of the quality assessment system was part of a broader new framework of government regulation of higher education. In 1985 a planning cycle was introduced in which the higher education institutions and the Ministry of Education would discuss national higher education objectives and subsequently develop a unified strategy to achieve them. These discussions and agreements were tied to 2-yearly (since 2000, 4-yearly) cycles of public *Higher Education and Research Plans*. These Plans review what institutions have accomplished and how funds were spent, and they also outline a new set of aims for higher education and research in the light of new social and economic conditions. These formal consultative processes between higher education institutions and the Ministry of Education have given institutions a more direct role in shaping the rules under which they operate.

It can be concluded that the Dutch Government has introduced several market-type elements in the Dutch higher education system. At present, higher education institutions have considerable autonomy to use their financial resources as they wish and to determine the type and content of programmes they offer. Students also have a large degree of freedom to choose their institution and programme. Market mechanisms are missing in the arrangements for tuition fees, and basic government funding of higher education is not strongly market-oriented. Several government regulations have promoted competition, while other regulations are aimed at securing equal access to higher education, protecting curriculum programmes that are the last of their type in the country, and assuring the quality of institutions and programmes.

11.3 Market-Framing of Higher Education in England

Compared to the Netherlands, higher education reforms in England were shaped very differently, and a different balance between market-framing and state intervention was developed. English higher education institutions traditionally selected their own students, appointed and employed their own staff, and decided on their own curricula. In England a test of 'macro-efficiency' – as exists in the Netherlands – was never introduced. Higher education programmes can be established but they are subject to the quality assessment rules of the Quality Assurance Agency. A well-known example of government attempts to encourage market competition by altering the basic conditions within which institutions compete is the removal (in 1988 by the Thatcher Government) of the legal right of universities to offer tenured appointments. Although the abolition of tenure was partly a response to financial pressures, it also was a clear step in the direction of a market-oriented system. It introduced greater competition into the UK higher education labour market, and it created a competitive higher education market that rewards entrepreneurial risk-taking and improvement of performance (Dill, 1997; Williams, 2004).

The financial autonomy of institutions has been increased. Government funding is allocated as a block grant: the institutions decide on internal funding allocations. In addition, by the mid-1980s the Government started to urge higher education institutions to generate income from external sources. Since then, there has been a clear increase in contract-based funding. In 1980 over 75% of income of British universities came directly from the Government, the corresponding figure is now less than 40% and in several universities much lower (HESA, 2003). Among the income-generating strategies pursued by many higher education institutions from the mid-1980s onwards were (i) recruitment of full fee-paying students, (ii) the establishment of university companies to sell teaching and research services, (iii) formalisation of consultancy services by members of academic staff and charging full costs for any services provided, (iv) the creation of science and business parks, and (v) renting out teaching and living accommodation at times when it was not required by students (Williams, 1992). In addition, the Higher Education Funding Council has recently established a third stream of public funding to emphasise links between higher education and business and society.

However, institutions and departments do not only compete for external income. The British Government has also constructed a market in which higher education institutions compete for government funding, either through the Funding Council or the research councils, or for budgets specific to particular government programmes. Institutions strongly compete for students because government funding for teaching follows the student very closely. Higher education institutions receive per-student income on the basis of student number contracts with the Funding Council. Each year the Funding Council determines the maximum number of students that each institution is allowed to recruit. Institutions are paid a 'price' for each student recruited up to this target. These prices are fixed by the Funding Council. There are four price bands: medicine, laboratory subjects, part laboratory subjects and other subjects. Under-recruitment is penalised and there is thus a direct incentive to max-imise student numbers up to the contract ceiling. Higher education institutions have to bid for additional student places at prices they hope the Government would pay (HEFCE, 2001). The market responses of the institutions were attempts to increase their funding by recruiting as many 'full-cost' students as the Funding Council allowed, and then as many 'fees-only' students as they could find (these include postgraduate and overseas students, who are not subsidised by the Government).

For research, each university is given a basic allocation according to the volume and 'quality' of its research as determined by a 4-year Research Assessment Exercise (RAE) in which its research during the previous 4 years and its future research potential, are evaluated. In the last assessment exercise each university department was given a score from 1 to 7 depending on the extent to which a national peer review panel considers its research to have met national and international standards during the previous 4 years. The formula that converts these scores into institutional funding is highly selective (in 2002/03, 75% of research money from the Funding Council went to 25 institutions) and depends heavily on government policy and priorities (HEFCE, 2002). The proportion of an institution's total income allocated by the Funding Council also depends on its activities and money raised from other sources. Thus, attracting external funding is doubly rewarded.

In the 1980s and 1990s the British Government introduced several programmes to make higher education more open to the needs of industry (no such programmes were developed in the Netherlands). Since the mid-1990s higher education institu-tions have also been eligible to receive 'third leg' funding from the Funding Council to strengthen links between higher education and business through short training courses and consultancy work. All higher education institutions are eligible to receive such funds, but they must be bid for and are allocated on a competitive basis depending on the amount of effort the institution appears to be willing to put into these activities. The funds are at present small in relation to those for teaching and research, but the 2003 White Paper announced that they would be increased considerably over the next few years.

The formula funding of higher education institutions by the Government is a clear indication of a very market-oriented approach to higher education funding. However, the market is firmly regulated through the conditions set on receipt of public funds (Williams, 2004). The funding for teaching and for research consists of a network of assessment scores linked to funding, 80 research assessment categories, four price bands for teaching subjects and individual institutional bids for 'third leg' funds. The details of the formulae and procedures are complex and they are changing regularly. It is partly through manipulation of the formulae that government policy is put into practice.

The British Government has also introduced clear market elements in the arrangements for tuition fees. The 1998 Teaching and Higher Education Act required full-time undergraduates to pay (means-tested) fees for the first time in nearly 40 years. This was a single-fee level determined by the Government (only postgraduate and overseas students paid variable fees). The Government also provided differential state support for students by type of course programme, with the highest amount for students in techno-science fields.

Recent legislation indicates a further step in the direction of market-framing. From September 2006 higher education institutions are allowed to determine their own tuition fees for undergraduate students, subject to a £3,000 price cap and an agreement with the Office for Fair Access of a plan to promote and protect access for less advantaged student groups (DfES, 2004). The government rhetoric is that variable fees are part of a broader strategy to encourage 'excellence' and innovation in higher education, and to give students more choice and institutions more autonomy. The Government wants to raise additional money for those institutions 'where the benefits can be justified by the offer and expected return to students' (DfES, 2004).

These proposals to introduce variable fees for undergraduates had raised enormous controversy in the popular press. Public opinion was almost equally divided on this issue. Many universities claimed that a maximum fee of £3,000 a year was insufficient to meet their financial needs. This claim was especially supported by the most popular universities, which were unlikely to have difficulty in filling all their available places even at much higher fee levels. On the other hand, many people believed that differential fees for first-degree studies would discriminate against students from less affluent backgrounds.

The Government thought that some universities would charge the maximum of £3,000 a year, while some would charge less. Soon, however, it became clear that the great majority of universities feared that charging anything less than the maximum would suggest that the quality of their programmes would be lower in the market. Most universities announced to charge the maximum fee. At the moment, it seems that the factor that will differentiate universities will not so much be the fees, but rather the level of bursaries (and scholarships for a few 'outstanding' students) that the institutions will offer. For students this means that, on top of evaluating a university's reputation, courses, location and facilities, they will have to calculate carefully which bursary package is best for them, and – in some cases – whether lower fees at one institution will be cancelled out by higher bursaries at another.

The level of fees under the new system is based on parental income (rather than on the future salaries of the graduates). Students will be able to defer payment of their tuition fees until after graduation: they are signing a contract to pay in the future after they have started to earn. On average, around 75% of the extra fee income is expected to improve institutional finances, while the other 25% will fund bursaries for less well-off students. The Government argues that the money is thus redistributed from the better off to the less well off. In 2006, for all new full-time students from lower income households the Government announced to provide a new income-assessed grant. Moreover, higher education institutions have been encouraged to target different 'markets'. For instance, institutions can opt to introduce special bursaries to attract students with top grades, students from low-income families and/or local students.

The introduction of differential tuition fees is a clear example of market-framing of higher education. Variable tuition fees encourage relationships between 'customers' and 'providers', and the bursaries and scholarships are recruitment tools intended to influence students' considerations of where to apply. Finally, there have been major changes in the state regulation of higher education. In England market-framing of higher education has been accompanied by the development of strong modes of government regulation. This can be illustrated by looking at the construction of a formal system of quality assessment for universities.

Traditionally, universities in England were autonomous in terms of quality assurance. However, by the end of the 1980s the Government thought that a quality assessment system of teaching would be needed. Most universities were keen to resist the imposition of external assessments. Afraid that the Government would take control over the quality assessment system, the universities set up their own agency to monitor and regulate the quality of their teaching. This agency, the Academic Audit Unit, had to ensure that suitable quality assurance mechanisms were in place in every university. However, the Government was not convinced that this agency would offer adequate accountability, and in 1992 established a new national Funding Council that was mandated to assess systematically the 'quality' of education in all universities. The Funding Council organised direct observation and evaluation of teaching in classrooms. For a few years, therefore, the universities, which had little previous experience of external evaluation of the quality of their teaching, had two competitive agencies monitoring their teaching quality. In 1997, the two agencies were combined into the Quality Assurance Agency (QAA) under close auspices of the State.

In the last 2 decades the British State has also taken a firm grip on quality assessment of higher education research. As mentioned earlier, the quantity and 'quality' of all university research is assessed on a 4-year basis, and the evaluation outcomes are linked to levels of government funding. The assessment criteria and working methods have been developed based on a common framework determined by the Funding Council. A major function of the Research Assessment Exercise (RAE) was to sustain stratification and selective state resource allocation between universities (Bauer & Henkel, 1999). However, the RAE was also important for the Government's aims to improve the performance and relevance of higher education research, and to reduce the universities' dependence on state funding and to introduce market mechanisms by encouraging competition between institutions and pressurising them to attract external income.

The imposition of quality assessment systems for higher education has been at the heart of much friction between higher education institutions and the Government. The Government has been effective in sidelining criticism and opposition from higher education staff by taking control over the development of quality assessment systems. It can be concluded that higher education institutions in England clearly have been framed within markets. Institutions are free to establish new programmes according to 'market demand', they have considerable financial autonomy, and there is fierce competition between institutions for state funding, external funding and students. The model of government funding of higher education in England is an example of a very market-oriented approach. In addition, market elements have been introduced in tuition fee arrangements and institutional bursary schemes. At the same time, the markets are closely regulated by the Government through a large number of regulations that set conditions on the receipt of government funding, and that regulate quality assessment criteria and quality management procedures.

11.4   Evaluation

It is evident that in several countries there has been a shift to market-framing of higher education. However, it is not possible to make quick generalisations about the market and the State. Local factors are important. Markets are not introduced everywhere, and the State is not changing everywhere in the same way (Zajda, 2006). Where markets have been introduced, they have been shaped and regulated differently. It is important to notice that there are crucial differences between the two countries examined above, depending on local contexts and the nature of resistance. This chapter shows that market elements in Dutch higher education are different and not as far-reaching and powerful as in higher education in England. A clear example of this is the market in which higher education institutions compete for government funding. While both countries have introduced a form of performance-related funding, in the Netherlands university research is still to a large extent dependent on government funding and the proportion of total public research income that institutions receive on the basis of competition is relatively low. In England the funding formula for research is more market-oriented: research assessment outcomes are directly linked to levels of institutional funding, funding is highly selective and competition for funding is stronger. Institutions in both countries compete for students, but the Dutch Government allocates teaching funding mainly on the basis of degrees awarded and students numbers, whereas in England the allocation of government funding for teaching is a more market-oriented system of bidding schemes and contracts between the institutions and the Funding Council.

Another example of more extensive market-framing in England lies in the decision by the British Government to introduce market elements in the form of differential tuition fees for undergraduates and variable institutional bursary schemes. Although some discussions on differential fees have emerged in the Netherlands, the Dutch Government still sets a uniform tuition fee rate. In the Netherlands resistance against the introduction of differential fees is strong, partly because there is no tradition of institutional hierarchy on the basis of quality. There have also been crucial differences between the countries in the ways in which relations between higher education and the State have changed in the past 2 decades (see Zajda, 2006; Zajda et al., 2006). In the Netherlands, a policy framework was constructed that stressed loosening rigid mechanisms of state regulation, while in

England the policy framework emphasised strengthening instruments of the State to regulate the higher education system more closely. This can be seen in the different ways in which forms of quality regulation were constructed. In both countries the universities and the Government competed to develop and control the quality assessment process. In both countries resistance by the universities against state imposition of a quality assessment system was strong, and in both cases the higher education institutions themselves took the initiative to establish their own quality assessment agency. However, an important difference was that the British Government largely sidelined academic resistance and took firm control over quality assessment arrangements, while in the Netherlands the struggle between universities and the Government ended up in an agreement that the universities should be responsible for the quality assessment system, within a very broad procedural framework set by the Government. Thus, in the Netherlands the universities' resistance against the state imposition of a quality assessment system was more successful than in England.

These differences in policy-making and market-framing can be explained partly by the fact that policy-making in England was much more ideological. It could be so because policy-making in England was based on a one-party political system and because it was heavily influenced by think-tanks that were closely linked to the market ideologies of the Conservative Party.

11.5   Conclusion

The above discussion demonstrates that some of the differences in the market-framing of higher education in the global culture can be explained by making a distinction between forms of market economy (see Hall & Soskice, 2001). The English case can be seen as a liberal market economy, which is strongly focused on realising effectiveness and efficiency. The Dutch case is an example of a more coordinated market economy, in which trade unions and welfare policies have not been weakened so strongly. In a liberal market economy public sector funding tends to be lower and higher education institutions are becoming more corporatised and more strongly urged to become entrepreneurial (see also Zajda, 2005; Zajda et al., 2008). To survive in an increasingly competitive environment, higher education institutions are developing closer ties with business and industry, and move towards a 'user-pays' philosophy for most services. Higher education institutions in a coordinated market economy tend to be more heavily funded by the Government, which still believes to a degree in keeping tuition fees low enough to guarantee student access (Currie, 2004). Thus, in the two countries there have not only been different policies of market-framing and quality management, but also different resistances against them. These forces of resistance have had consequences for the ways in which higher education policies and practices in each country have been shaped. Clearly, a fuller study would explore the politics of that resistance or the historical trajectory of higher education reforms.

References

Bauer, M. & Henkel, M. (1999). Academic Responses to Quality Reforms in Higher Education. In M. Henkel & B. Little (Eds.), *Changing Relationships Between Higher Education and the State* (pp. 236–262). London: Jessica Kingsley.

Boer, H. de & Huisman, J. (1999). The New Public Management in Dutch Universities. In D. Braun & F.-X. Merrien (Eds.), *Towards a New Model of Governance for Universities? A Comparative View* (pp. 100–118). London: Jessica Kingsley.

Butera, F. (2000). Adapting the Pattern of University Organisation to the Needs of the Knowledge Economy. *European Journal of Education,* 35(4, 403–419.

Clark, B. R. (1998). *Creating Entrepreneurial Universities: Organizational Pathways of Transformation.* Oxford: Pergamon Press for International Association of Universities.

Cowen, R. (1991). The Management and Evaluation of the Entrepreneurial University: The Case of England. *Higher Education Policy*, 4(3), 9–13.

Cowen, R. (2000). The Market-Framed University: The New Ethics of the Game. In J. Cairns, R. Gardner, & D. Lawton (Eds.), *Values and the Curriculum* (pp. 93–105). London: Woburn Press.

Currie, J. (2004). The Neo-Liberal Paradigm and Higher Education: A Critique. In J. K. Odin & P. T. Manicas (Eds.), *Globalization and Higher Education* (pp. 42–62). Honolulu: University of Hawai'i Press.

Deem, R. (2001). Globalisation, New Managerialism, Academic Capitalism and Entrepreneurialism in Universities: Is the Local Dimension Still Important. *Comparative Education*, 37(1), 7–20.

Department for Education and Skills (DfES) (2004). *Why Not a Fixed Fee?* London: HMSO.

Dill, D. (1997). Higher Education Markets and Public Policy. *Higher Education Policy*, 10(3–4), 167–185.

Fulton, O. (2002). Higher Education Governance in the UK: Change and Continuity. A. Amaral, G. A. Jones, & B. Karseth (Eds.), *Governing Higher Education: National Perspectives on Institutional Governance* (pp. 187–211). Dordrecht: Kluwer.

Fulton, O. (2003). Managerialism in UK Universities: Unstable Hybridity and the Complications of Implementation. In A. Amaral, V. L. Meek, & I. M. Larsen (Eds.), *The Higher Education Managerial Revolution?* (pp. 155–178). Dordrecht: Kluwer.

Goedegebuure, L. C. J. & Westerheijden, D. F. (1991). Changing Balances in Dutch Higher Education. *Higher Education*, 21(4), 495–520.

Gordon, L. & Whitty, G. (1997). Giving the 'Hidden Hand' a Helping Hand? The Rhetoric and Reality of Neoliberal Education Reform in England and New Zealand. *Comparative Education*, 33(3), 453–467.

Great Britain (2004). *Higher Education Act 2004.* London: HMSO.

Hall, P. A. & Soskice, D. (2001). *Varieties of Capitalism.* Oxford: Oxford University Press.

Henkel, M. & Little, B. (Eds.). (1999). *Changing Relationships Between Higher Education and the State.* London: Jessica Kingsley.

Henry, M., Lingard, B., Rizvi, F., & Taylor, S. (2001). *The OECD, Globalisation and Education Policy.* Oxford: Pergamon.

Higher Education Funding Council for England (HEFCE) (2001). *Funding Higher Education in England: How the HEFCE Allocates Its Funds*, No. 01/14. Bristol: HEFCE.

Higher Education Funding Council for England (HEFCE) (2002). *Funding Higher Education in England: How the HEFCE Allocates Its Funds,* No. 02/18. Bristol: HEFCE.

Higher Education Statistics Agency (HESA) (2003). *Resources of Higher Education Institutions 2001–02. Reference Volume.* Cheltenham: HESA.

Huisman, J., Verhoeven, J., & de Wit, K. (2004). Change in Study Programmes: The Low Countries. *Higher Education Policy*, 17(3), 269–285.

Jongbloed, B. (2003). Marketisation in Higher Education, Clark's Triangle and the Essential Ingredients of Markets. *Higher Education Quarterly*, 57(2), 110–135.

King, R. (2004). *The University in the Global Age.* Basingstoke: Palgrave Macmillan.

Kogan, M. & Hanney, S. (2000). *Reforming Higher Education*. London: Jessica Kingsley.

Maassen, P. (2002). Organisational Strategies and Governance Structures in Dutch Universities. In A. Amaral, G. A. Jones, & B. Karseth (Eds.), *Governing Higher Education: National Perspectives on Institutional Governance* (pp. 23–41). Dordrecht: Kluwer.

Maassen, P. A. M., Goedegebuure, L. C. J., & Westerheijden, D. F. (1993). Social and Political Conditions for the Changing Higher Education Structures in the Netherlands. In C. Gellert(Ed.), *Higher Education in Europe* (pp. 135–151). London: Jessica Kingsley.

McNay, I. (1999). Changing Cultures in UK Higher Education: The State as Corporate Market Bureaucracy and the Emergent Academic Enterprise. In D. Braun, & F.-X. Merrien (Eds.), *Towards a New Model of Governance for Universities? A Comparative View* (pp. 34–58). London: Jessica Kingsley.

Ministerie van Onderwijs, Cultuur en Wetenschappen (OECW) (1999). *Financiële Schema's 2000–2004* [Financial Schemes 2000–2004]. Den Haag: Sdu.

Neave, G. (1998). The Evaluative State Reconsidered. *European Journal of Education*, 33(3), 265–284.

Salerno, C. (2004). Rapid Expansion and Extensive Deregulation: The Development of Markets for Higher Education in the Netherlands. In P. Teixeira, B. Jongbloed, D. Dill, & A. Amaral (Eds.), *Markets in Higher Education: Rhetoric or Reality?* (pp. 271–290). Dordrecht: Kluwer.

Schugurensky, D. (1999). Higher Education Restructuring in the Era of Globalisation; Toward a Heteronomous Model?. In R. F. Arnove & C. A. Torres (Eds.), *Comparative Education: The Dialectic of the Global and the Local* (pp. 283–304). Oxford: Rowman & Littlefield.

Slaughter, S. & Rhoades, G. (2004). *Academic Capitalism and the New Economy: Markets, State, and Higher Education*. Baltimore, MD: Johns Hopkins University Press.

Vossensteyn, J. J. (2002). Shared Interests, Shared Costs: Student Contributions in Dutch Higher Education. *Journal of Higher Education Policy and Management*, 24(2), 145–154.

Vught, F. A. van (1993). *Quality Management and Quality Assurance in European Higher Education: Methods and Mechanisms*. Luxembourg: Office for the Official Publications of the European Communities.

Vught, F. A. van (1997). Combining Planning and the Market: An Analysis of the Government Strategy Towards Higher Education in the Netherlands. *Higher Education Policy*, 10(3–4), 211–223.

Weert, E. de (2001a). Pressures and Prospects Facing the Academic Profession in the Netherlands. *Higher Education*, 41(1–2), 77–101.

Weert, E. de (2001b). The End of Public Employment in Dutch Higher Education?. In J. Enders (Ed.), *Academic Staff in Europe: Changing Contexts and Conditions* (pp. 195–216). London: Greenwood Press.

Weiler, H. (2000). States, Markets and University Funding: New Paradigms for the Reforms of Higher Education in Europe. *Compare*, 30(3), 333–339.

Williams, G. (1992). *Changing Patterns of Finance in Higher Education*. Buckingham: The Society for Research into Higher Education & Open University Press.

Williams, G. (1997). The Market Route to Mass Higher Education: British Experience 1979–1996. *Higher Education Policy*, 10(3–4), 275–289.

Williams, G. (2004). The higher education market in the United Kingdom. In P. Teixeira, B. Jongbloed, D. Dill, & A. Amaral (Eds.), *Markets in Higher Education: Rhetoric or Reality?* (pp. 241–269). Dordrecht: Kluwer.

Willmott, H. (2003). Commercialising Higher Education in the UK: The State, Industry and Peer Review. *Studies in Higher Education*, 28(2), 129–141.

Zajda, J. (Ed.). (2005). *International Handbook of Globalisation and Education Policy Research*. Dordrecht: Springer.

Zajda, J. (Ed.). (2006). *Decentralisation and Privatisation in Education: The Role of the State*. Dordrecht: Springer.

Zajda, J. Majhanovich, S., & Rust, V. (Eds.). (2006). *Education and Social Justice*. Dordrecht: Springer.

Zajda, J. Biraimah, B., & Gaudelli, W. (Eds.). (2008). *Education and Social Inequality in the Global Culture*. Dordrecht: Springer.

Name Index

Subject Index